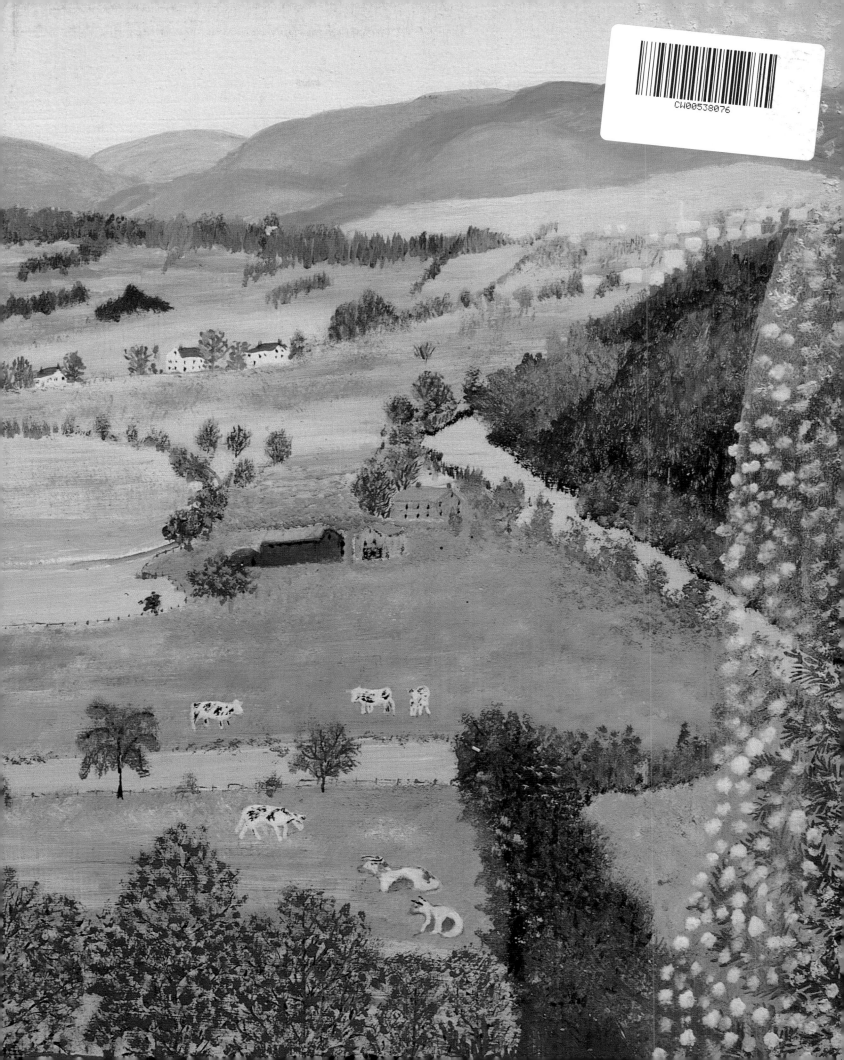

Grandma Moses

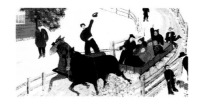

Groun m

Grandma Moses

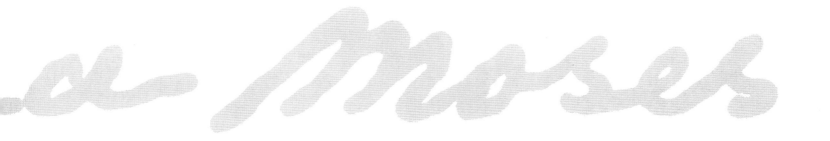

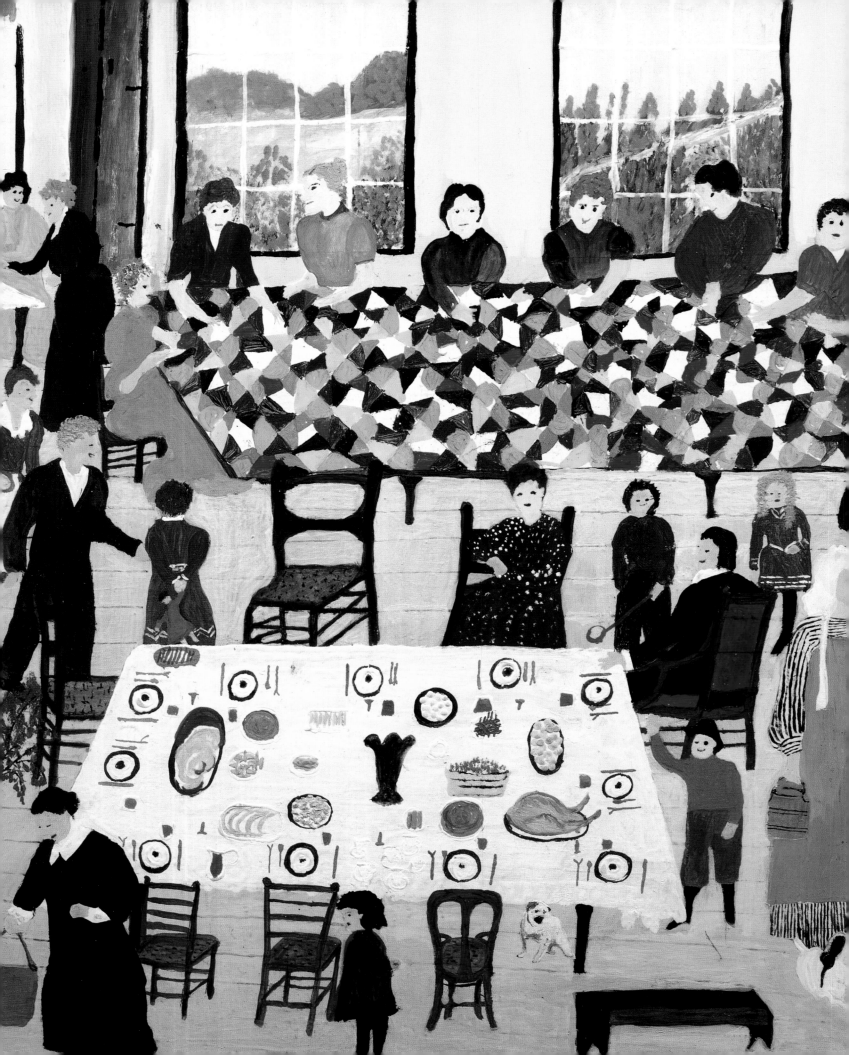

Grandma Moses in the 21st Century

Jane Kallir

with contributions by

Roger Cardinal

Michael D. Hall

Lynda Roscoe Hartigan

Judith E. Stein

Art Services International
Alexandria, Virginia
2001

in association with
Yale University Press

This volume accompanies an exhibition
organized and circulated by
Art Services International, Alexandria, Virginia.

The national tour has been generously
sponsored by AARP.

Clothbound edition distributed by
Yale University Press.

LIBRARY OF CONGRESS CATALOGING-IN-PUBLICATION DATA
Kallir, Jane.
        Grandma Moses in the 21st century / Jane Kallir; with essays by
Roger Cardinal . . . [et al.].
                        p.   cm.
        Catalog of an exhibition held in the National Museum of Women
in the Arts, Washington, D.C., and six other museums between March 15,
2001 and December 1, 2002.
        Includes bibliographical references and index.
        ISBN 0-88397-133-X (pbk.)
        1. Moses, Grandma, 1860–1961—Exhibitions. 2. Primitivism in
art—United States—Exhibitions. I. Title: Grandma Moses in the twenty-first
century. II. Moses, Grandma, 1860–1961. III. Cardinal, Roger. IV.
National Museum of Women in the Arts (U.S.). V. Title.
ND237.M78 A4 2001
759.13—dc21
                                                    00-038990

Editor	Sharon R. Herson
Designer	Watermark Design Office
Typeset in	Mrs. Eaves Roman
Printed on	Biberist Demi Matte 150 gsm
Printed by	Dai Nippon Printing, Inc.
Printed in	Hong Kong

Cover	Grandma Moses, *Moving Day on the Farm*, detail of plate 28
Endpages	Grandma Moses, *Hoosick Valley (From the Window)*, detail of plate 42
Title page	Grandma Moses, *The Quilting Bee*, detail of plate 66
Contents	(*above*) Grandma Moses at Work, 1958, photograph by Hildegard Bachert
	(*below*) Grandma Moses, *Waiting for Santa Claus*, detail of plate 75
Catalogue	(*pages 106–107*) Grandma Moses, *The Old Checkered House*, detail of plate 40

Photo Credits
Geoffrey Clements: plates 43, 45, 59
Eric Pollitzer: plates 7, 15, 17, 75, 80
Jim Strong: plates 1, 4, 8, 9, 11, 13, 20, 31, 34, 38, 58, 79, 81, 83, 84

Contents

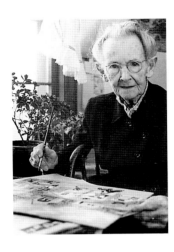

Acknowledgments

The biography of Anna Mary Robertson Moses spins like an authentic American folk tale. With maternal and paternal ancestors who arrived on the Mayflower, Grandma Moses appears to have led the quintessentially American life. Nevertheless, her career defied the norm—not only for her own era but also for ours, more than sixty years after her first exhibition. Before she "took up art," Anna Mary's life was devoted to her husband, her children, and the farmland surrounding her upstate New York home. In her seventies, she began to paint. Her bucolic works quickly became popular, in part because they evoked nostalgia for this American way of life and its optimistic values, and she became a national darling almost without leaving her front porch. Still, even a novelist might be hard-pressed to create a believable character who retained such humility after being catapulted into the national spotlight. Her advanced age at the time of her artistic "discovery" may have hindered her acceptance within the established art world, contributing to her dismissal by some art critics, yet it was a positive factor in her immediate appeal to the American public, who came to adore and respect the rural, self-taught artist and saw her paintings as valid art. In our contemporary review of Grandma Moses, however, her lifestyle and age should not be allowed to overshadow her contributions to the art culture of the 1940s and 1950s. Moses invented a unique style that, while distinct from the American avante-garde then in its ascendancy, incorporated a wealth of traditions, ranging from nineteenth-century folk art and popular art to the Regionalist and American Scene movements that flourished during the Depression era. Art Services International is delighted to present this retrospective, which highlights Moses' natural artistic abilities and documents her esteemed and well-deserved place within the history of American art.

This exhibition would not have been possible without the passionate and efficient guidance of Jane Kallir, who has graciously served as lead scholar and guest curator for this endeavor. Following in the path of her grandfather, Otto Kallir, whose early recognition of Grandma Moses' work was key to the artist's ultimate success, she is the foremost authority on the artist. It is an honor to recognize her personal initiative to reexamine Moses' work, four decades after the peak of her popular appeal. Together with Hildegard Bachert, co-director of Galerie St. Etienne, who worked closely with the artist for over twenty years, Ms. Kallir has contributed significant new scholarship, and we are proud to collaborate once again with these valued colleagues on this major project.

In recognition of this exhibition's importance, the AARP is generously supporting the national tour, and for this we express our appreciation.

We are enormously grateful to the lenders who have entrusted their precious works to us and, in doing so, have created this synergistic look at the artist's oeuvre that would have been lost without the cooperation of each. Our appreciation is extended to Galerie St. Etienne, New York, and its staff, and to Grandma Moses Properties Co., New York, which not only loaned paintings but also were instrumental in securing other key loans. In addition, we thank the respected institutions of Seiji Togo Memorial, Yasuda Kasai Museum of Art, Tokyo; Hallmark Fine Art Collection, Hallmark Cards, Inc., Kansas City, Missouri; The Montclair Art Museum, New Jersey; The Phillips Collection, Washington, D.C.; and Miss Porter's School, Farmington, Connecticut. We also recognize the personal commitment of individual lenders: Anne C. Brower, Brock H. Brower, and Charles N. Brower; G. Arnold Haynes; John and Dorothy Levy; Roy W. Moses and Harry L. Moses; Al M. Nakamura; Richard D. Della Penna, M.D., and Mearl A. Naponic, M.D.; Bruce and Alice Ivy Weiss; and private collectors in several states for sharing these icons of American culture with the nation.

It is a great pleasure to recognize our dedicated museum colleagues who enthusiastically endorsed this novel review of an American folk tradition and have generously made Moses' work accessible to a large audience. We send our special thanks to: Nancy Risque Rohrbach, Director, and Dr. Susan Fisher Sterling, Chief Curator, The National Museum of Women in the Arts, Washington, D.C.; Dr. Don Bacigalupi, Director, and D. Scott Atkinson, Curator of American Art, San Diego Museum of Art; Marena Grant Morrisey, Executive Director, and Hansen Mulford, Curator, Orlando Museum of Art; J. Brooks Joyner, Director, and Dr. Dan Swan, Senior Curator, Gilcrease Museum, Tulsa; Irvin M. Lippman, Executive Director, and Nannette V. Maciejunes, Senior Curator, Columbus Museum of Art, Ohio; and John E. Buchanan Jr., Executive Director, and Donald Jenkins, Chief Curator and Curator of Asian Art, Portland Art Museum, Oregon. These professionals have collectively advanced the appreciation of Moses' art, and we are truly in their debt.

Led by Jane Kallir, the contributing scholars have triumphed in reevaluating the textbook perspective on self-taught, naïve artists. Their analyses have redefined Grandma Moses with a contemporary approach, considering her work in relation to regional art, the cultural and political setting, "memory painting," and the influence of feminism in a grandmother's work. For their outstanding research and eloquent essays, we are indebted to Dr. Roger Cardinal, Professor of Literary and Visual Studies, University of Kent at Canterbury; Michael D. Hall, artist and independent curator, formerly head of the sculpture department at Cranbrook Academy of Art, Michigan; Lynda Roscoe Hartigan, Chief Curator, Smithsonian American Art Museum (formerly National Museum of American Art), Washington, D.C.; and Dr. Judith E. Stein, independent curator, formerly curator at the Linda Alter Collection of American Women Artists, Philadelphia, and professor at the Pennsylvania Academy of Fine Arts.

The technical realization of this publication was in the experienced hands of several outstanding professionals: Sharon R. Herson, editor; Lynne Komai, Watermark Design Office; and Dai Nippon Printing, Inc., printer. We thank them for their efforts in creating a framework that will enable this volume's scholarship to effectively serve a broad community long after the conclusion of the tour.

Finally, we are delighted to have yet another opportunity to congratulate the staff of Art Services International for their exemplary completion of the detailed arrangements for this multi-lender exhibition, specifically recognizing Douglas Shawn, Sheryl Kreischer, Catherine Bade, Kathryn Evans, Heather Schweizer, Sally Thomas, and the assistance of William MacDonald.

LYNN K. ROGERSON
Director

JOSEPH W. SAUNDERS
Chief Executive Officer

ART SERVICES INTERNATIONAL

Lenders to the Exhibition

Anne C. Brower, Brock H. Brower, and Charles N. Brower

Galerie St. Etienne, New York

Grandma Moses Properties Co., New York

Hallmark Fine Art Collection, Hallmark Cards, Inc.,
Kansas City, Missouri

The Collection of G. Arnold Haynes

John and Dorothy Levy

The Montclair Art Museum, New Jersey

Mr. Roy W. Moses and Mr. Harry L. Moses

Mr. Al M. Nakamura

Private Collection in honor of Mr. J. B. Olstein

From the Collection of Richard D. Della Penna, M.D., and
Mearl A. Naponic, M.D., San Diego

The Phillips Collection, Washington, D.C.

Miss Porter's School, Farmington, Connecticut

Seiji Togo Memorial, Yasuda Kasai Museum of Art, Tokyo

Bruce and Alice Ivy Weiss

Private Collections

Participating Museums

The National Museum of
Women in the Arts
Washington, D.C.

San Diego Museum of Art
California

Orlando Museum of Art
Florida

Gilcrease Museum
Tulsa, Oklahoma

Columbus Museum of Art
Ohio

Portland Art Museum
Oregon

Introduction

Rethinking Grandma Moses

Jane Kallir

The art history of the twentieth century will surely be remembered for its curious chain of "isms." Artists over the course of the past hundred years have been ranked according to their place in such movements as Fauvism, Cubism, Expressionism, and Conceptualism, and the movements themselves were ranked in accordance with their relationship to one another. There was a general assumption that these labels told us almost all we needed to know about modern art history, and that there was a logical, immutable progression from one movement to the next. At times it seemed that artists were subject to "branding" no less than soft drinks and designer jeans. An artist's stylistic label determined where he (or, more rarely, she) was placed in the hierarchy of our nation's museums and galleries, just as the manufacturer's label determined whether a product would be sold at Nieman Marcus or K-Mart.*

The growing suspicion that art-historical labels, while still useful, do not tell us everything, is reinforced by a serious encounter with Grandma Moses. Although Moses and her art changed relatively little over a twenty-odd-year career, the labels applied to her underwent a marked transformation. Moses' initial "discovery" was part of an art-world trend favoring self-taught or folk artists, and there was nothing intrinsic to her paintings or the circumstances of their creation to distinguish her from such contemporaries as John Kane, Horace Pippin, or Morris Hirshfield. Unlike these folk artists, however, Moses went on to become enormously popular. One of the first artists to be hailed as a media superstar, and possibly the most successful female artist of her era, Moses is nevertheless surprisingly invisible when it comes to histories of postwar American painting. While her relative neglect may in part be attributed to the fact that her work does not conform to any of the accepted modernist "isms," it is interesting to note (as Judith Stein does elsewhere herein) that even feminists—so quick to denounce conventional art-historical hierarchies because of their male bias—have failed to claim

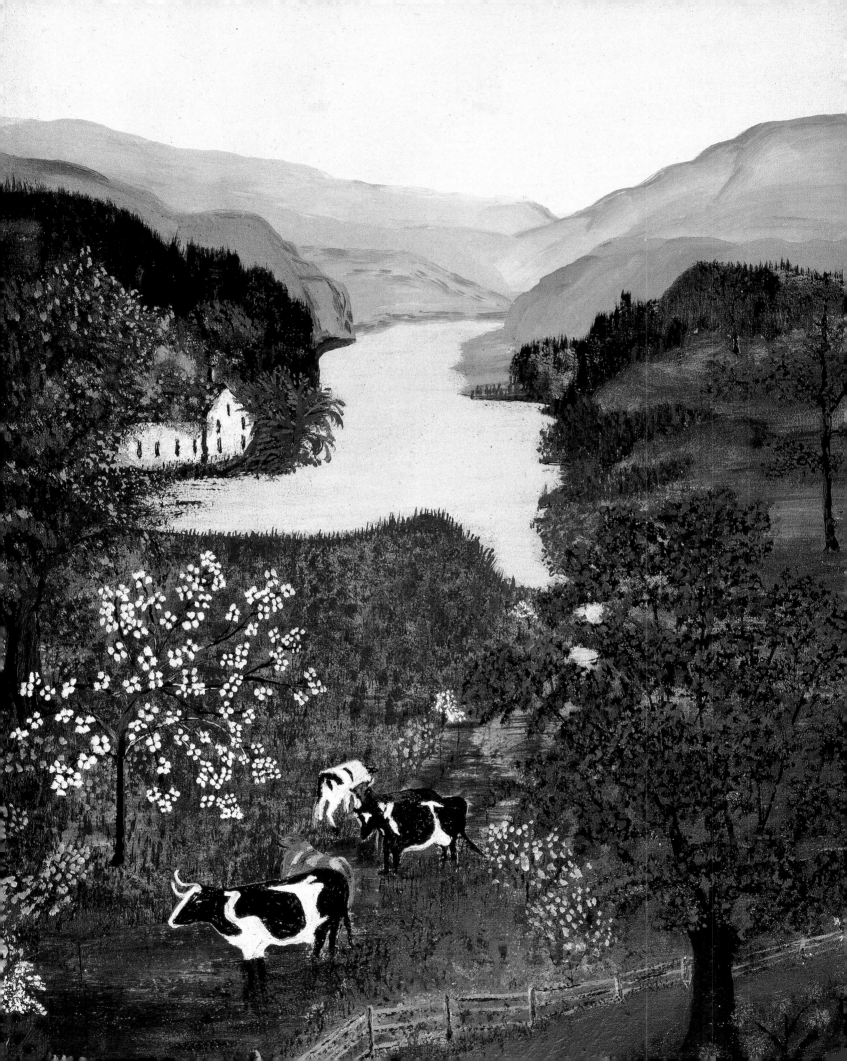

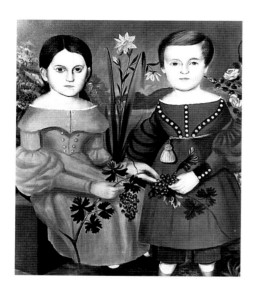

Fig. 1. Anonymous American Artist,
Portrait of Two Children, ca. 1835.
Oil on panel, 35 ¹/₂ x 30 ¹/₄ inches
(90.2 x 76.8 cm). Photograph courtesy
Galerie St. Etienne, New York

Grandma Moses. Nor has Moses received much attention from advocates of so-called Outsider Art, perhaps because her work is seen as being too cheerful and conventionally pretty to qualify. The principal reason for Moses' relative neglect may be found, paradoxically, in the extremity of her success: Moses was a folk artist until she became famous, but then she became a popular painter, and her art was dismissed because of its mass appeal.

Few designations within the schema of art-historical labeling have proved as volatile as the categories of folk and popular art. The high–low dichotomy haunted the twentieth century from its inception and in recent decades has proved the nemesis of more than one curator.[1] Although folk and popular art are closely related and at times indistinguishable from one another, modernists often chose to define them as mutually exclusive categories. Whereas popular art was considered to be tainted by commerce and mechanization, folk art was believed to represent everything that was pure. True folk art in the twentieth century was an elusive yet much cherished ideal, the surviving evidence of a pre-industrial expressive Eden.

When examined closely, however, folk art often fails to live up to the idealized standards that have been set for it. Certainly, folk art has not historically been anti-commercial; many folk artists earned income from their work. Nor is folk art "pure" in the sense of being uninfluenced. Traditional folk crafts were tightly bound by inherited forms, and even the more independent painters eagerly copied one another, as well as popular prints. As industrialization became increasingly pervasive over the course of the nineteenth century, cultural objects that would once have been made by hand were instead produced by machine. And so folk art shaded into and was largely supplanted by popular commercial art. To suggest that the former is "good" and the latter somehow "bad" seems rather arbitrary; and yet it is precisely this widespread prejudice that shaped art-world perceptions of Grandma Moses.

If the trajectory of Moses' career—with its transition from obscure farmwife to media darling—sent off conflicting signals, the history of folk art in America has proved no easier to comprehend. In fact, to this day, no one is quite sure what is meant by "folk art" in the United States, and debates continue to rage about the term's proper definition.[2] The principal reason for this problem lies in the fact that folk art was not originally an American concept. Literally the art of the common people, European folk art reflected the age-old socioeconomic divide between peasantry and aristocracy. The advent of European folk art can loosely be dated to the Renaissance, when the often anonymous craftsmanship of the medieval guild system was replaced by a two-tiered structure in which "high" artists, serving the ruling elite, were elevated to a realm separate from those humbler creators who catered to the masses. Not only were such extreme class distinctions absent in ostensibly egalitarian America, but also the attendant cultural apparatus was several thousand miles away. Until the establishment of the first American art schools and museums in the second half of the nineteenth century, only a handful of American artists managed to cross the Atlantic to study at the European academies. The knowledge they brought back was then passed down, through a series of apprenticeships (often brief) and through engravings. As in the children's game "telephone," much got lost in the transmission of the aesthetic message from the European capitals to the towns and villages of the New World. It was this set of circumstances—inherently free-flowing and individualistic—that shaped the ad hoc character of American folk art, which is on some fundamental level the direct antithesis of its rigidly circumscribed European counterpart.

"True" folk art, along the European model, is oriented toward and defined by the needs of a specific (usually rural) community; it is traditional in form and often utilitarian or religious in function. America did produce plenty of folk art—quilts and weathervanes and such—that conformed to this definition, though today these works are more highly prized for their quirky idiosyncrasies than for the rote parroting of conventional patterns. However, America also produced, in far greater number than any European nation, a plethora of folk paintings that were neither strictly utilitarian nor religious (fig. 1). The creators of these paintings were fully the equals, in ambition if not in education, of the artistic servants of the European aristocracy. In the days before photography, American folk painters serviced the infant nation's need to see itself, as reflected in portraits of upstanding citizens, of farms, prized livestock, and magnificent sailing ships. Imperfect training in many cases became the mother of invention, leading to surprising pictorial solutions that would later be much admired by the modernists. But in their day the so-called limners and their ilk were more frequently criticized for ineptitude by better-educated Americans. And herein lay the double-edged nature of American folk art: while the genre could be lauded as proof of American ingenuity and individualism, it could equally be taken as evidence of America's cultural inferiority and inability to measure up to a more sophisticated European standard. America's attitude toward folk art would thus be colored by an innate ambivalence, even as

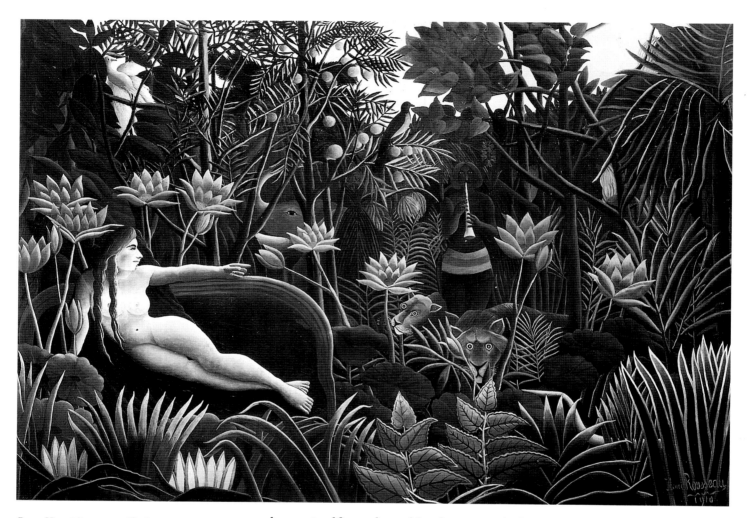

Fig. 2. Henri Rousseau, *The Dream*, 1910.
Oil on canvas, 80 ¹/₂ x 117 ¹/₂ inches
(204.5 x 298.5 cm). The Museum
of Modern Art, New York. Gift of
Nelson A. Rockefeller. Photograph
copyright © 2001 The Museum of
Modern Art, New York

the art itself was shaped by this nation's democratic structures.

Appreciation of folk art began, in nineteenth-century Europe, as an anthropological interest in rural folkways that were being destroyed by the relentless tide of industrialization. This seemingly objective, scientific interest partnered cozily with the Romantic distrust of "civilization" that had been afoot since the late eighteenth century, as well as with a more recent loathing for the corrosive effects of bourgeois capitalism. The art-historical legitimacy of folk art was crowned by the early-twentieth-century modernists, who in addition to sharing the aforementioned political values, felt that self-taught art offered an aesthetic escape from hidebound tradition. In their search for "pure" sources of artistic inspiration, however, the modernists were themselves hardly purists: they collected folk art, children's art, tribal art, and the art of mental patients indiscriminately, with scant attention to the very different origins of

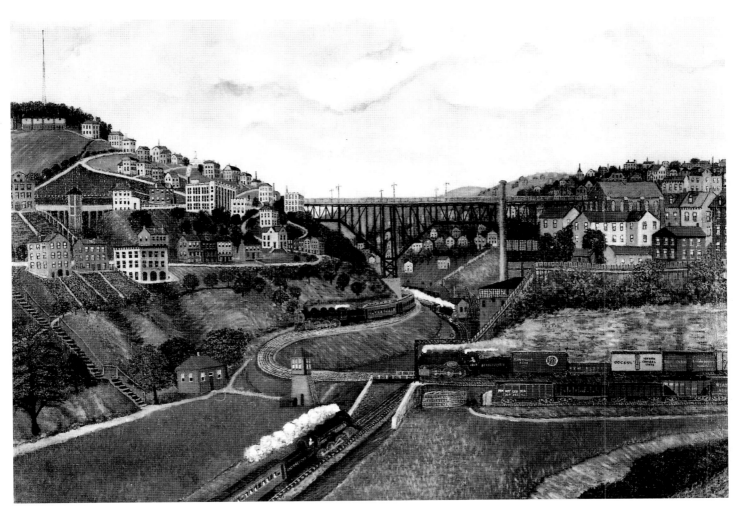

each sort of expression. Contemporary art by self-taught adults—
commonly called naïve art in Europe—was of a piece with this generic
search for untainted creativity.

As is well known, the French toll-collector Henri Rousseau (fig. 2)
was the first contemporary "naïve" to win the support of the avant-garde,
but he was soon followed by other kindred spirits. And when the avant-
garde aesthetic began to penetrate the United States in the wake of World
War I, it was only a matter of time until the discovery of the first
"American Rousseau": a one-legged housepainter named John Kane
(fig. 3), who was admitted to the prestigious Carnegie International
Exhibition in Pittsburgh on his third try, in 1927. It quickly became
evident, however, that Kane was no Rousseau—not only because his work
was visually quite different, but chiefly because the myth of the "naïve"
in America strayed fundamentally from its European prototype.

Fig. 3. John Kane, *Crossing the Junction,*
1933–34. Oil on canvas, 35 ¹/₂ x
47 ¹/₂ inches (90.2 x 120.7 cm).
H. J. Heinz Company, Pittsburgh

American self-taught art immediately triggered a comparatively broad popular response because the genre was so fortuitously compatible with the national self-image. John Kane could readily be perceived as a personification of the American dream: an uneducated Scottish immigrant who finally made good amongst the cultural elite. That elite itself was of two minds about Kane. He had his protectors, to be sure, but the droves of contemporary trained artists who had failed to gain admittance to the International seethed with resentment. Some even plotted revenge. An enterprising art critic purchased a Kane painting and cleaned off half of it with paint thinner, exposing a photograph beneath. Although today, in our post-Warhol era, manipulation of photographic sources is entirely acceptable, in the early 1930s it was seen as a sacrilege. More to

Fig. 4. Morris Hirshfield, *Girl with Pigeons,* 1942. Oil on canvas, 30 x 40 ⅛ inches (76.1 x 101.7 cm). The Museum of Modern Art, New York. The Sidney and Harriet Janis Collection. Photograph copyright © 2001 The Museum of Modern Art, New York

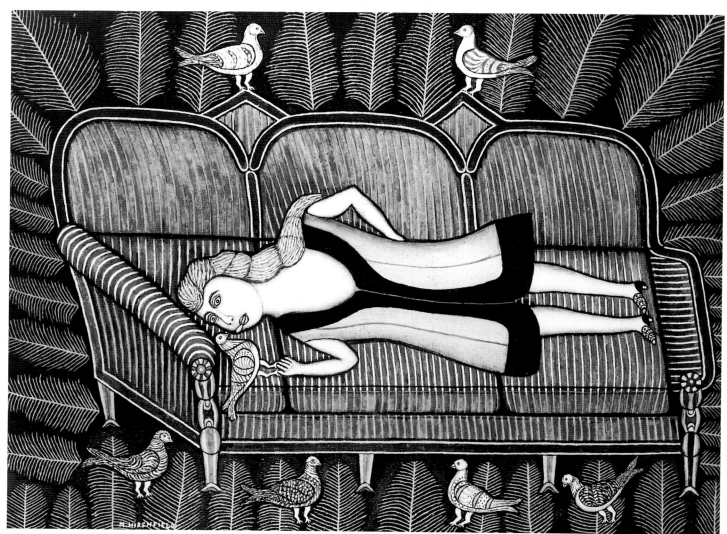

the point, Kane's use of photographs completely dashed the fantasy of artistic purity that was the naïve artist's raison d'être.

If genuine artistic purity was an ideal unattainable to Kane or, indeed, to any artist living in the modern world, the left-wing political edge ascribed to European naïve art seemed particularly irrelevant in the United States. On the contrary, the "Horatio Alger" aspect of the typical folk artist's story lent credence to the myth of American egalitarianism and offered an appealing antidote to the threat of revolutionary social unrest raised by the Great Depression. It is probably no coincidence that the heyday of the American self-taught painter coincided with the Depression. Self-taught art defused the labor issues that were addressed more pointedly by some of the contemporaneous Regionalist artists.

Fig. 5. Horace Pippin, *Sunday Morning, Breakfast,* 1943. Oil on canvas, 20 x 16 inches (50.8 x 40.6 cm). Private collection. Photograph courtesy Galerie St. Etienne, New York

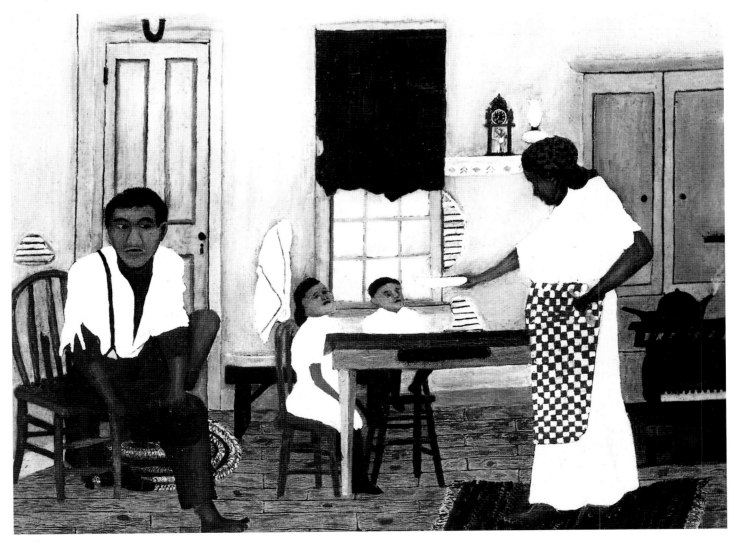

Nevertheless, as Michael Hall discusses in his catalogue essay, self-taught art can also be seen as a natural adjunct to Regionalism, which exemplified a parallel turn to grassroots, bootstrap efforts. The four greatest American folk artists to emerge during the prewar period—Kane, Morris Hirshfield (fig. 4), Horace Pippin (fig. 5), and Moses—represented an ideal demographic sampling: respectively, two immigrant laborers, an African-American war veteran, and a Yankee farm woman.

Anna Mary Robertson Moses, born on a farm in upstate New York in 1860, led a life marked by hard work and the common tragedies of her time and place. Married at the then relatively late age of twenty-seven to Thomas Salmon Moses, Anna Mary would give birth to ten children, five of whom did not survive infancy. She and her husband worked as tenant farmers in the post-Civil War South, sometimes barely skirting financial ruin but finally accumulating enough money to buy their own farm. After the family returned to Eagle Bridge, New York, in 1905, and after the deaths of Thomas in 1927 and of her daughter Anna in 1932, "Mother Moses" (as she was known locally; the nickname "Grandma" replaced "Mother" by and by as she aged) found herself with time on her hands. Never one to sit idle, she began to paint. Later she would write: "If I didn't start painting, I would have raised chickens. I could still do it now. I would never sit back in a rocking chair, waiting for someone to help me."[3]

Her need to be productive and her love of beauty were strong motivating forces for Grandma Moses, as they have been for countless self-taught artists before and since. Roger Cardinal's catalogue essay analyzes in depth the manner whereby Moses gradually combined local lore, memory, and observation to craft a unique folk idiom. Still, the initial response to her homespun paintings was not especially encouraging: the artist gave them to family and friends, and sent a few to the country fair, along with her jams and preserves. Moses won a ribbon for the preserves, but her paintings went unnoticed. Finally, in the spring of 1938, her work was discovered by a traveling collector in the window of a local drugstore, where she had sent it as part of a "woman's exchange." The collector, Louis Caldor, bought everything the druggist and Moses herself had on hand, and went home to New York City resolved to introduce the artist to the urban art world. Many months of discouragement lay ahead of him.

In 1939, Caldor achieved a modest success when the Museum of Modern Art agreed to include Moses in a show called *Contemporary Unknown American Painters.* This exhibition (which also marked the debut of Morris

Hirshfield) was not open to the general public, however, and thus had virtually no impact. Caldor's attempts to solicit commercial gallery support were largely stymied by Moses' advanced years. Seventy-nine in 1939, the artist seemed unlikely to live long enough to merit the investment of time and money entailed by gallery representation. Finally, in 1940, Caldor managed to interest the art dealer Otto Kallir, who presented Moses' first one-woman show at his Galerie St. Etienne in October of that year.

By this time, self-taught art had become an integral component of the more sophisticated art scene (a topic discussed at some length in Michael Hall's essay). The seriousness accorded the new field of folk art may be demonstrated by the progress of John Kane's career: during the 1930s, the Museum of Modern Art featured him in no fewer than four surveys of contemporary trends; he appeared as well in "annuals" at major museums such as the Art Institute of Chicago, in the first and second Biennial exhibitions of the Whitney Museum, and in every Carnegie International until his death. The Museum of Modern Art's *Contemporary Unknown American Painters* show in 1939 was, in fact, a follow-up to a far more significant 1938 exhibition, *Masters of Popular Painting*, a survey of European and American naïve art that featured, among others, Rousseau, Kane, and the recently "discovered" Horace Pippin. Moses was initially received within the context of this larger phenomenon. Reviewing her show at St. Etienne, the *New York Times* noted, "The 'Primitive' which has been much to the fore . . . in the early season crops out again."[4] The magazine *Art News* commented that Moses' work had "the freshness of some of the early folk painting in this country."[5] In 1942, Moses was featured in the first survey of contemporary folk art, Sidney Janis's *They Taught Themselves*.[6]

If critics were already schooled in recognizing genuine "primitives" (then the term of choice in the United States for contemporary self-taught artists), Judith Stein has remarked elsewhere herein that some members of the press seemed at least as interested in Grandma Moses' personality as in her art. "Grandma Moses Just Paints and Makes No Fuss About It," proclaimed one headline;[7] "Widow, 80, Hailed for Art Eagle Bridge Spurned," declared another;[8] and "'Land Sakes' Says Grandma Moses, 80, As Critics Rave About Her Art."[9] This interest in the artist's persona really took off when, shortly after the St. Etienne show closed, Moses came down to New York City to attend a special Thanksgiving festival featuring her work at Gimbel's department store. While a department store may seem an unlikely venue for art, the Gimbel's event presaged the broad-spectrum accessibility so fundamental to Grandma Moses' appeal. As forthright and down-to-earth in person as she was in her paintings, Moses immediately charmed both press and public. From here, her career would head into largely uncharted territory: out of the elite museums, and into the homes of millions of ordinary fans all over the world.[10]

Grandma Moses' rise to fame was predicated on the same confluence of political, economic, and art-historical circumstances that had fostered other self-taught artists during the Depression years. The tabloid press lionized painters such as Kane and Moses because they were seen as exemplars both of native ingenuity and of the triumph of talent and perseverance over adversity. The art world, meanwhile, was looking for homegrown artists who could hold their own on European turf. And whereas the work of America's trained artists was, at the time, relatively provincial by comparison with that of their European colleagues, American self-taught painters were fully the equals of the European naïves. The problem was that the populist agenda was fundamentally at odds with the art world's agenda, and in the roughly ten years that passed between the advent of John Kane and the debut of Grandma Moses, these once-overlapping agendas began to pull apart. Moses was to become an unwitting pawn in the battle to define modern American art.

Some of the problems that would soon confront Grandma Moses are foretold in America's historical attitude to nineteenth-century folk painting. "Slander of the family in oil," was Mark Twain's notorious description of a typical cycle of limner portraits.[11] Modernism in the twentieth century gave a new edge to America's aesthetic inferiority complex. For modernism was originally a European invention in which relatively few American artists participated. The jealousy that had colored some artists' reactions to John Kane's triumph at the Carnegie International found an even more compelling target in the programs of New York's Museum of Modern Art, whose founding director, Alfred H. Barr Jr., initially identified three "major divisions or movements of modern art": Cubism and abstraction, Dada and Surrealism, and self-taught art.[12] Of the three divisions, only the last had many American representatives in the 1930s. Once again, America's trained artists would complain that inept amateurs were usurping their rightful place.

The evident European bias of the Museum of Modern Art was a source of friction throughout its early years, but matters really came to a head in 1943, when the museum gave Morris Hirshfield a retrospective. Barr was excoriated for glorifying "a fumbling old man,"[13] and one critic scathingly dubbed Hirshfield "the master of the two left feet."[14] The scandal grew so serious that Barr was temporarily forced from his job by the museum's board.[15] Once reinstated, he dropped his pioneering advocacy of self-taught art forever. If America were to develop an art capable of competing with European modernism, the solution clearly would not be found in the work of retired laborers or farmers' wives.

After World War II, America's lack of cultural hegemony became a political as well as an artistic problem. The United States now needed an art befitting her new stature as a world power. Although that role would eventually fall to Abstract Expressionism and its various stylistic descendants, such an outcome seemed far from assured in the late 1940s and 1950s. Most Americans detested abstract art, and President Harry Truman was not above broadcasting his own populist philistinism. "Ham and eggs art," he called the work of Jackson Pollock and his cohorts.[16] Nor did Truman shy away from cultivating Grandma Moses, who by the late 1940s had become the darling of the popular press. In 1949, he invited her to Washington to receive the Women's National Press Club Award, took full advantage of a classic photo opportunity (fig. 6), and even played the piano for her.

Grandma Moses was perceived as a welcome antidote to the rising tide of modernism. Her popularity, one critic hopefully opined, might permanently "lead us out of the lanes of abstraction and intellectualized distortion."[17] Another pundit put it this way: "When [Grandma Moses] paints something, you know right away what it is—you don't need to cock your head sideways like when you look at some modern dauber's effort and try to deduct [sic] if it is maybe a fricassee of sick oyster, or maybe an abscessed bicuspid, or just a plain hole in the ground."[18] Moreover, Moses—a double descendant, through both her maternal and paternal lines, of ancestors who came to the United States on the Mayflower—was quintessentially American. She tapped into the groundswell of patriotism that rose under the duress of the Depression and crested after the nation's triumph in World War II. Whereas modern art was still largely a European phenomenon, Moses was as American as apple pie.

It is therefore not surprising that, during the early Cold War period, some American government officials saw Grandma Moses as democracy's ideal cultural ambassador. In 1950, the United States Information Agency circulated an exhibition of her work through six European cities. In allying itself with popular tastes, however, the government inadvertently riled the art-world elite, which by this time had firmly coalesced around America's burgeoning avant-garde. Furthermore, the U.S.I.A.'s

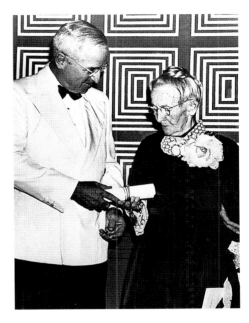

Fig. 6. Grandma Moses receiving the Women's National Press Club Award from President Harry S. Truman, May 14, 1949

choice of a folk painter inflamed America's lingering inferiority complex. "Europeans like to think of Grandma Moses . . . as representative of American art," wrote one disgruntled reporter in the *New York Times*. "They praise our naïveté and integrity, . . . but they begrudge us a full, sophisticated artistic expression. Grandma Moses represents both what they expect of us and what they are willing to grant us."[19] The *Times*, however, misjudged the European bias. In reality, Europeans received Moses respectfully and welcomed her as the antithesis of soulless American capitalism.[20] Nor were Europeans exactly clamoring for American abstract art, which did figure in later government-sponsored exhibition tours.[21] As one British critic commented: "Grandma Moses' art is more likely to endure than the misshapen and demented ravings of the second generation of psychological and abstract painters."[22]

Despite the widespread hostility to American abstraction, the art-world elite's failure to support Grandma Moses eventually doomed her to second-class status. By the time Moses came on the scene in the 1940s, the elite's flirtation with folk art was waning. Moses may have debuted in a private showing at the Museum of Modern Art, but she never made it into the public galleries or the permanent collection. And while her work toured constantly during the 1940s and 1950s, turning up in museums everywhere from Abilene, Texas, to Zanesville, Ohio, she was for the most part shunned by the major big-city institutions. In the nation's cultural capital, New York, Moses was shown at the behest of maverick entrepreneurs—at Thomas J. Watson's IBM Gallery of Arts and Sciences and Huntington Hartford's Gallery of Modern Art—but never in the mainstream museums.

The more famous Grandma Moses became, the more the art world distanced itself from her. Critics who had been charmed by Moses when she was "just" a folk artist began to question her integrity when she became a marketing phenomenon.[23] Greeting cards by the millions, best-selling books, radio interviews, television shows, an Academy Award-nominated documentary, and a comprehensive licensing program that included everything from drapery fabric to collector plates— these and other miracles of the technological age brought Grandma Moses into more American homes than almost any other artist.[24] Her story of achievement late in life and her no-nonsense reiteration of rural American values seemed only to increase in appeal as America came to terms with the harsh realities of the nuclear age. The miracle of Moses' achievement was matched by a miracle of longevity, and an adoring public stuck with her, holding its breath in admiration as she passed 90, then 95, and finally 100, dying in 1961 at the age of 101.

By comparison with the standards prevalent today, the marketing of Grandma Moses seems tame, almost quaint. For one thing, she herself had no truck with celebrity: disliking the urban environment, she preferred to remain on her remote farm in upstate New York. She was polite to the many interviewers who courted her but never actively courted them. Neither her work nor her forthright manner was affected by all the public attention. Of her fame, she said: "That I am too old to care for now."[25] The sundry Moses reproductions and products were nothing compared to the items now routinely found in every museum gift shop. Otto Kallir, who oversaw the Moses licensing program, made sure that each reproduction did justice to the original, and was inherently tasteful and consistent with Moses' own sensibilities.

While debates still rage regarding where to draw the line when it comes to licensing reproductions of art, the propriety of such reproductions per se is no longer questioned. In Moses' day, however, a sharp divide still obtained between the art world and the mass market, the art museum and the department store. This divide was maintained by an assortment of interrelated prejudices and questionable assumptions. Foremost among them was the widely held belief that "good" art is by nature difficult and therefore accessible to a limited few. According to this theory, the American public's aversion to abstraction was de facto proof of abstraction's high quality; the corollary was that anything the masses liked could not be worthwhile.[26] America's cultural inferiority complex played into this equation as well, encouraging those with "highbrow" pretensions to disdain all association with the "low."

European attitudes to popular art, while paralleling those in the United States, were somewhat more conflicted. On the one hand, European intellectuals initially had more respect for such "lowbrow" American art forms as film and jazz (just as they did for Grandma Moses) because these art forms seemed to offer an alternative to the aesthetic values favored by the aristocracy and the bourgeoisie. On the other hand, the European avant-garde's efforts to promote an "art of the people" proved to be at odds with the artists' own elitist sensibilities. From Victorian England to Weimar-era Germany, attempts to produce enlightened art for the masses failed. The British Arts-and-Crafts movement, the Austrian Wiener Werkstätte, and the German Bauhaus all manufactured objects that were too costly for the majority, while the political posters of the Russian Constructivists and the Dadaists were too obscure to be generally effective. And while American popular art might look good from the opposite side of the Atlantic, seen up close it was indelibly marked by the commercial hand of capitalism.[27] Left-leaning European artists finally had to concede that, far from being harbingers of a new socialist aesthetic, popular tastes were generated via a symbiotic relationship with the marketplace.

With the end of the Cold War, the notion that art is supposed to serve as a bulwark against capitalism has become as antiquated as the other ideological trappings of the socialist dream. Far from tainting art, money now adds to its allure, and contemporary art stars are hardly less glamorous than rock or movie stars. As "high" artists increasingly absorb influences from "low" culture, which in turn draws inspiration from above, the categories "high" and "low" become almost impossible to separate. There is no way back to an expressive Eden where art was untouched by power, commerce, and civilization. In acknowledging this, we must also accept that such an Eden never did exist. Perhaps for the first time, we can recognize that the barrier of popularity that separated Grandma Moses from the "serious" artists of her day was nothing more than an illusory conceit, with no bearing on the substance of her art.

Every generation rewrites history in its own image and in the process sets its own standards of quality. Yesterday's ironclad hierarchy of artist-heroes has today been replaced by a comparatively undifferentiated flow of cultural artifacts. While some deplore this leveling as an abdication of qualitative standards, it must be remembered that the earlier standards were abandoned because of their inherent inadequacy. An artist like Grandma Moses virtually disappeared from the art world because of the shifting labels that were applied to her—"naïve," "primitive," "folk," "popular," "commercial"—and those, associated with the major modern movements, that were not. Amidst the general sorting-out of values and historical narratives taking place at the dawn of the twenty-first century, the story of Grandma Moses is ripe for re-examination.

It is hoped that the present exhibition will provide the impetus for a more thorough evaluation of Moses' achievement than has previously been possible. The authors whose contributions appear in this catalogue have tackled the myth and reality of Grandma Moses from various angles. Roger Cardinal meticulously analyzes Moses' working methods, in the process providing an illuminating view into the mind of the self-taught painter. Lynda Hartigan investigates the nature of memory and imagination, exploring the ways in which the two merge in Moses' paintings.

Michael Hall and Judith Stein focus on the manner whereby the artist's public image was constructed. Stein looks in particular at the role that gender played in shaping her reputation. Hall concludes that Moses, far from being anomalous, was in some respects very much a product of the art and social framework of her era.

To be sure, the paintings of Grandma Moses lie at the heart of the present effort. The exhibition is divided into five principal groupings, bookended by sections devoted, respectively, to Moses' early and late work. One prevalent myth has it that folk artists do not develop, but as the exhibition shows, just about all artists of merit do grow and change, given the time and opportunity. The three central portions of our presentation—titled "Work and Happiness," "Place and Nature," and "Play and Celebration"—explore the most important themes that recur in Moses' work. Collectively, these themes champion the fundamental American values that made Moses such a potent force at the dawn of the nuclear age. Much twentieth-century art was riddled with anxiety; Moses was one of the few to speak optimistically. Linking "memory and hope" (as she phrased it in her autobiography),[28] Moses put forth the daring proposition that the past might after all be used to secure the future, because the basic human virtues of work, home, and community do not change. These are the terms that Moses' art set for itself, and by which the work must ultimately be judged. ❧ ✢ ❧

NOTES

* I would like to thank Hildegard Bachert, Fay Duftler, and Elizabeth Marcus for patiently following this manuscript through its various drafts and providing innumerable insightful comments along the way, and Ann Barbaro for her superb work on the catalogue entries.

1. The attempt to delineate the interrelationship between modern art and its lowborn brethren inspired the Museum of Modern Art to present two exhibitions, *Primitivism in 20th-Century Art* (1984) and *High/Low* (1990), both of which were subjected to protracted critical assaults. The exhibition *Parallel Visions* at the Los Angeles County Museum of Art (1992–93) focused specifically on the connection between modern art and *Art Brut* (or Outsider Art, as it is commonly known in the United States). Less controversial than the Museum of Modern Art's shows, *Parallel Visions* was notable chiefly for the strength of the *Art Brut* pieces.

2. Two of the leading American institutions devoted to folk art, the Museum of American Folk Art in New York and the Abbey Aldrich Rockefeller Folk Art Center in Williamsburg, Virginia, apply a very liberal interpretation of the term. Both exhibit a variety of paintings in addition to the sort of group-oriented artifacts that conform to a traditionalist's definition of the folk genre. But many theorists object to such a catholic approach to folk art, especially when the field is stretched to include the extremely marginal work popularly known as Outsider Art. Often the issue of definition is skirted by using the neutral generic term "self-taught," even though the field does include some artists who received rudimentary training. In this essay, the terms "folk" and "self-taught" are used more or less interchangeably.

3. Grandma Moses, *My Life's History*, edited by Otto Kallir (New York: Harper and Row, 1952), 138.

4. Howard Devree, *New York Times*, October 13, 1940.

5. *Art News*, October 26, 1940.

6. Sidney Janis, *They Taught Themselves: American Primitive Painters of the 20th Century* (New York: Dial Press, 1942; reprint, Hudson River Press, 1999).

7. *New York World-Telegram*, November 15, 1940.

8. *New York Journal American*, October 8, 1940.

9. *Washington Daily News*, January 10, 1941.

10. In this, Grandma Moses' career parallels that of Norman Rockwell, an artist whom she knew personally and with whom she is frequently compared. The ongoing re-evaluation of Rockwell's achievement has bearing as well upon our current reconsideration of Moses' artistic legacy.

11. Mark Twain, *Life on the Mississippi* (New York: Random House, 1994), 287.

12. Alfred H. Barr Jr., "Preface and Acknowledgment," in *Masters of Popular Painting* (New York: The Museum of Modern Art, 1938), 9.

13. "Tailor-Made Show Suits Nobody," *Art Digest* (July 1943): 15.

14. "Master of the Two Left Feet," *Art Digest* (July 1943).

15. René d'Harnoncourt replaced Barr as Director in 1943, but since Barr persisted in showing up for work every day, he was eventually made Director of Museum Collections.

16. Jane Kallir, *Grandma Moses: The Artist Behind the Myth* (New York: Clarkson N. Potter, 1982), 21–23.

17. "About Grandma Moses," *New York World-Telegram*, May 21, 1947.

18. "The Low Down," *Oakland [Cal.] Neighborhood Journal*, November 23, 1949.

19. Aline B. Louchheim, "Americans in Italy—Biennale Representation Raises Many Issues," *New York Times*, September 10, 1950.
20. Jane Kallir, *Grandma Moses*, 21.
21. The American government eventually came to support abstract art because abstraction did not have the leftist political taint of Depression-era social realism; abstract art, therefore, could be more readily hailed as a banner of democratic freedom in the fight against Communism. For an in-depth discussion of these issues, see Frances Stonor Saunders, *Who Paid the Piper? The CIA and the Cultural Cold War* (London: Granta Books, 1999), 252–78.
22. *Art News and Review* (England), April 28, 1956.
23. Jane Kallir, *Grandma Moses*, 28–29.
24. Grandma Moses was the beneficiary of a number of technological innovations, such as the first live-remote radio broadcast (in 1946), an early television "docu-drama" (in 1952), and a rare use of color television (for an Edward R. Murrow interview in 1955, when very few Americans actually owned color television sets).
25. Moses, *My Life's History*, 138.
26. André Malraux expressed this widespread prejudice when he wrote: "It would be rash to assume that the emotions the modern crowd expects from art are necessarily profound ones; on the contrary, they are often superficial and puerile and rarely go beyond a taste for violence, for religious or amatory sentimentalism, a spice of cruelty, collective vanity and sensuality" (*The Voices of Silence* [Garden City, N.Y.: Doubleday, 1953], 515). More recently, Tom Wolfe, reviewing the twentieth century's standard of taste, noted: "Art worldlings regarded popularity as skill's live-in slut. Popularity meant shallowness. Rejection by the public meant depth. And truly hostile rejection very likely meant greatness" ("The Artist the Art World Couldn't See," *New York Times Magazine*, January 2, 2000, 10).
27. This reality was particularly disillusioning to the European intellectuals who came to the United States in the 1930s and 1940s seeking refuge from Hitler. Foremost among these was the sociologist Theodor W. Adorno, who flogged the topic constantly. See, for example, his "Scientific Experiences of a European Scholar in America," in Donald Fleming and Bernard Bailyn (eds.), *The Intellectual Migration* (Cambridge: Harvard University Press, 1969), 338–70.
28. Moses, *My Life's History*, 3.

Picturing Myth and Meaning for a Culture of Change

Michael D. Hall

"Bring me Moses!"
(Pharaoh Rameses II, 13th century B.C.)

"Bring me Grandma Moses!"
(President Harry S. Truman, 1949)

What's in a name, anyway? Maybe more than one might think, especially if the name is Moses. In fact, the Moses name, with all its attendant lore and belief, provides a frame of reference for this whole essay—one that probes the sociocultural history wherein a little old farm lady became a unique and mythic figure in the landscape of American art (fig. 1).*

Let's start out with a short synopsis of the biblical Moses story. It commences with a recounting of the prophet's birth among the oppressed people of a humble, pastoral clan. Then there is the "discovery" episode (bulrushes and the Pharaoh's daughter). Next, there are the years of favor at court, followed by an exodus—change sweeps over the land. Ultimately, a great sea divides and a lot of people drown. Finally, Moses grows very old, regaling the faithful with endless visions of a Promised Land. At the conclusion of the story, the ancient seer dies, the people find a home, and a myth begins.

It turns out that the biblical Moses and Grandma Moses have a lot more in common than just their names. Grandma Moses began life as a humble farm wife. She rose to glory as an artist after the age of eighty. She survived a flood of change in the world around her and grew very old painting vistas of her promised land. She was very much a Moses in the great tradition of her name. Though she never found herself building pyramids and overseeing throngs of slaves, Grandma Moses, in her own right, did play a role in a real-life cultural drama as sweeping as any that might have been concocted by Cecil B. De Mille. The life and career of

Grandma Moses, *The First Automobile*, detail of plate 13

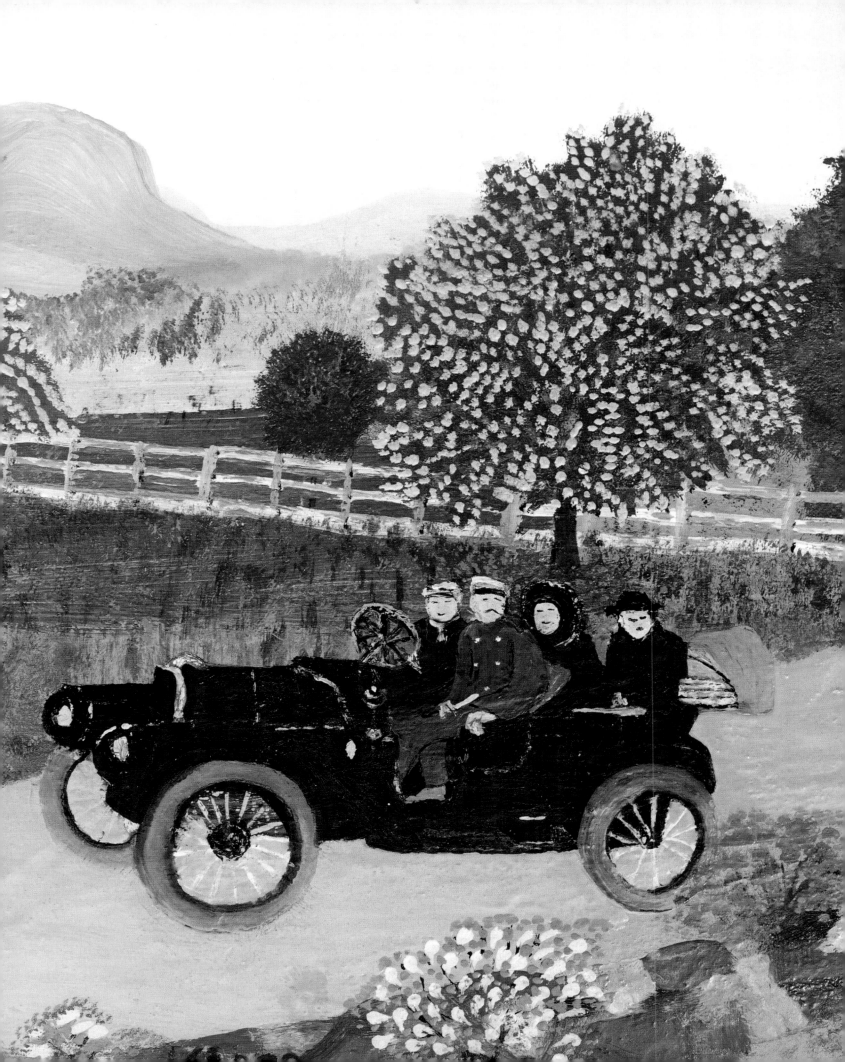

Grandma Moses are epic because they intertwine so completely with the epic story of twentieth-century America.

The Grandma Moses story always references the humble circumstances from which she came. Humble beginnings provide the key to a proper understanding of her success. Biographies of individuals who rise to prominence from humble beginnings strike a deep chord in the American popular imagination: the "up from nothing" stories of Abraham Lincoln, Thomas Edison, and Elvis Presley come to mind. In this country, we tend to place a higher value on good things that seem to come from nothing than on good things that come from something. We esteem things of seemingly autogenous character because we deem them inherently "clean" and miraculous in nature. They bespeak authenticity and we appreciate them as "real." Maybe this is why the popular American mind has had such a durable love affair with the idea of folk culture—the humble, "natural," unself-conscious culture we imagine as the antithesis of our own artificial technological society. We cyclically rediscover folk music, folk art, folk medicine, and all manner of folk customs and foodways—stuff we perceive as innately tied to a generative and good earth.

Long before the twentieth-century popular press discovered Grandma Moses, it found one of its first great humble folk celebrities in the figure of Charles Lindbergh. Lindbergh's story showed the modern press just how well the humble hero scenario played to the American people. The aviator's 1927 transatlantic flight became folkloric and mythic as the press exploited the image of Lindbergh—the humble, high-flying, heart-land mail-carrier—grabbing the glory of the first solo Atlantic crossing from a pack of rich, highborn competitors. Lindbergh's roots in the stolid mid-west, his closeness with his mother, and his shy boyishness all fed the American appetite for things "real," down-home, and humble. Affectionate feelings come easily for such traits because their perceived "commonness" renders them nonthreatening. After Lindbergh, the popular media became ever more watchful for any and all humble heroes who might wander down the American road.

In the world of American art culture, something clearly separate from but decidedly related to the idea of "the humble" evolved at just about the time that Lindbergh was first flying the mail. In modern art circles, the idea of the humble, with its attendant connotations of simple, earthy, and naïve, came to resonate with the idea of the primal, a central construct in the modernist canon. Modern artists sought (among other things) to rebuild art from the base of its raw, primal essence. They

Fig. 1. Grandma Moses on cover of *LIFE* magazine, September 19, 1960. Courtesy Time, Inc.

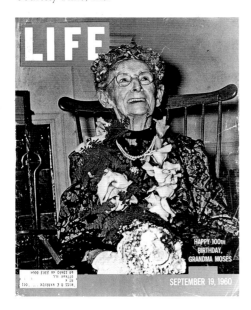

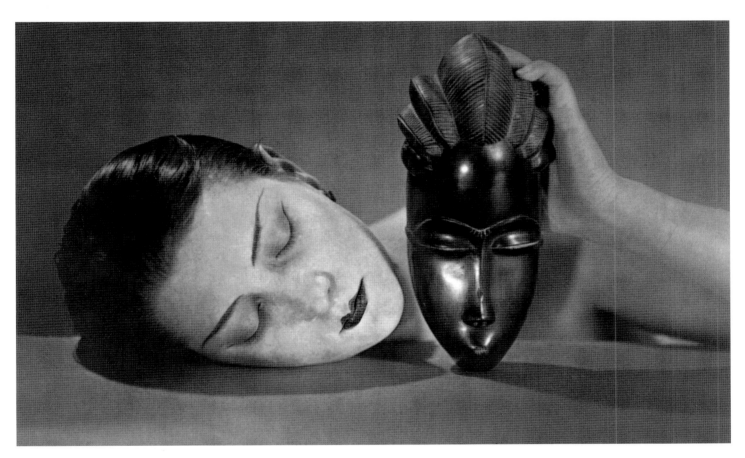

believed that this essence could be found in the art of "primitive" cultures and in the art of naïves and children. As a consequence, they appropriated "primitive" art (fig. 2) as "a means to dignify their own use of simplified forms, arbitrary perspective, and unmixed color."[1] By the beginning of the twentieth century, several of the most famous French Post-Impressionists had already "discovered" and collected the naïve paintings of their contemporary Henri Rousseau. In the United States, modern artists were a bit slower to admire folk and naïve art, but when they did, their interest created a conduit that transported works by a number of folk and naïve artists into the world of American modern art.

As early as 1923, the New York art dealer Stephan Bourgeois declared: "For the first time in its history, America is on a sound foundation of thought. The future belongs to the Naïve and the children."[2] Curiously, Bourgeois at that time was exhibiting works by a group of modernist painters in his gallery and had singled out the precisionists George Ault and Stefan Hirsch to identify as "Naïves." By 1928, however, works by bona fide naïves came into the art marketplace as New York's Downtown

Fig. 2. Man Ray, *Noire et Blanche*, 1926. Gelatin silver print, 6 ³/4 x 8 ⁷/8 inches (17.1 x 22.4 cm). The Museum of Modern Art, New York. Gift of James Thrall Soby. Copy Print © 2000 The Museum of Modern Art, New York. © Man Ray Trust/Artists Rights Society (ARS), New York/ADAGP, Paris

Gallery, under the direction of Edith Halpert, began showing nineteenth-century American "primitive" portraits and landscapes alongside contemporary modernist works created by artists such as Charles Sheeler, William Zorach, and Stuart Davis. Halpert had been inspired to introduce this work into her gallery after seeing folk art in the collections of such American modernists as Robert Laurent, Yasuo Kuniyoshi, and Elie Nadelman.

By 1930, the humble genre of folk and naïve art had so thoroughly impacted the thinking of the art public that major museums in several American cities began to mount full-scale exhibitions of this work. Foremost among these were the Newark Museum in New Jersey and the Museum of Modern Art in New York. Humble things (including humble art) were definitely a part of the emerging art life of modern America. In a brief foreword to the catalogue for a 1931 exhibition of folk sculpture, Newark's director, Arthur Egner, presented the case for folk art as both a cultural affirmation and a critique. His foreword then proceeded to endorse the exhibition as exemplary within the scheme of folk art interpretation first brought to the museum by his predecessor, John Cotton Dana:

> *What is so stimulating about the present exhibit is that we have in it a truer and more indigenous expression of the American artistic sense because of its very absence of pretense and importance. . . . Here is another persuasive example of the truth of John Cotton Dana's constant assertion that articles of common and humble character may well be as significant expressions of Art as products of cost and circumstance.*[3]

Still another cultural phenomenon suffused with the idea of humbleness sprouted from American soil in the 1920s and 1930s: it might be described as the "dream of home"—the cultural imaginings of a nation reconsidering its own proud but humble domestic identity. The dislocations Americans experienced after World War I and on through the Depression no doubt engendered and amplified this dream. The consequences of this cultural preoccupation were many. American antiques became a rage. Local historical societies sprang up everywhere. Country music emerged to find its popular audience and, most important for our study here, the art movement called Regionalism was born. In the Regionalist period, artists all across the United States became part of their country's efforts to strengthen its shaky sense of national identity. They began painting works intended to celebrate the variegated American landscape as well to record the traditions and daily activities of Americans residing in the country's many distinctive locales.

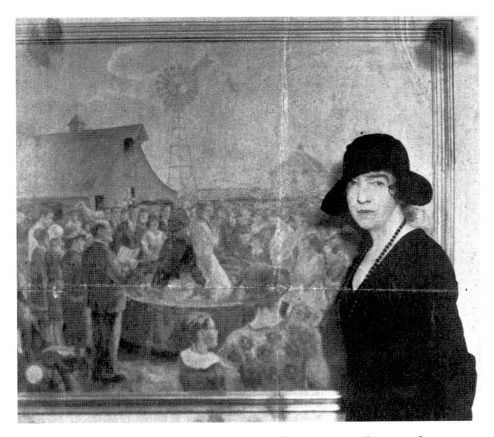

Fig. 3. Newspaper clipping from the *New York Times*, November 22, 1931. Photograph of Gertrude Vanderbilt Whitney standing beside the painting *Baptism in Kansas* by John Steuart Curry in the Whitney Museum of American Art. Maynard Walker papers, Archives of American Art, Smithsonian Institution, Washington, D.C. Photograph of clipping by Lee B. Ewing

Regionalism and its dream of home took root everywhere as the 1930s unfolded. Grant Wood began painting the rolling farmlands of his Iowa at the same moment that Reginald Marsh started recording street life in his New York. Simultaneously, Charles Burchfield became famous for his moody watercolor depictions of the industrial and rural landscape in and around his Buffalo, New York. Acknowledging the appeal of the American Scene movement, Gertrude Vanderbilt Whitney posed for press photographers in front of a Regionalist painting by the Kansas-born painter John Steuart Curry as she opened her new Whitney Museum of American Art (fig. 3). The picture, *Baptism in Kansas*, portrays a country preacher, knee-deep in a stock-watering trough, poised to immerse a prayerful Kansas girl into the baptismal waters of the makeshift Jordan River that swirls around the tails of his frock coat. The Regionalist movement provided a displaced and disheartened America with a collage of home. On canvas and on the walls of many of the nation's post offices and other public buildings, some of the most talented artists of the era set themselves to the task of creating and enriching this collage.

Thus, a set of cultural vectors was poised for convergence prior to Grandma Moses' first solo exhibition in New York in 1940. The modern art world was searching out the raw, the uninhibited, and the primal in various forms of nonacademic art. The popular press was looking for yet another "up from nothing" real-life hero to celebrate in tomorrow's early edition. And a Depression-shocked society, obsessed with dreams of home, was seeking to recast its national identity in the easel paintings and public murals produced by the artists of the American Scene.

In retrospect, it seems almost inevitable that this convergence produced the discovery of a little old lady folk artist (a jam-maker-cum-painter) who painted her memories of home in the very particular terms of her own regional/local life experience and whose painting style could be called "primitive." There was destiny in the discovery of Grandma Moses just as there had been in the discovery of the biblical Moses in the bulrushes along the Nile. As we have seen, a critical assessment of the cultural and artistic milieu of the period leading up to the discovery of Grandma Moses seriously challenges the claim by one of her early "discoverers" that her paintings "contain nothing that would seem 'interesting' to a modern public [and that] they have no connection with what we like to call 'the artistic expression of our time.'"[4]

The discovery of Grandma Moses came right on cue. In the mid-1930s Grandma Moses was an unknown. She was a "hobby" painter, unaware of possessing any special talent. Although a visitor to Hoosick Falls could have purchased Moses' early pictures out of the exhibit she maintained at the local drugstore, there is no record that any of them ever did so. The circle of early Moses collectors seems to have been made up exclusively of friends and family who shared the artist's regional life experience and who received their pictures as gifts. All this changed in 1938 when Louis Caldor, a sophisticated collector with a strong interest in modern art, chanced upon the paintings in this very drugstore. His familiarity with trends in the New York art world inclined him to understand Moses' paintings as art rather than as memorabilia—as "primitive" rather than as merely quaint. The newcomer quickly shared his discovery with others whom he knew in the New York art gallery scene. The more astute among them reinforced his conviction that Grandma's pictures did, indeed, have value as primitive art. The "discovery" process culminated with the introduction of the works to an art public already primed to admire and consume them. In short, Grandma Moses' emergence as an artist turned on a shift in the awareness of her work from one arena of perception to another. It was not the work that changed, but rather the context within which it was seen and understood.

No less a figure than the renowned dealer and collector Sidney Janis became a Moses booster early on. Janis was an important spokesman for modern art's embrace of the primitive. In his book *They Taught Themselves: American Primitive Painters of the 20th Century* (1942), Janis summed up the modernist view of the art produced by Moses and other naïves who were being exhibited at that time in New York:

> *Paradoxically, although the self-taught artist does not make a selection from the complex and developed painting tradition of today, he often independently achieves isolated results that parallel those of cultivated expressions. . . . For instance, knowing nothing of Cubism, he may paint a picture in which a circulating viewpoint is used, or one that is counterpoised like a cubist painting. Knowing nothing of Surrealism, he may create enigmatic surface textures, use literary ideas and fantasies that are closely akin to Surrealism. . . . With many of the self-taught painters, psychological factors which are tied up with inner conflicts of various kinds are of primary importance. . . . On the other hand, there is a primitive character and a true primitive synthesis in the work of certain very advanced moderns, for they too embody the force and austerity of purpose that accompany any initial struggle with art forms. . . . Léger is a primitive poet of the machine as Rousseau is of nature.[5]*

Grandma Moses was selected as one of only thirty artists to be featured in Janis's book. Face to face with the artist, Janis was captivated by the Moses persona. Adopting the writing style and tone of a popular journalist, the author recalled his impression of the artist on the day he first visited with her on her farm: "Small and slim, Mother Moses is a tiny dynamo. Darting about with a surprisingly springy step, she is always ready for fun; her keen wit and animated response are trigger-fast."[6] Turning to Moses' work, however, Janis employed the more formal language and objective tone that inflected his earlier discourse on the primitive and the modern. In his assessment of Grandma Moses as a painter in the modern American grain, Janis wrote: "Possessed of a spontaneous and ingenuous compositional sense, a fresh spirit and an aptitude for color luminosity, she gives to her best work a pictorial quality that is sprightly and distinctively American."[7]

Moses' rise to favor in the popular press followed soon after her discovery by the art world. The media made Grandma Moses its new barefoot hero and the public couldn't get enough. Grandma, for her part, obviously had the right blend of pluck, self-effacing modesty, and coy charm to beguile the press and thus to feed the celebrity machine of which she so quickly became a part. At any rate, from the day she first made headlines in the press, Grandma Moses attracted reporters and commentators who fixated their accounts on the "humbleness" of all things Grandma. An excerpt from a *New York Journal American* news story published in the fall of 1940 is fairly brimming over with the sort of homilies the popular media endlessly reconfigured to describe Grandma's amazing rise from humbleness to the pinnacle of a still humble greatness:

> *In 1936 Anna Mary Robertson Moses, then 76, exhibited strawberry preserves and paintings at the Cambridge, N.Y. fair. For her strawberries she won a blue ribbon. For her paintings she got no more than the razz-berry. But today in New York those same paintings, praised by art critics, are bringing as high as $200 each.*[8]

Announcing "Grandma Moses in person" at the Gimbel's department store's Thanksgiving festival in 1940, the *New York Herald Tribune* trumpeted: "She's the white-haired girl of the U.S.A. who turned from her strawberry patch to painting the American scene at the wonderful age of 80. You'll see her."[9] Within twenty years, the white-haired girl had become a legend. In 1960, the *New York Journal American* reported that "the story of Grandma Moses will undoubtedly go down in the folk lore of our nation, along with Casey Jones and Carry Nation."[10]

But let's not get ahead of ourselves. Beyond the avant-garde's fascination with the primitive and the popular media's delight in "the white-haired girl," we still need to consider the third of the cultural permissions that catapulted Grandma Moses into the American spotlight: the appealing nature of the subject matter of Moses' work. This entails a look at the forces that folded Moses' paintings into the American Scene and the movement identified as Regionalism.

It is important to understand that the art world of the Regionalists was decidedly not the art world of Robert Laurent, Stuart Davis, Edith Halpert, and other pioneers of American modernism. It was the world of Grant Wood, Thomas Hart Benton, and a host of painters committed to an idea of American art as a figurative/narrative/landscape expression, fully pluralist, democratic, and populist in its outlook. In fact, one could say that Regionalism formed a bridge between a popular culture that viewed Moses as a folk hero and a high culture that sought nascent modernism in the style of her paintings. The Regionalists admired the way she threaded the theme of home throughout her work. As the new postwar hegemony grew, Americans became predictably nostalgic about the regional pluralism they felt was eroding around them. Having arrived on the scene in 1940, Moses fit immediately into the Regionalist model created by the coterie of writers and painters who, "when addressing

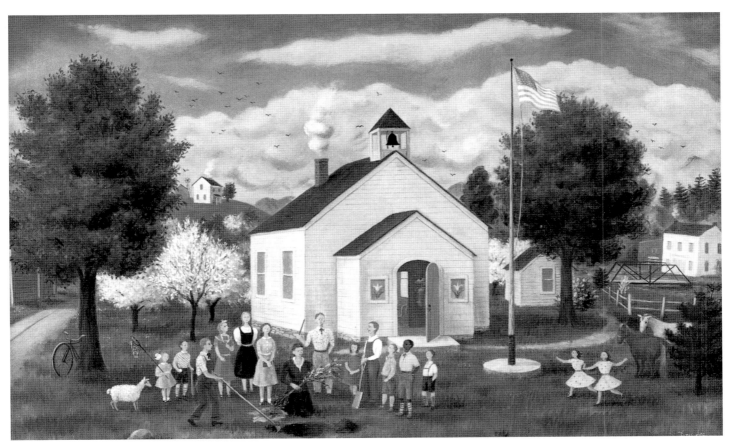

Fig. 4. Doris Lee, *Arbor Day*, 1941.
Oil on canvas, 22 x 34 inches
(55.9 x 86.4 cm). Ostrove-Klein Collection.
Photograph by Charles Cloud III

New England subjects during the 1930s were similarly inclined to register the present in terms of an old-fashioned rural past."[11]

While Moses became a part of the Regionalist scene late, she managed to outlive it by more than a decade. Canonic Regionalism had grown out of the prolonged and serious economic privation of the Depression. It reflected the notion of the 1930s that industrial capitalism "was deeply flawed, a system both stifling and inhumane and, most disturbing of all, virtually impossible to control."[12] Moses came to the movement at precisely the moment when the economic stress that had engendered the creation of the idiom was about to be relieved by the boom created by World War II. By the 1940s, Regionalism had lost some of its social urgency and was being transformed into a kind of "feel good" form of cultural tourism. Grandma Moses (keeping the good old days alive) found her paintings hanging comfortably with those of the 1940s pantheon of Regionalist greats. For example, in the fall of 1947, the Rockford (Illinois) Art Association opened its exhibition season with an October showing of new works by the renowned Michigan Regionalist

Zoltan Sepeshy; its November calendar featured a solo exhibit of the paintings of Grandma Moses. Earlier that same year, Moses received a special merit award from the Art Directors Club of New York in the company of three very well-known American Scene masters: Thomas Hart Benton, Adolf Dehn, and Doris Lee. Moses' selection for this citation becomes all the more interesting when we note that Doris Lee was a fully trained artist who had become well known for her own distinctive "neo folk art" style (fig. 4). A 1948 exhibition at the gallery at the University of Kansas presented a grouping of Moses' paintings alongside those by still other painters of the American Scene, including Gladys Rockmore Davis, Isaac Soyer, Waldo Pierce, and Philip Guston. Most significantly, the major survey exhibition *Painting in the United States, 1948*, held at the Carnegie Museum in Pittsburgh, displayed Moses' paintings in the company of a virtual "who was who" of Regionalism: Charles Rain, Thomas Hart Benton, Charles Burchfield, Peter Hurd, Andrew Wyeth, and Millard Sheets among them.

American political culture also recognized a good thing when it came along. The great Moses moment may well have been the day in 1949 when, at a ceremony in Washington, D.C., Harry S. Truman, as president of the United States, stepped up to present an outstanding achievement award to a self-taught painter who, in a single decade, had found her way from the less-than-auspicious environs of Eagle Bridge, New York, into the very center of American life. A short time later the *Voice of America* published an article entitled "Grandma Moses—Primitive but Modern." The article confirmed what the public, the art world, and the president had all come to understand and admire:

> In these paintings Americans see their native land in characteristic moods, but stripped of pretense or glamor. Grandma omits the superfluous features of a landscape; in painting it she reveals the fundamental harmony between life and nature. Such work inspires many people with a desire to return to a simple existence.[13]

The following year, Moses marked her ninetieth birthday at a special celebration in Arlington, Vermont, attended by a host of friends, including her famous admirer Norman Rockwell. Like her biblical namesake, Grandma Moses had risen far above her humble beginnings to find favor and celebrity amidst the political and cultural nobility of her time.

Nothing, however, lasts forever. Even as Moses received her award from President Truman, the art world, which had sought her out and admired her, was quickly being dismantled and replaced by a radically different art culture and marketplace. The popular culture that had so adored Grandma Moses was also changing. In the 1950s Americans would become obsessed with Hollywood, cars, suburbs, kitchen gadgets, the Cold War, and their own newly invented "youth culture." Aged celebrities, provincial art, and the old homestead were not the stuff of the new.

As the waters of American culture parted at mid-century, the first casualty was the American Scene. From the early 1940s on, various critics began denouncing Regionalism as a "low brow" art of nostalgia. Typical of these was Samuel Kootz, who took occasion in 1943 to publicly lambaste the "paint America" credo of the Regionalists:

> *I consider this belated discovery of America a rather narrow ecstasy. I distrust the genial camaraderie. News reporting of this sort, which is propaganda at its lowest state, seems to me as dead as yesterday's headlines—because painting should be concerned with ideas and sensations far removed from this methodical theft of America's ostentatious surfaces.*[14]

Convinced that American artists should express an international rather than a regional perspective in their work, Kootz asserted that the true painters of America's new age should be "concerned with what is going on in the world, rather than in some regional prairie or other local rabbit-warren."[15]

The denunciations of Regionalism became even more shrill in the 1950s. The very same Regionalist vision that had inspired the Hallmark Card company to print and merchandise 16,000,000 Grandma Moses Christmas cards in 1947, was thoroughly passé in the art world by the year 1950. In 1951 Moses' work was rejected for inclusion in an exhibition of American art assembled by the Metropolitan Museum of Art in New York. The art world was changing rapidly, and all the artists who had been associated with the American Scene movement found themselves in trouble professionally. The entire category of art involving regional, narrative, and expositive subject matter (the very category that had once extended artistic credibility to Grandma Moses' paintings of New England life) came under heavy fire. The Regionalists and their paintings were branded conservative, xenophobic, and even fascist. In response, many of the artists abandoned their figurative-landscape styles and "went abstract." Still others, like Charles Burchfield, turned their work inward toward a more personal or mystical form of expression. Such change was not an option for Grandma Moses. She just kept on painting the stories and places she had always known.

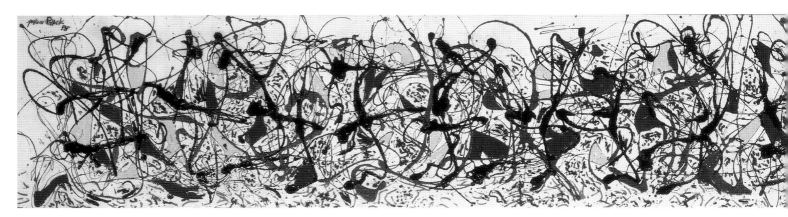

Fig. 5. Jackson Pollock, *Summertime, Number 9a*, 1948. Oil, enamel, and house paint on canvas, 33 ³/₈ x 218 ¹/₂ inches (84.8 x 555 cm). Tate Gallery, London, Great Britain. Copyright © 2000 Pollock-Krasner Foundation/Artists Rights Society (ARS), New York

A second change in the American art world (connected to the collapse of Regionalism but still separate from it) also impacted Moses' artistic viability in the 1950s. The same postwar optimism that inclined Americans to newly imagine themselves as important players on the global stage created a condition wherein many in the nation's art community became embarrassed by the taint of provincialism so evident in their modern art. Somehow, it seemed that American painters were always playing catch-up when it came to the modern. They had always come late to every radical style from Impressionism to Fauvism and Cubism. Vitalized by the postwar challenge, a new and aggressive generation of painters, critics, and museum professionals set out to create an art style that would befit America's new global preeminence.

If the old art had been derivative, provincial, intimate, and accessible, the new would be original, cosmopolitan, grand, and difficult. If the old art celebrated community and the specifics of place, the new would explore the self and the universals to be discovered beyond the particulars of the local. By 1955, the art style known as Abstract Expressionism had fully evolved to become just such an art. As a style and as a cultural statement, it quickly became an art form that America's official art culture could tout as its own original creation. In 1958, the Museum of Modern Art organized an exhibition featuring the new style and titled it *The New American Painting.* Sponsored by the museum, the show then toured for two years through eight European countries. For the first time—ever—the United States was exporting modern art rather than importing it. The museum's longtime champion of American modernism, Alfred H. Barr Jr., wrote the introduction to the exhibition's catalogue. In the spirit of high expectation that surrounded the exhibition, Barr wrote of having watched with great pride and excitement the "development of the artists here represented, their long struggle—with themselves even

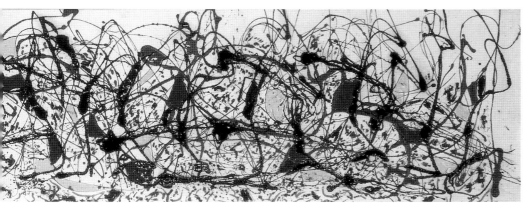

more than with the public—and their present triumph."[16] Along the way, Jackson Pollock, Mark Rothko, Barnett Newman, Franz Kline, and the rest of the Abstract Expressionist group became the new art heroes of a new age (fig. 5).

Splashing paint across a room-sized canvas was not an option for an elderly folk artist. And as for humble, pastoral folk landscapes? They had suddenly become quite uninteresting to an audience both confounded and transfixed by the agitated mindscapes conjured up by the new expressionists.

All of this, however, begs the question: Whatever happened to Grandma Moses through all of this turmoil? Was she really just left to wander in the desert? No, she was not. She could have been, but she found a safe harbor where the Regionalists and even the other naïves of her era could never have gone. She found it in the popular culture that had so adored and mythicized both her and her work over so many years. As the art world convulsed, Grandma Moses found herself privileged to be an artist no longer in need of the art world. Some of this may have been just dumb luck, but I suspect that it is more realistic to credit Moses' special durability to the Moses magic and to the instincts and brilliance of Otto Kallir, the astute dealer-manager who shaped and guided her career from the beginning.

Kallir's instinct seems to have been that Grandma Moses was an artist who need not be assigned to a particular niche in some fixed system of an art ecology. It also seems that Moses herself was disinclined to being neatly packaged and pigeonholed. The two were well matched. Thus it was that when a museum, organizing an exhibition of modern primitives, requested a Moses painting, Kallir obliged. At the same time, however, he was fully willing to provide a Moses picture to another exhibition featuring Regionalist works. The same breadth of perspective

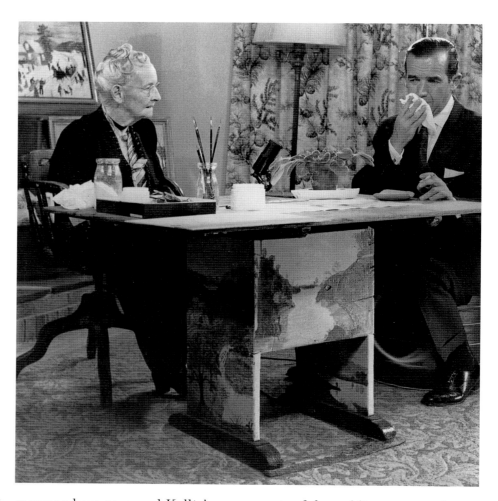

Fig. 6. Grandma Moses being interviewed by Edward R. Murrow for the CBS program *See It Now*, June 29, 1955. Photograph by Otto Kallir

seems to have governed Kallir's assessments of the public exposures he orchestrated in Moses' interest. He knew when to have her show up in Washington for her award, but he also knew when to have Edward R. Murrow travel to Eagle Bridge to film his famous interview in Moses' own living room (fig. 6). The historical record strongly suggests that Kallir grew to understand that Grandma Moses was more than just a painter of rural scenes and certainly more than just a topical personality to parade through the media circus. His genius was that he seems to have appreciated (and represented) Moses as a cultural property to be shared.

To understand the Moses career in this way is to comprehend just what it was that Otto Kallir set in motion when he first presented Grandma Moses at the Galerie St. Etienne in 1940: an artist who could be understood as a grandmother, who painted pictures that could be understood as memories, entered the life of a nation that would endlessly find new utility for just such an artist and just such an art. As early as 1947,

Kallir recognized Grandma Moses' unique capacity to exist as an artist beyond the boundaries of the art culture of which he himself was so much a part. Seemingly in awe, he wrote: "Grandma Moses speaks in her simple words and through her untaught pictures. Hers is a small voice in the great chorus of America, yet it is clear and true, and it is lifted in praise of life and of enduring, humble beauty."[17]

In the confluence of American desires that made a place for a Moses painting on the walls of the White House, we discover the chorus of America finding its small voice. The painting entitled *July Fourth* was shipped from Eagle Bridge to Washington, D.C., in 1952. Other paintings found their way to exhibitions in Europe, where they were received as goodwill ambassadors from the United States. Eight years before the Museum of Modern Art's Abstract Expressionist show went abroad to represent the American avant-garde, Grandma Moses had already presented Europeans with her own brand of Americanism. The painter and her pictures were news, and dailies all across the United States regularly printed the latest Moses update. She became so well known that in 1958, the *Chicago Sun Times* led off its story on the paintings of 69-year-old Jennie Siporin with the pronouncement: "Chicago's art world has its own Grandma Moses (junior style)."[18]

As her 100th birthday approached, Grandma Moses experienced another of the displacements that had regularly marked her life as an artist. Neither she nor her work had changed, but, once again, the context within which they were seen and understood was different. Beyond her Hoosick Valley farm, beyond folk art, Regionalism, modernism, and Abstract Expressionism, even beyond celebrity, Grandma Moses had arrived at a place where both her persona and her idea of art had become a part of the self-imaginings of a nation. The honorary committee sponsoring her 100th birthday party included "former President and Mrs. Truman, Eleanor Roosevelt, Irving Berlin, Jean Cassou, Walt Disney, Lillian Gish, and Thornton Wilder."[19] The list speaks volumes. So too does a short note in the *Los Angeles Times* from 1960 in which the writer instructs his readership that Moses' 100th birthday "provides the occasion for a display of the paintings and other hobbies of the old people of your community."[20] Thus, the artist had even found her way into America's conversation on aging and the problems of the elderly. At the age of 100, Grandma Moses had become many things for many people.

In his greeting to Moses on the occasion of her 101st birthday, President John F. Kennedy wrote: "Your painting and your personal

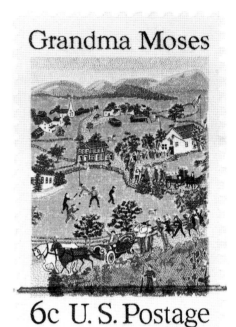

Fig. 7. Grandma Moses commemorative postage stamp with a detail of the painting *July Fourth*; issue date May 1, 1969. Photograph by Fay Duftler

influence continue to play a large and valuable role in our national life."[21] And it is precisely Moses' indelible imprint on our national life that remains. Her passing in 1961 was, in many ways, only a footnote in a life that continues today. The Grandma Moses postage stamp was issued in 1969 (fig. 7). Her work became an important part of the folk-art revival of the 1970s and then resurfaced as a point of reference in the debate on Outsider Art that began in the 1980s and continues into the present. Recent scholarship on art and cultural values has also occasioned a rethinking of Grandma Moses. Her work persistently informs discussions in which artists, curators, and historians consider the ways in which images and memories are connected to our perceptions of meaning. As one commentator has noted, her paintings "established a link between the past and the present that seemed to guarantee the future."[22] Filtering the specifics of time and place through the vagaries of memory and imagination, Grandma Moses successfully transformed her own life into a text on living.

It is interesting to speculate on Moses' potential utility for the future. Surely, the idyllic world she depicted in her paintings slips further and further away. Still, the dream of humble roots, homelands, families, and peace endures. As the Internet becomes yet another force favoring the globalization of culture, issues of self-identity continue to shape our cultural politics—the politics of difference. Our idea that a person or a community can (and should) have a recognizable and distinct identity will ensure our ongoing search for the "selfness" manifest in things local, regional, tribal, "primitive," and even, provincial. The Promised Land to which Grandma Moses leads us is not a mythic place flowing with milk and maple syrup. Instead, it is a real place with identity and character—a place where this twentieth-century Moses tells us that we can be comfortable with ourselves and still find ways to be fully engaged in the world around us. Penning her own story, the painter at one point briefly mused on the way dreams and life entwine. Rhetorically, she asked: "Did that dream cast its shadows before?"[23] Painting at the table in her bedroom on the farm, she assured us that it did—and that it will again. ❧ ❀ ❧

NOTES

*   I would like to thank Hildegard Bachert at the Galerie St. Etienne in New York for making the gallery's extensive clipping files on Grandma Moses available for this research on a summer weekend when she surely had better things to do.

1.   Beatrix T. Rumford, "Uncommon Art of the Common People: A Review of Trends in the Collecting and Exhibiting of American Folk Art," in *Perspectives on American Folk Art*, edited by Ian M. G. Quimby and Scott T. Swank (New York: W. W. Norton, 1980), 23.

2.   Martin L. Friedman, *The Precisionist View in American Art* (Minneapolis: Walker Art Center, 1960), 12.

3.   Holger Cahill, *American Folk Sculpture* (Newark: The Newark Museum, 1931), 9.

4.   Otto Kallir (ed.), *Grandma Moses: American Primitive* (New York: The Dryden Press, 1946), 15.

5.   Sidney Janis, *They Taught Themselves: American Primitive Painters of the 20th Century* (New York: Dial Press, 1942; reprint, Hudson River Press, 1999), 10–11.

6.   Ibid., 130.

7.   Ibid., 131.

8.   *New York Journal American*, October 8, 1940.

9.   *New York Herald Tribune*, November 14, 1940.

10.   *New York Journal American*, September 7, 1960.

11.   William H. Truettner and Roger B. Stein (eds.), *Picturing Old New England: Image and Memory* (New Haven: Yale University Press, 1999), 112.

12.   Ibid., 118.

13.   "Grandma Moses—Primitive but Modern," *Voice of America*, September–October 1949.

14.   Samuel M. Kootz, *New Frontiers in American Painting* (New York: Hastings House, 1943), 14.

15.   Ibid., 57.

16.   *The New American Painting* (New York: The Museum of Modern Art, 1959), 19.

17.   Otto Kallir, *Grandma Moses: American Primitive*, 36.

18.   David Anderson, "'Go Ahead, Paint Ma' and She Really Did," *Chicago Sun Times*, April 6, 1958, 28.

19.   Otto Kallir, *Grandma Moses* (New York: Harry N. Abrams, 1973), 185.

20.   *Los Angeles Times*, June 3, 1960.

21.   Otto Kallir, *Grandma Moses* (1973), 191.

22.   Jane Kallir, "Grandma Moses," in *Self-Taught Artists of the 20th Century: An American Anthology* (New York: Museum of American Folk Art, 1998), 79.

23.   Otto Kallir, *Grandma Moses* (1973), 271.

The White-Haired Girl: A Feminist Reading

Judith E. Stein

Grandma Moses, *Baking Bread*, detail of plate 20

Fig. 1. Window display at Scribner's, a bookstore in New York, 1952. Photograph by Otto Kallir

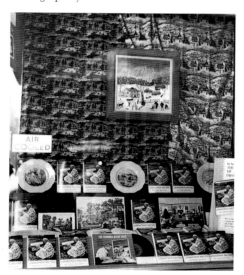

"If asked about lady artists in America," *Cue* magazine wrote in 1953, "most Americans would probably mention one, Grandma Moses."*[1] Indeed, such was Moses' phenomenal popularity in the 1950s that her exhibitions broke attendance records all over the world. A cultural icon, the spry, productive octogenarian was continually cited as an inspiration for housewives, widows and retirees. Her images of America's rural past were transferred to curtains, dresses, cookie jars, and dinnerware (fig. 1), and used to pitch cigarettes, cameras, lipsticks (fig. 2), and instant coffee. Cole Porter, one of her collectors, alluded to the "big dough" pursuing the artist in his lyrics for a 1950 Broadway play.[2] She was a drawing attraction at parades and political rallies, courted by presidents and awarded honorary degrees. At the time of her death at age 101 in 1961, it was estimated that Americans had exchanged over 100 million Christmas cards bearing reproductions of her paintings.[3]

Born a decade past the middle of the nineteenth century, Anna Mary Robertson was raised amidst traditional notions of woman's domestic duties. Hired out as a maid at age 12, she married farmer Thomas Moses at age 27 and bore 10 children, 5 of whom died in infancy. Her adult life was defined by her multiple duties as a farmwife. For three-quarters of her 101 years, art was a luxurious pastime she could not afford. In 1943 she confessed to an interviewer, "I had always wanted to paint, but I just didn't have time until I was seventy-six." Russell Robertson, her farmer father, painted as a hobby, introducing her to grape and berry juice pigments as a young child. She called these girlish efforts "lambscapes."[4]

Her father was a strong influence on the young girl in a variety of ways, giving her a sense of her own powerful potential. Moses often told interviewers: "I was along about 9 years old when my father said one morning at the breakfast table, 'Anna Mary, I had a dream about you last night.' 'What did you dream, pa?' 'I was in a great, big hall and it was full of

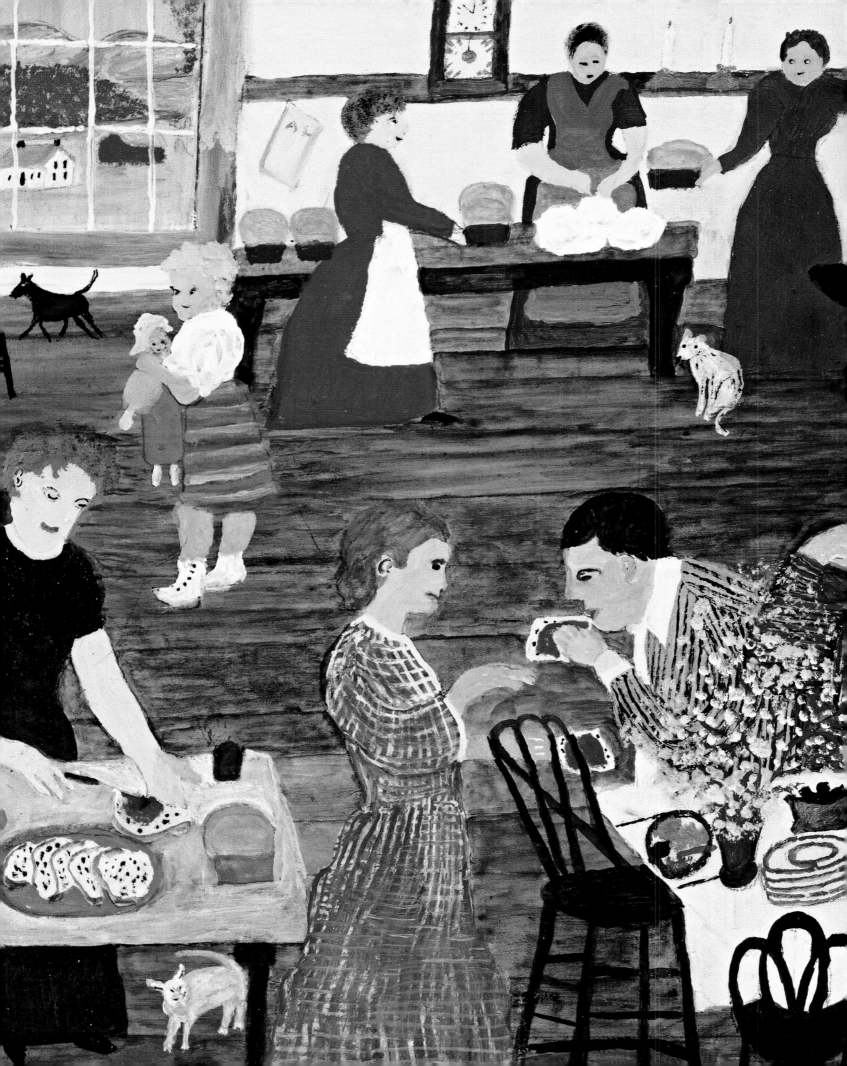

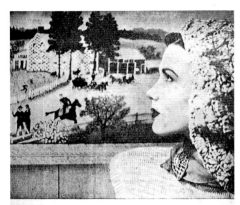
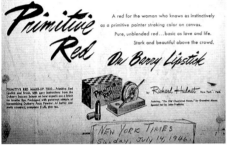

Fig. 2. Advertisement for "Primitive Red" lipstick, published in the *New York Times*, July 14, 1946. Photograph by Fay Duftler

people. And you came walking toward me on the shoulders of men.' As of now, I have often thought of that since."

Russell Robertson also inspired his daughter in ways he could not have imagined. She confided to a writer who had asked about a candy-pink house in one of her canvases: "'Oh, that. Once when I was a little tyke I asked Pa why he couldn't paint our house pink, and he said houses just didn't come pink. 'Well,' with a little twinkle, 'that's a pink house, isn't it?'"[5] To another reporter she related a story that obliquely revealed the power of her father's approval: "[As a child] I used to like to make brilliant sunsets, and when my father would look at them and say: 'Oh, not so bad,' then I felt good. Because I wanted other people to be happy and gay at the things I painted with bright colors."[6]

Like most women raised in the nineteenth century, and in much of the twentieth century, Moses was taught that one of woman's virtues is to please. She seemed to embody the old gender recipe of "sugar and spice and all things nice." For example, in 1946 she commented: "I like pretty things the best, what's the use of painting a picture if it isn't something nice? So I think real hard till I think of something real pretty, and then I paint it."[7] Practical at heart, she returned to painting in her seventies after working with worsted wools for embroidered compositions (see plates 2 and 3): "I did not want my pictures to be eaten by moths, so when my sister, who had taken lessons in art, suggested I try working in oils, I thought it was a good idea. I started in and found that it kept me busy and out of mischief."[8]

She took pride in her own thrift and ingenuity, painting on things that were left over, in her left-over time. She recalled that in the 1930s, she had made her first painting by pulling together a fragment of thrasher canvas, house paint remains, and an old frame. Her sense of accomplishment in her painting was rooted in her ability to make "something from nothing," as Lucy Lippard defined the aesthetic of women's "hobby art" in 1978,[9] and was akin to her quilting work, where she transformed cloth scraps into useful and beautiful objects. Curiously, Lippard is silent on the subject of Moses.

Indeed, feminist critics and scholars were uninterested in Anna Mary Robertson Moses when, in the 1970s, they first began reappraising women's art work, and factoring gender into the analysis of artists' oeuvres and careers.[10] It may be that the artist's very success counted against her. She was neither forgotten nor neglected, and therefore could not be rediscovered. Society in general tends to desexualize elders, and Moses' womanly identity took a backseat to her visibility as a visual bard of the

American rural experience. Too, within the art world, self-taught artists were much more marginalized than they are now. She was neither part of the canon nor the object of revisionist attention.[11]

Forty years after her death, it is more than timely to investigate how gender influenced the course of her extraordinarily successful career. The story begins with collector Louis J. Caldor, who happened upon her paintings in a drugstore in upstate New York. He introduced them to the Manhattan dealer Otto Kallir, who soon gave Moses her first solo exhibition. Kallir mounted *What a Farm Wife Painted* at his recently opened Galerie St. Etienne in October 1940. The matter-of-fact, if infelicitously worded, title communicated both the artist's rural identity and her status as an unschooled "primitive." The *Herald Tribune* reviewer, for example, "went away with the feeling that the most evident thing about the show is the artist's delight in painting the simplicity of the rural country."[12]

In his *New York Times* review of the show, art critic Howard Devree picked up on the title's other implication, namely that she was a self-taught painter. He began by noting that "the 'primitive,' which has been much to the fore in the early season, crops up again."[13] Commenting on her artworks' "simple appeal" and "simple decorative effects," Devree pronounced Mrs. Moses' exhibit "a very creditable show of its kind."[14] *World-Telegram* critic Emily Genauer wrote a singularly thoughtful critique, insightfully noting that Mrs. Moses' "colors are fresh and clear (perhaps because she found expression first through bright embroidery). . . ."[15]

Genauer did not dwell on Moses' status as an unschooled artist. Rather she honed in on the visual strength of her paintings. Describing Moses as possessing "an extraordinary natural talent," she noted that "her textures are rich. Even her drawing is loose and fluid. And her conceptions are at once daring and imaginative." She was particularly taken with a painting entitled *A Fire in the Woods* (see plate 9), which she saw as "a challenge to scores of more sophisticated painters. I think especially of a George Grosz canvas in which a similar theme was handled no more excitingly and with no more assurance and success than Mrs. Moses handled it here."[16] These favorable comments by a respected critic would be cited again and again in the succeeding months, in a variety of publications.

Few early writers looked as carefully at Moses' paintings as had Genauer. In general, the New York press distanced the artist from her creative identity. They commandeered her from the art world, fashioning a rich public image that brimmed with human interest. The Galerie St.

Etienne's debut invitation had referred to the octogenarian artist as "Mrs.," but it was the *New York Herald Tribune* that had called her "Grandma."[17] Although the artist's family and friends addressed her as "Mother Moses" and "Grandma Moses" interchangeably, the press preferred the more familiar and endearing form of address. And "Grandma" she became, in nearly all subsequent published references. Only a few publications by-passed the new locution: a *New York Times Magazine* feature of April 6, 1941; a *Harper's Bazaar* article; and the landmark *They Taught Themselves: American Primitive Painters of the 20th Century*, by the respected dealer and curator Sidney Janis, referred to the artist as "Mother Moses," a title that conveyed more dignity than the colloquial diminutive "Grandma."

But "Grandma Moses" had taken hold. The avalanche of press coverage that followed had little to do with the probity of art commentary. Journalists found that the artist's life made better copy than her art. For example, in a discussion of her debut, an *Art Digest* reporter gave a charming, if simplified, account of the genesis of Moses' turn to painting, recounting her desire to give the postman "a nice little Christmas gift."[18] Not only would the dear fellow appreciate a painting, concluded Grandma, but "it was easier to make than to bake a cake over a hot stove." After quoting from Genauer and other favorable reviews in the New York papers, the report concluded with a folksy supposition: "To all of which Grandma Moses perhaps shakes a bewildered head and repeats, 'Land's Sakes.'" Flippantly deeming the artist's achievements a marker of social change, he noted: "When Grandma takes it up then we can be sure that art, like the bobbed head, is here to stay."

A month after her New York gallery debut, Gimbel's department store made Moses the focus of its Thanksgiving festival, and invited the artist to speak at its Thanksgiving forum. Although she had seen no reason to attend her October opening at the Galerie St. Etienne, she now agreed to journey to the city for the first time since 1917. Addressing an audience of Long Island, Westchester, Staten Island, and Queens club women who had been assembled at Gimbel's for a Thanksgiving table-setting contest, she talked about Thanksgiving customs in her childhood.[19] "'Artist Just by Hobby 'Doesn't Mind Fuss,'" declared a headline reporting the event in the *New York Times* of November 15. The press began to favor a "just us folks" approach to Moses, reveling in examples of her "uncitified" ways.

Besides featuring Moses as a speaker, Gimbel's mounted an exhibition in its auditorium of fifty of her paintings (fig. 3). Store officials capitalized on her identity as a farmwife, and the press followed suit.

The *New York World-Telegram* led off its coverage with the tantalizing observation that "El Greco and Raphael and Van Gogh couldn't have done it; Picasso and Wood and Dali couldn't do it. But Grandma Moses did it."[20] *It* was the simple demonstration of domestic skills. Gimbel's had supplemented Moses' art display with "a table beneath the paintings spread [with] samples of Grandma's culinary talents—home-baked bread, rolls and cake, plus some of the preserves which won her prizes at the county fair." The public ate it up, so to speak.

When, weeks later, her paintings were shown at the Whyte Gallery in Washington, D.C., one writer would make the same point with words: "She concocted these paintings much as she made her prize-winning jams, with care, with naturalness and using the homely ingredients that she found about her."[21] The press loved to pair and contrast her art and her cooking,[22] and the writer Eugenia Sheppard would cleverly conflate these spheres by commending Moses for her "delicious paintings."[23] It is interesting to contemplate this kind of commentary when recalling that in 1950, the young Lee Krasner chose to be engaged in making currant jelly when a *New Yorker* writer came for a visit at the home she shared with her husband Jackson Pollock.[24]

Gimbel's savvy publicists had a field day writing copy for the newspaper advertisements alerting New Yorkers to Moses' visit. The ad in the *New York Herald Tribune* on November 14 enthused:

> *Grandma's the biggest artistic rave since Currier & Ives hit the country. She's* <u>the white-haired girl of the USA</u> *who turned from her strawberry patch to painting the American scene at the wonderful age of 80. You'll see her. You'll see the first complete loan exhibition of her wool paintings and American primitive paintings. Come hear what gave her the urge to buy paints and try her brushes on her threshing cloth. Gimbel's Eleventh Floor.*
> *[emphasis added]*

Framed as an antiquated "girl next door," New Yorkers took the all-American Grandma to their hearts.

In the years following Moses' debut, the popular press often underscored her identity as a simple farmwife. For example, a *Harper's Bazaar* feature of 1942 noted: "Daughter and wife, she's been a farm-woman all her life. She has five children, eleven grandchildren, one great-grandchild; still takes prizes at the county fairs for her jams and pickles; and her cakes stack up with any in Washington county."[25] A year later, a story in a woman's magazine praised her "farm wife's adaptability for turning her hand to anything."[26] A contemporary article in *The Pathfinder* first

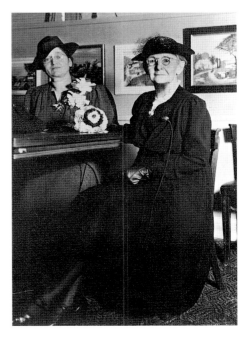

Fig. 3. Grandma Moses and Carolyn Thomas at Gimbel's auditorium, New York, on November 14, 1940. Photograph by Louis J. Caldor

recounted the accolades of such New York art critics as Genauer and then reminded readers that "she still doesn't paint until she's swept the house and done the chores, just as she has been doing for many years."[27] The apotheosis of this characterization may be the Mother's Day feature in *True Confessions* (1947) entitled "Just a Mother," which noted: "Grandma Moses remains prouder of her preserves than of her paintings, and proudest of all of her four children, eleven grandchildren and four great-grandchildren."[28] People adored this simple and ordinary woman whose public presence as "Grandma" had been invented by feature writers.

When Anna Mary Moses spoke at Gimbel's Thanksgiving forum in mid-November 1940, much of Europe was at war. Against this backdrop of distant conflict, the seasoned copywriters in the store's publicity department emphasized enduring national values in their ad for the event published in the *New York Times* (November 14, 1940). They pitched Moses as an old-fashioned American homemaker and only once referred to her status as an artist. Their copy hit more than a note of nostalgia, it struck a whole harmonic chord:

> *"Over the river and through the woods to Grandmother's house we go." We couldn't go to grandmother's house so grandmother came to us. Grandmother who? Grandma Moses, the American girl who made good at 80. You'll meet Grandma herself today. <u>She's more than a great American artist. She's a great American housewife.</u> The sort of American housewife who has kept the tradition of Thanksgiving alive. Fussing with cranberry sauce may seem a bit useless in these turbulent times. It's not. A woman can't do much about wars or rumors of wars. She <u>can</u> [sic] fight to make the world a pleasanter place by perfecting her cranberry sauce. As long as American housewives busy themselves with cranberries and chrysanthemums there'll always be Thanksgiving! [emphasis added]*

However traditional her earlier years had been, Anna Mary Moses' life was more complex than that of a housewife who fussed over cranberry sauce. Nonetheless, she was presented as an authentic embodiment of hearth and home, a dear sweet lady who was not going to bother her pretty little head with thoughts of distant crises. What appealed to Gimbel's were Grandma's memory pictures of the holiday, where the only dead creature was the unfortunate turkey (fig. 4).

Thanks to old-fashioned gender politics, Gimbel's found a perfect fit between Moses' feminine hand and the glove of Thanksgiving. Indeed, it was a woman who "invented" the holiday as we know it. While it may have seemed in 1940 that Thanksgiving had been celebrated continuously since the Pilgrims first landed, this was not so. Its history in the intervening

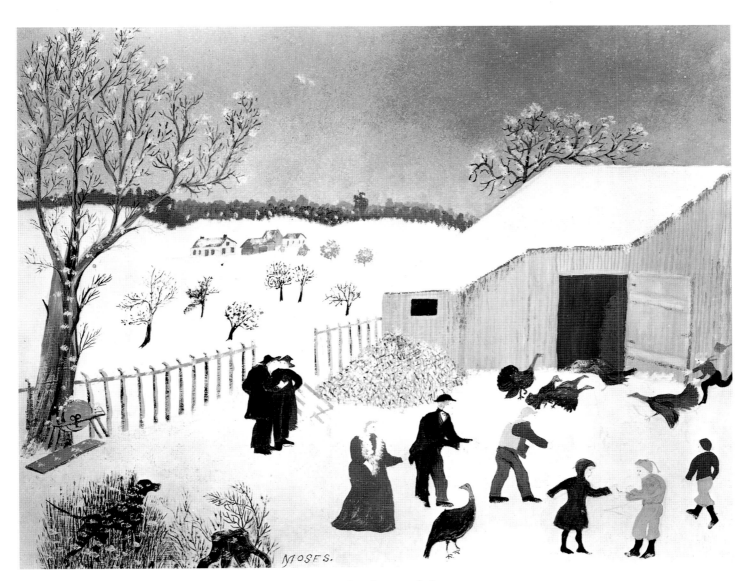

centuries reveals ephemeral initiatives and periods of widespread disinterest. Although George Washington had twice proclaimed a day of Thanksgiving, Thomas Jefferson had actively condemned it. Then largely a religious observance, the day was officially adopted by the state of New York in 1817, for example, and by the state of Virginia in 1855.[29] Were it not for the work of Sarah Josepha Hale, there likely would be no national holiday, nor would it have had such strong patriotic connotations.

In 1827, as editor of Boston's *Ladies Magazine*, Sarah Hale began a one-woman campaign to have Thanksgiving celebrated across the nation. Today she would be described as an essentialist, one who believes that women are innately more moral than men. For over thirty years, she waged a passionate crusade for a national holiday, enjoining her country to express gratitude by sharing a meal together. She believed that this moral act of family solidarity would lessen the likelihood of civil war.[30] Later, when she was the influential editor of *Godey's Ladies Book*, her efforts finally prevailed. It was Abraham Lincoln who acceded to her petition and promulgated Thanksgiving Day three years after Anna Mary Robertson was born.

That the legal celebration of the holiday had been formalized only in 1863, helps explain a curious story that Moses told the *New York Times Magazine* in 1948 when she was asked to recall her first Thanksgiving. While professing the difficulty of the task—she had seen so many Thanksgivings—she nonetheless was able to bring her thoughts back to the year 1864. She recollected that one day, when her father was going to town to buy boots, he told her he would bring her back a red dress. In turn, she promised to be a good girl all day long:

> But when candlelight came, Father came in from the flax mill, and said he could not get his Boots. Because it was Thanksgiving day, and the Stores were closed. I was heart broken, to think I did not get my red dress. I could not eat my supper. Mother said it was too bad as I had been a good girl, that day.[31]

A few days later, her Dad again went shopping and this time brought back a dress that "was not red, it was more of a brick red, or brown. I was awfully disappointed but said nothing, so I never got what I call a red dress."[32]

The anecdote is interesting in at least two regards. The young Anna Mary was so taken with the exact color red fixed in her mind's eye that she could not be satisfied with a neutralized version of the hue. Like the tale of the princess and the pea, which revealed royal sensitivity through a stack of mattresses, the little girl's specialized desire bespeaks the particular eye of an artist.[33] Too, once it is realized that her father's trip into town occurred on the second instance of the newly legalized national holiday, it is more understandable that he might have been unaware or had forgotten that stores would not be open on that day.

Just as the New York press had been quick to forge a link between Moses and the seasonal festivities she frequently depicted in her paintings, the national news media followed suit. By the end of the 1940s, Moses had become "indisputably associated with certain traditional holidays," as Jane Kallir has previously noted.[34] It became standard practice for the media to run features on her work at Thanksgiving and Christmas.

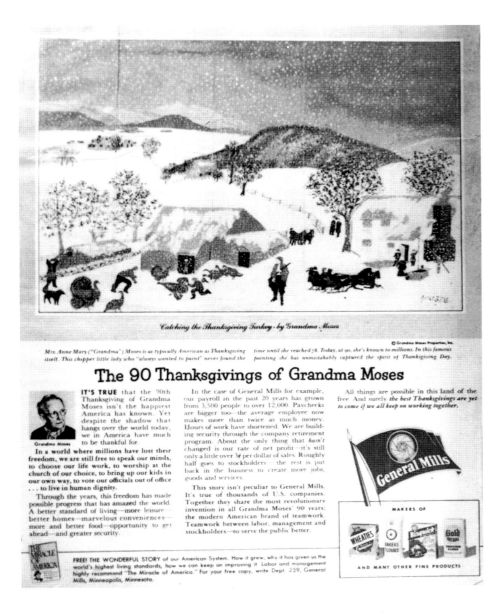

Fig. 5. Grandma Moses' painting, *Catching the Thanksgiving Turkey* (1943; Kallir 260, private collection), featured in a General Mills advertisement in 1950. Photograph by Fay Duftler

In November 1950, during the Korean War, the cereal manufacturer General Mills issued an advertisement that reproduced the artist's *Catching the Thanksgiving Turkey* (fig. 5). The accompanying copy harked back to the Gimbel's ads of the preceding decade: "It's true that the 90th Thanksgiving of Grandma Moses isn't the happiest America has known. Yet despite the shadow that hangs over the world today, we in America have much to be thankful for. . . ."[35] Grandma had become almost as much of an institution as the holidays themselves.

As her fame and popularity grew, so did the accolades bestowed upon

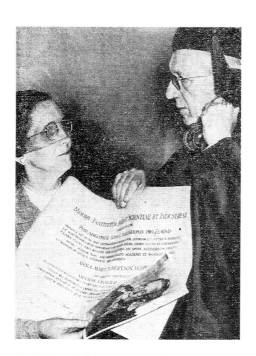

Fig. 6. Dorothy Moses receiving honorary doctorate for her mother-in-law, with Judge Edwin O. Lewis, Chairman of the Board of Directors of Moore College of Art, who is on the telephone with the honoree. *The Philadelphia Inquirer*, March 16, 1951. Archives of Moore College of Art and Design, Philadelphia, Pennsylvania

her. They came from diverse quarters—the National Press Club cited her as one of the five most newsworthy women in 1950, and the National Association of House Dress Manufacturers honored her as their 1951 Woman of the Year. Along with a group of women in their twenties and thirties, *Mademoiselle* named Grandma Moses as a "Young Woman of the Year" in 1948, awarding the artist a Mademoiselle Merit Award "for her flourishing young career and the youth of her spirit."[36] She was the only recipient to say that marriage and a career could not mix, a fact that was noted by the New York press.[37] Interestingly, this immiscibility was the emotional theme of Michael Powell and Emeric Pressburger's 1948 film *The Red Shoes*, about a ballerina fatally torn between her art and her life.

With comments such as those that she made to *Mademoiselle*, the untutored Grandma Moses may not seem the most natural choice as a role model for young women art students in mid-twentieth-century America. But who else was there? No other woman artist even approached her level of renown. As a celebrity, she disarmed and charmed potential detractors in countless interviews, in which she related:

> *I didn't have an opportunity to study art, . . . but if a thing seems right to me, I do it. Art is like the Bible. Everyone reads the Bible and has a different opinion. Everyone looks at pictures and has a different opinion, so I go on my own. I love bright colors so I use bright colors. I don't know much about perspective and things like that. But I paint because I like to and I know what I want to paint.*[38]

Philadelphia's Moore College of Art awarded Moses an honorary doctorate in 1951. Established as the Philadelphia School of Design for Women in 1848, Moore College was the nation's first school of design,[39] and remained a school with no male students. Founder Sarah King Peter had decided to educate women, to provide a means for supporting themselves, "should the necessity occur," as her friend, *Godey's Lady's Book* editor Sarah Hale had phrased it.[40] Peter chose a design-arts curriculum in part because "these arts can be practiced at home, without materially interfering with the routine of domestic duty, which is the peculiar province of women."[41] Even after the fine arts were added in the ensuing decades, the school continued to offer a rigorous education in design.

In March 1951, a little more than a century after its founding, Moore College decided to award its first honorary doctorates. They singled out five individuals: Anna Mary Robertson Moses topped the list of four men who were civic leaders.[42] It is not known if the impetus to include Moses originated with the celebrated Reginald Marsh, then head of Moore's

Department of Painting. Perhaps the idea came from Moore's recently retired Dean Harriet Sartain, who had a long-standing commitment to women's art education. Despite the fact that Moses was unschooled in her art, the school keenly understood the usefulness of the highly successful woman artist as a role model for its students, faculty, and staff.

Although she had initially indicated that she would attend the ceremony, Moses received her Doctor of Fine Arts degree in absentia. Due to a lingering cold, the artist remained in upstate New York, her daughter-in-law Dorothy journeying to Philadelphia to represent her. Moses gave her acceptance speech via a special telephone hookup (fig. 6). "Grandma Moses Regrets 'Not Being with Girls,'" read the headline reporting the event in the *Evening Bulletin*. She expressed gratitude for the honor and mentioned that she would have enjoyed being at the school, "especially with the girl students."[43]

Another *Evening Bulletin* article focused on the artist's textile work. Days in advance of the Moore awards ceremony, five local department stores had featured displays of drapery fabrics reproducing her paintings. Two of the designs had been introduced the year before, but two were making their debut that week. Although the report did not say so, textile design was a major offering at Moore since its founding. The newspaper account did emphasize the appropriateness of Moore's award to Moses: ". . . the oldest woman artist will be awarded an honorary degree by . . . the oldest women's art school in the country."[44]

A third *Evening Bulletin* story previewed the award from a "human interest" angle. Describing the artist as "a little old lady with a fastidious knot perched on top of her head as if it belongs there, and nowhere else," the writer Polly Platt recounted the well-known story of the artist's discovery. Platt recycled such decade-old quotes from Moses as her expressed preference for her preserves over her paintings, and her initial and inimitable response to news that her creations were fetching four-figure prices, namely that the buyers were crazy. Platt's feature also contained material she gleaned from a visit to the artist's home. In response to a question about her process, Moses explained how she would shape a canvas with a saw to fit the frame she had chosen: "A picture without a frame is like a woman without a dress, in my way of thinking."[45] To the Victorian-reared artist, good girls were only presentable with dresses, and nice pictures were best presented with frames, which completed and contained their painted image.

In August 1949, *LIFE* magazine published a photo essay on Jackson Pollock, audaciously subtitled "Is he the greatest living painter in the

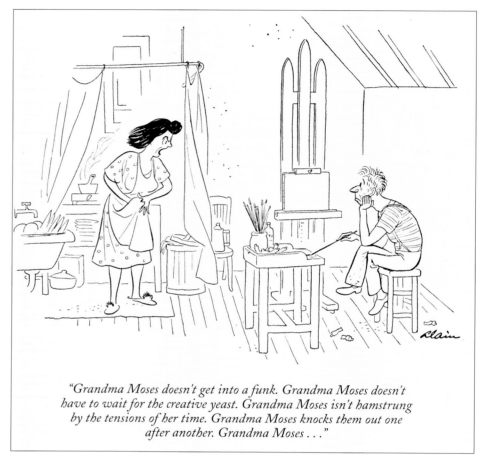

"*Grandma Moses doesn't get into a funk. Grandma Moses doesn't have to wait for the creative yeast. Grandma Moses isn't hamstrung by the tensions of her time. Grandma Moses knocks them out one after another. Grandma Moses . . .*"

United States?" Had the editors taken a poll in that year, it is likely that most Americans would have responded, "No, Grandma Moses is" (fig. 7). A quaint and homespun nonagenarian, blissfully inattentive to avant-garde developments, Moses painted accessible subjects that fed a national nostalgia for a simpler time in our history. In a world of postwar expansion and burgeoning technologies, here was a visual poet of rural America who could recall hearing about President Lincoln's assassination. In the decade of the 1940s, this endearingly cheerful Grandma from New York State managed to swallow the wolf of the male-dominated art world. At least for a time. ✤

NOTES

* Virtual bouquets are due to Rebecca Kelly, who cleared a path for me by working her way through the entire rich territory of the Grandma Moses scrapbooks, where most of the cited periodical clippings may be found; to Hildegard Bachert, an experienced hiker in this terrain; and to the indefatigable Traci Weatherford-Brown, for innumerable kindnesses as I processed what I found. Hildegard, Jane Kallir, and Rachel Stein offered valuable comments after reading an earlier draft of this essay.

1. Emory Lewis, "About New York," *Cue*, January 1953.

2. The song, "Nobody's Chasing Me," was written for *Out of This World*.

3. Editorial, *Allentown [Pennsylvania] Call*, December 15, 1961.

4. Always fond of color, she once told reporters that she used to squeeze elderberry juice to dye otherwise drab dresses (Nancy Davids, "To Grandmother's House We Go," *Collier's Magazine*, January 6, 1945, 48.

5. Ibid.

6. *The Newark Star-Ledger*, July 23, 1948.

7. Grandma Moses, 1946, quoted in *Grandma Moses*, promotional booklet published by Calhoun's Collectors Society, Inc., 1980, title page (Grandma Moses Scrapbook, vol. 8, Galerie St. Etienne).

8. S. J. Woolf, *New York Times Magazine*, December 2, 1945.

9. Lucy R. Lippard, "Making Something from Nothing (Toward a Definition of Women's 'Hobby Art')," first published in *Heresies* 4 (Winter 1978) and reprinted in her compilation of feminist essays on art, *The Pink Glass Swan* (New York: The New Press, 1995).

10. The sole mention of Moses in a feminist context is found in C. Kurt Dewhurst, Betty MacDowell, and Marsha MacDowell, *Artists in Aprons: Folk Art by American Women* (New York: E. P. Dutton, in association with the Museum of American Folk Art, 1979), 132, 166.

11. Interestingly, another self-taught "Grandma" did capture the attention of feminists in the 1970s, the living artist Grandma Tressa Prisbey. From 1958 to 1978, she made daily trips to the local dump in search of discarded bottles, automobile headlights, and other "treasures," working alone without formal plans to fabricate 22 structures for her Bottle Village in Santa Susana, Simi Valley, California. Prisbey, a North Dakota transplant, began to build the miniature community when she was 60 years old. See Cynthia Carlson, "Grass Roots Art," *Ms.*, October 1977, 65. Grandma Prisbey's 1975 exhibition at the Los Angeles Women's Building was accompanied by a stapled catalogue, *Grandma Prisbey's Bottle Village*, consisting of 14 pages of her own text, with photos by Irv Goodnoff and Mike Herman, printed by Dickranz Corporation.

12. *Tribune* reporter Carlyle Burrows, quoted in *Art Digest*, October 15, 1940.

13. This was probably an oblique reference to the concurrent exhibition by the black self-taught painter Horace Pippin, who was enjoying his own New York debut at the nearby Bignou Gallery. Pippin's show ran through the middle of October. For an account of that exhibition, see Judith E. Stein, "An American Original," *I Tell My Heart: The Art of Horace Pippin* (New York: Universe, 1993), 20.

14. Howard Devree, *New York Times*, October 13, 1940, 10.

15. Emily Genauer, "The Galerie St. Etienne," *New York World-Telegram*, October 12, 1940, 10.

16. Ibid.

17. Galerie St. Etienne founder Otto Kallir credited the first published reference of "Grandma" to the *Tribune* (October 8, 1940), which noted: "Mrs. Anna Mary Robertson Moses, known to the countryside around Greenwich, New York, as Grandma Moses, began painting three years ago, when she was approaching 80" (quoted in Otto Kallir, *Grandma Moses* [New York: Harry N. Abrams, 1973], 26).

18. This and the following quotations are found in "Grandma Moses," *Art Digest,* October 15, 1940.

19. Information given in a caption to a photo of the artist in the *New York Post,* November 15, 1940, 17.

20. These comments and the following description of the food table are from the *New York World-Telegram,* November 15, 1940.

21. Alice Graeme, "Rural Scenes by Anna Moses Have Flavor of Early U.S. Art," a review (from an unidentified publication) of Moses' January 1941 exhibition at the Whyte Gallery in Washington, D.C. (unpaged clipping, Grandma Moses Scrapbook, vol. 1, Galerie St. Etienne).

22. A few months earlier, the *New York Journal American* had recounted the fate of Moses' 1936 display of preserves and paintings at a fair in Cambridge, N.Y.: "For her strawberries she won a blue ribbon. For her painting she got no more than the razzberry!" (*New York Journal American,* October 8, 1940).

23. Eugenia Sheppard, *New York Herald Tribune,* November 14, 1945.

24. This example of Krasner's conscious construction of her womanly identity is insightfully discussed by Anne Wagner in "Krasner's Fictions," *Three Artists (Three Women)* (Berkeley: University of California Press, 1996), 122.

25. "She Picked Up Her Paintbrush at Seventy-Seven," *Harper's Bazaar,* December 1942, 42.

26. Robert M. McCain, "She Took Up Art at 76," *The Woman with Woman's Digest,* May 1943, 18.

27. *The Pathfinder* (after December 1943).

28. Eleanor Early, "Just a Mother," *True Confessions,* May 1947, 47.

29. Robert J. Myers, *Celebrations: The Complete Book of American Holidays* (Garden City, N.Y.: Doubleday, 1972), 278–80.

30. Frank N. Magill (ed.), *Great Lives from History,* American Women Series, vol. 3 (Pasadena, Cal.: Salem Press, 1995), 799.

31. Grandma Moses, "My First Thanksgiving," *New York Times Magazine,* April 14, 1996, 91; originally appeared in issue of November 21, 1948 (artist's punctuation).

32. Ibid. Eighty-four years later, she could still recall her unfulfilled desire and draw a moral for her readers: "I have found in after years it is best never to complain of disappointments, they are to be."

33. Moses' early sensitivity to color is also revealed in the anecdote about the candy-pink house that she related to Nancy Davids in the 1940s (see notes 4 and 5 above).

34. Jane Kallir, *Grandma Moses: The Artist Behind the Myth* (New York: Clarkson N. Potter, 1982), 19.

35. Advertisement in the *New York Herald Tribune,* November 19, 1950.

36. *Mademoiselle,* December 30, 1948.

37. *New York Post,* December 30, 1948.

38. McCain, "She Took Up Art at 76" (see note 26 above).

39. For the early history of the school, see Judith Stein, "The Genesis of America's First School of Design: The Philadelphia School of Design for Women," 1976, unpublished paper (in the library of Moore College of Art and Design).

40. Sarah Josepha Hale, "Editor's Table," *Godey's Lady's Book* 48 (March 1854): 271. She was of the opinion "that every young woman should be qualified by some accomplishment which she may teach, or some art or profession she can follow, to support herself creditably, *should the necessity occur*" (*emphasis added*).

41. Sarah King Peter [ca. 1850], quoted in Bruce Sinclair, *Philadelphia's Philosopher Mechanics: A History of the Franklin Institute* (Baltimore: Johns Hopkins University Press, 1974), 3.

42. The other recipients listed behind Moses' name on the program were: Edward Hopkinson Jr., an investment banker who was chairman of the City Planning Commission; Leroy Edgar Chapman, a doctor and state senator; Israel Stiefel, a state senator; and Henry Klonower, a Pennsylvania educator.

43. Grandma Moses, quoted in Gertrude Benson, "Grandma Moses Regrets 'Not Being with Girls,'" *Evening Bulletin*, March 16, 1951 (unpaged clipping, Archives of Moore College of Art and Design).

44. Barbara Barnes, "Grandma Moses Sees Her Work Enter Textile Field," *Evening Bulletin*, March 12, 1951 (unpaged clipping, Archives of Moore College of Art and Design).

45. Polly Platt, "A Little Old Lady of 90, Grandma Moses, Due for Philadelphia's Homage This Week," *Evening Bulletin*, March 11, 1951 (unpaged clipping, Archives of Moore College of Art and Design).

Grandma Moses and the Implications of Memory

Lynda Roscoe Hartigan

"Memory is life."

Narrator in Saul Bellow's *Bellarosa Connection*

The lengthy entry for "memory" in the *Oxford English Dictionary* cites "memory image," "memory picture," and "memory sketch" as references published in the fields of literature, metaphysics, and psychology between 1887 and 1906. But no mention of "memory painting" or "memory painter" appears in this authoritative compendium. Something, it seems, is amiss in the lexicon of American folk art or in the realm of my own expectations, at the very least.*

A survey of the voluminous literature on folk art and on Grandma Moses confirms that "memory painting" and "memory painter" are not the prevalent or time-honored terms we assume them to be. From the 1920s to the 1960s, "primitive" was the adjective of choice, followed by "naïve," in the popular press and in seminal folk art publications, including those of Otto Kallir, champion of Grandma Moses. Then, in the 1970s and early 1980s, Bert Hemphill, Robert Bishop, and Florence and Julius Laffal, pioneering supporters of twentieth-century folk art, published a flurry of references to memory painting as a type of modern folk art.[1] Their matter-of-fact discussions give no hint of coining a new phrase, perhaps because it rings with a certain familiarity. The source, it appears, is Grandma Moses herself, who observed that "memory is a painter" in the opening paragraph of her autobiography, published in 1952.[2] Tracking the history of the term has yielded some surprises, but it has also led back to another longstanding belief—that American memory painting (painting memory) originated with Grandma Moses. But did it? This question is at the heart of my impulse to shake up our snow globe of assumptions about memory painting.

Temporarily, then, set aside what this phrase and this artist's name evoke—decorative, nostalgic imagery rendered nonacademically.

Grandma Moses, *Waiting for Santa Claus,*
detail of plate 75

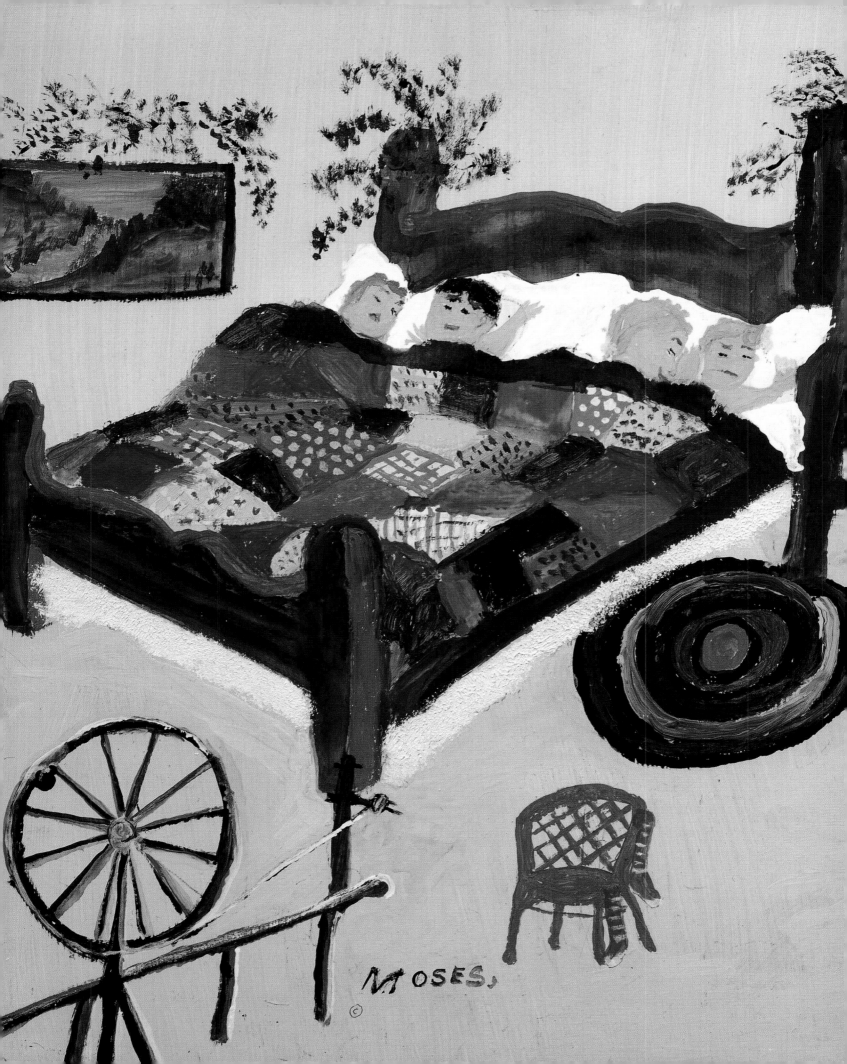

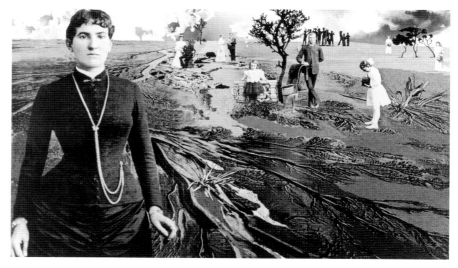

Acknowledge that artists across time and place work from personal and
cultural touchstones, forging an inevitable relationship between art and
memory. Take into account that we ourselves are in the midst of a highly
retrospective period—the turning of a century, the beginning of a new
millennium—and that memory is a conspicuous motivational presence in
contemporary art, especially photography (fig. 1). And consider that the
greatest concentration of memory-based images in Western art has traditionally appeared in either highly romantic times that foster optimism
and introspection or in periods involving enormous social, technological, and political change.[3]

The biography and career of Grandma Moses have been rehearsed at
length, usually from a perspective awed by her age and lack of formal art
training. The ten decades of her life—from just before the Civil War to
the Civil Rights era—coincided, however, with America's experience of
romanticism and change, in spades. Prince Hubertus of Loewenstein
asserted in 1957 that "you have to know America well" in order to appreciate Grandma Moses as an artist.[4] This provocative comment has
escaped notice, partly because of its foreign origin, but largely because
the artist's viewpoint has been circumscribed as that of an elderly woman
looking back at her rural life—nothing more, nothing less. Both the
praise and the disdain heaped on her paintings cite her attachment to
America's vanishing rural idyll as the source of their appeal. Although
this estimation is not incorrect per se, it is shortsighted in its failure to
link Moses to the continuum of America's fascination with understanding the past, in the guise of history and memory, as building blocks for
the present and future.

Plotting one segment on this continuum—from the 1880s, when Moses reached maturity, married, and had children, to the 1930s, when she began painting in earnest as a widow during the Depression— is revealing. "As though currents in the culture had thrown a switch," interpretations of memory proliferated in the fine and popular arts in America during this time.[5] By 1880 the country had come to terms with the rebuilding process after the Civil War, taken proud stock of itself for the Centennial, and settled into its Gilded Age of economic prosperity, all overlaid with a Victorian sensibility that pitted progress against nostalgia and even decadence. Some artists, like the poetically inclined painters Elihu Vedder and Albert Pinkham Ryder, dealt with memory as a theme or process for personal discovery. Others, sculptor Daniel Chester French (fig. 2) and Frederic Remington in his role as illustrator, for example, considered memory a source of historical knowledge that illuminated the country's evolving collective experience.

In the 1930s, these two threads—the personal and the collective— converged around the concept of survival, as Americans struggled with economic decline that tested individual dignity and democratic ideals to an unprecedented degree. In 1938, a muralist for the Depression era's federal art projects summed up the heavy responsibilities that the government as well as many artists and citizens assigned to memory at this time: "The spiritual reservoir of society has countless memories which have given man faith, courage, strength, and a sense of the abiding goodness of life" (fig. 3).[6]

Bright colors and quiltlike compositions for regional landscapes and cheery vignettes of people at work, worship, and play in rural America: what more could one ask of paintings during the Depression and through the war years? Moses tapped into and visualized a spiritual reservoir that was not hers alone. Her life as a young, industrious farmwife who liked to decorate her environment had little to do with the splendors of the Gilded Age, yet her love of family and handwork and her sensitivity to mortality and memento are unmistakably Victorian in

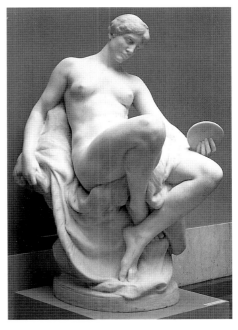

Fig. 2. Daniel Chester French, *Memory*, 1919. Marble, 57 1/2 x 25 x 42 1/2 inches (146.1 x 63.5 x 108 cm). Gift of Henry Walters, 1919 (19.47)

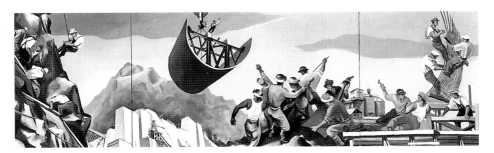

Fig. 3. William Gropper, *Construction of the Dam* (study for mural, the Department of the Interior, Washington, D.C.), 1938. Oil on canvas, 27 1/4 x 87 1/4 inches (69.3 x 221.7 cm). Smithsonian American Art Museum. Transfer from the U.S. Department of the Interior, National Park Service (1965.18.11A–C)

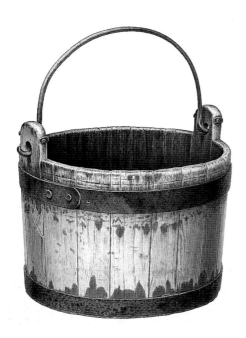

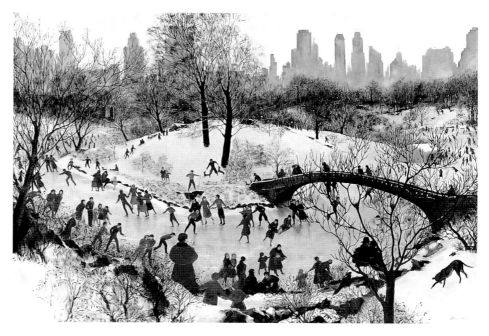

Fig. 4. Edward Bashaw, *Bucket*, ca. 1940. Watercolor, pen and ink, and graphite on paperboard, 18 3/8 x 14 7/16 inches (46.7 x 36.7 cm). Index of American Design. Copyright © 2000 Board of Trustees, National Gallery of Art, Washington, D.C. (1943.8.16592)

Fig. 5. Agnes Tait, *Skating in Central Park*, 1934. Oil on canvas, 33 7/8 x 48 1/8 inches (85.8 x 121.8 cm). Smithsonian American Art Museum, Washington, D.C. Transfer from the U.S. Department of Labor (1964.1.15)

sensibility. When she began painting at home around 1935, this elderly widow was hardly exempt from New York State's share of economic hard times or the pathos that enveloped America. Yet her assertion that "I would never sit back in a rocking chair, waiting for someone to help me"[7] has the ring of a person who would not have gone on relief, even within the orbit of federal projects that documented craft traditions for the Index of American Design (fig. 4) or created uplifting paintings and murals for public buildings across the nation (fig. 5).

"Pretty," "nice," and "pleasant"—these are the effects that Grandma Moses wanted to achieve in her paintings, and she succeeded. The absence of negativity in the works has suggested that this woman blithely painted in a suspended state of nostalgia because of her age. Setting aside the relationship between aging and memory, consider that Moses chose subjects and goals in keeping with her character as well as with the tenor of the times and a prospective audience in mind.

In print and on film, Moses comes across as a plucky, no-nonsense personality, as someone oriented toward the work ethic and survival (fig. 6). She was, trite as it sounds, the epitome of the "can do" attitude frequently associated with the American drive toward achievement rather than resignation in the face of adversity and challenge. Moses was simply not predisposed to dwelling on the down and out. To do so would have contradicted her sense of personal worth and her belief in striving for something. In the midst of the Depression, it is unlikely that this type of personality would have rushed to create negative images for paintings she gave to friends and relatives or tried to sell at church bazaars, country fairs, and local stores.

No, whatever sense of urgency Moses felt revolved around the notion that "things get lost," as she told Edward R. Murrow during her interview for his television series, *See It Now*, in 1955. A little more than a century earlier, American artists and writers, "tempted to fix these few memorials of a transient state of things fast passing into oblivion," had embraced narrative to document and interpret the history of a country predisposed toward constant change.[8] Moses herself would never have claimed any connection to this historicizing, narrative tradition. Nonetheless, many of her contemporaries, American and European, perceived her penchant for recording "old-timey" costumes, architecture, and mores as that of a history-sensitive storyteller with firsthand experience of a vanishing scene. "Memory is history recorded in our brain" is the way Moses put it.[9] Vivid, abundant detail, accompanied by her equally vivid autobiographical anecdotes in print, offered reassuring preservation of the past during a troublesome present. Before America's very eyes, Moses had pictured an inherent tension—between truth and fiction, perception and imagination—that characterizes not just narrative and history but the process of memory itself.

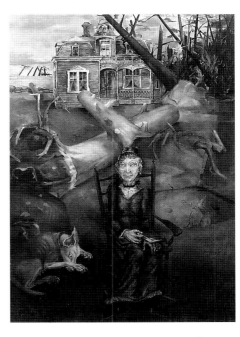

Fig. 6. Philip Evergood, *My Forebears Were Pioneers*, 1939. Oil on canvas, 50 x 36 inches (127 x 91.4 cm). Georgia Museum of Art, University of Georgia, Athens. University purchase GMOA (74.3190)

If the American psyche in the 1930s and 1940s placed its confidence in memory, it would seem to follow that the period's scientific community was similarly invested in the study of memory as a cognitive phenomenon. In fact, nothing could have been further from actuality. By the 1920s, American psychologists interested in human learning no longer emphasized memory and consciousness, as they had until the turn of the century, but favored behaviorism instead. Memory and introspection were considered subjective states of mind and were, therefore, suspect as resources. Examining and analyzing behavioral events using objective observation and quantifiable methods were deemed pursuits that would yield accurate results. In providing a historical perspective on theories of memory, one recent writer went so far as to suggest that America's emphasis on behaviorism represented "the dark ages for memory research" well into the late 1960s.[10]

How this orientation toward behavior as the measure of learning infiltrated the country's wider culture is a subject beyond my expertise. Is it mere coincidence, however, that a marked decline in memory research occurred during a period in which artists like Moses were not described as memory painters and were characterized instead as primitive and naïve? Traditionally, art historians and connoisseurs of European art have applied the term "primitive" to early phases of the historical development of painting and sculpture throughout Europe but especially in relation to the art and artists of pre-Renaissance Western Europe. A quality or style considered early, or even ancient, has either been commended or downplayed in the hierarchy of European achievement. This distinction, however, has not rested on training as a standard-bearer of learning.

By contrast, modern historians and connoisseurs of American art have emphasized the absence of formal training when describing artists as primitive or naïve. Their perception of the primitive has also incorporated the term's more anthropological applications, which stress isolation as a determining factor in stages of achievement and behavior. Consequently, terms like "untrained" and "isolated" have been used to link America's primitive artists to a repertoire of stereotypical behaviors. These include improvising, working without restraint, and calling upon (recalling) personal experiences. The title of Sidney Janis's historic book, *They Taught Themselves* (1942), epitomizes the association of modern primitive artists with alternate forms of learning.[11] It may not be feasible to quantify or make objective observations about how and why artists manifest creativity, at least in the sense that behaviorism intended. The study of America's primitive artists, however, reflects an abiding fascination with behavior, which recommends exploring the provocative possibility that behaviorist concepts of learning contributed to the evolution of this fascination at mid-century.

Memory, then, was simultaneously embraced and disavowed in different quarters during Moses' lifetime. By the 1970s, when the term "memory painting" gained currency, scientific study of memory was on the rise again. Today, after three decades of remarkable advances in theory and research, memory is considered a constellation of processes and systems that connect and activate different parts of the brain. This implies the existence of different types of memory that affect retaining and retrieving information, forming skills, habits, and concepts, and integrating our intellectual and emotional lives. In its most basic scientific sense, memory facilitates the brain's desire to impose order on the environment. In its broadest cognitive sense, memory fuels continuous learning; it enables us to reuse and reevaluate past experience in order to interpret current situations and to modify what we do in the future. Our capacity for consideration, flexibility, planned control of behavior,

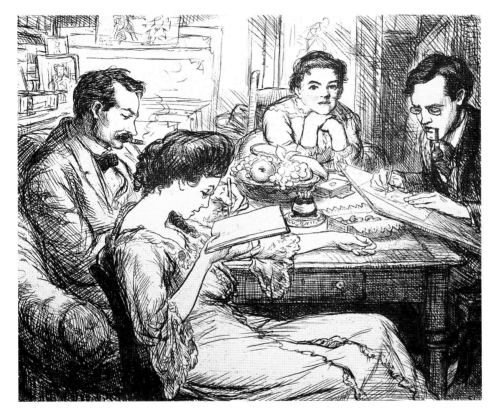

Fig. 7. John Sloan, *Memory*, 1906. Etching, 7 ^{1}/8 x 8 ^{5}/8 inches (18.1 x 21.9 cm). Amon Carter Museum, Fort Worth, Texas (1986.13)

and social interaction owes much to the multicomponent processes now identified with memory.

Navigating contemporary memory research without a firm grasp of its specialized theories, knowledge, and vocabulary represents a calculated risk for any layperson. Settling for the persistent simplification of memory painting as sentimental busywork for elderly people like Moses also risks misunderstanding. That Moses described memory metaphorically—as a painter, as history, as writing on the brain—suggests that she understood it as a multifaceted phenomenon and recommends that we tease out a few salient points derived from current memory studies (fig. 7).

Like language, memory makes us human, providing a foundation for our most strongly held beliefs about ourselves as individuals. Only recently, however, has the importance of subjective experience, our point of view, gained credence in memory studies. This has stimulated a sharp upswing in attempts to understand autobiographical memory— an experience remembered because we believe that it played a significant part in our life, an experience in combination with other autobiographical memories that help define our sense of self. Using the terms "autobiographical" and "recollective" interchangeably, W. F. Brewer provided this working definition from a philosophical perspective in 1996:

> *Recollective memory is memory for a specific episode from an individual's past. It typically appears to be a "reliving" of the individual's phenomenal experience during the earlier moment. Thus, these memories typically contain information about place, actions, persons, objects, thoughts, and affect. . . . The information in this form of memory is expressed as a mental image. . . . They are accompanied by a belief that the remembered episode was personally experienced. . . . Recollective memories give rise to high confidence in the accuracy of their content.*[12]

Brewer's mention of mental image alludes to the idea that imagery plays an important role in autobiographical memory for several reasons. Since ancient times visual imagery has been recognized as a powerful means of improving memory. And, as Brewer also notes, vivid memories—images rich in concrete detail, according to psychology's lexicon—go beyond improving memory and take on persuasive connotations. Correct or not, details increase the perception of accuracy, intimacy, immediacy, and effectiveness.

If this suggests that the communication of details assumes a narrative structure, it should, since the brain takes in and gives back experience as word as well as image. Autobiographical memories, according to one of its leading researchers, David Rubin, "are usually recalled as narrative. They are told to another person and to oneself."[13] Memories rehearsed and elaborated form the core of our life stories, and we convey these stories in narrative structures familiar to those around us, whether in conversation, letters, written and spoken stories, memoirs, or formal autobiography. Memory painting can be readily added to this list as a visual cousin of written and spoken narrative.

Certainly Moses is not the only American self-taught artist who painted from the vantage afforded by memories. She is, however, the only American self-taught artist, memory painter or otherwise, who has explored autobiography in an extended and very public alliance between images and words. Otto Kallir's masterful promotion of her career in print, exhibitions, commissions, and documentaries cannot be underestimated, yet entrepreneurship does not account for the appeal of her paintings and her autobiography, *My Life's History*. The key to their appeal is the convincing and inviting impression that she is telling a story that values memory.

Accumulated details—about places, events, people, customs—endow her works with a plausible intimacy and immediacy, yet Moses was not motivated by a desire to provide a passive or literal record of her world.

Acknowledging that her paintings combined elements derived from pictorial ephemera, direct observation, and recollections, Moses also described her works as "complete in my mind's eye before I put a stroke of paint on the canvas."[14] Frankly, I believe that she understood painting and writing as imaginative ways to reconstruct memory more than we have been willing to acknowledge. Perceptions of her aspirations instead remain divided between the documentary and the idealized, the real and the imagined.

Cambridge philosopher Mary Warnock has written cogently about why we value memory so highly, citing imagination and memory as "two powers" that "are impossible to separate."[15] She maintains that

> whether we are imagining or recalling, we are thinking of something that is not before our eyes and ears, and of something that has meaning for us, and may be imbued with strong emotions. We could say that, in recalling something, we are employing imagination; and that, in imagining something, exploring it imaginatively, we use memory.[16]

This assertion of a partnership between memory and imagination frees us to consider that fact and fiction are complementary rather than contradictory aspects of the autobiographical orientation.

To connect Moses with the narrative structures of autobiographical memory suggests that the appeal of her work could be described as literary. Early in her career, at least one writer, Louis Bromfield, did, although without noting any potential relationship to the art of auto-biography as a literary genre.[17] A relationship that would appear to be tenuous, however, takes on intriguing relevance for the appeal and significance of Moses if we entertain a question posed by the autobio-graphical writer Jill Ker Conway: "Why is autobiography the most popular form of fiction for modern readers?"[18]

Characterizing autobiography or memoir as fiction is another way of aligning memory with imaginative reconstruction, a fluid rather than static glimpse into the external events and inner life experienced by the auto-biographer. The desire to tell one's life story can imply self-absorption and a compulsion toward the confessional, especially in modern Western society. The telling and our receptivity to the telling have more to do, however, with forging connections between the self and the world. Autobiographical writers commonly hope that their experiences will enlighten others, and Conway's eloquent answer to the question from the reader's perspective reveals a reciprocal desire: "We want to know how

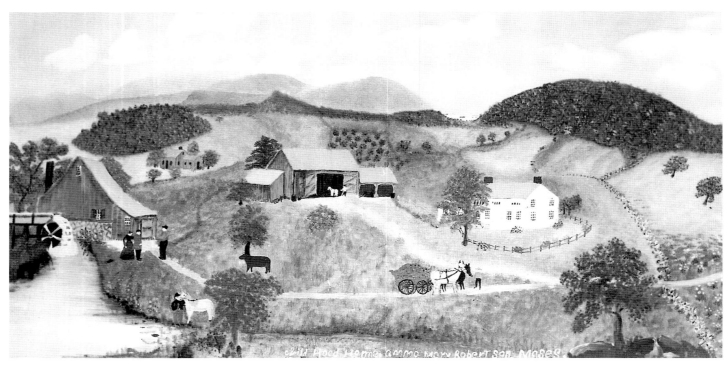

Fig. 8. Grandma Moses, *The Childhood Home of Anna Mary Robertson Moses,* 1942. Oil on pressed wood, 14 x 28 inches (35.6 x 71.1 cm). Titled, lower center. Kallir 160. Private collection

the world looks from inside another person's experience, and when that craving is met by a convincing narrative, we find it deeply satisfying."[19] Echoing David Rubin's description of autobiographical memory as a narrative "told to another person and to oneself," this reciprocity is at the heart of the satisfaction, or broad popular appeal, that Moses has consistently elicited because she paints convincing narratives.

If we think of memory as an evolving source of human-interest stories, this suggests that social and cultural factors affect their drafting, timing, and viewpoint. Historically, the personification of Memory has been a beneficent woman—the goddess Mnemosyne for the ancient Greeks and Minerva for the Romans—and memory has retained this gender-specific association to this day. Recent studies have even delineated significant differences between how women and men form autobiographical memories through social interaction initiated during early child–parent relationships.

With so little actually known about how Moses interacted with her father and mother, it is fruitless to dwell on the child–parent relationships tested in these studies. The salient point is that parents do not discuss the past with their sons as much as they do with their daughters. From this follows the suggestion that women develop more elaborate structures for talking and thinking about the past. Their memories of past events tend to be richer and more embellished and extend further back in time, facilitating the onset of a life story at an earlier age. Women, these same studies assert, are usually more interested in past events on a lifelong basis, reminisce more often, and assign greater significance to past events than men do. Women, in effect, place greater value on autobiography and the past as sources of knowledge and ways to understand oneself and others. This apparently reinforces for women their early appreciation of communication as an integral aspect of social interaction.[20]

As these types of gender-based autobiographical studies have unfolded over the past two decades, Florence Laffal and Julius Laffal have initiated the first attempts to gather what they call "demographic perspectives on twentieth-century American folk art."[21] The Laffals presented their findings at the annual convention of the American Psychological Association in 1984. Surveying the literature for folk artists active between 1900 and 1984, the Laffals obtained information on 486 American and 75 Canadian folk artists active as painters and sculptors rather than craftspeople. They estimated that this pool represented sixty percent of the artists they had identified in publications. Although they found that men outnumbered women as folk artists, more women were involved with painting and drawing. Almost one-third of American women folk artists pursued memory as a theme or subject while their male counterparts preferred religious, historical, and political topics. Noting that American women displayed a greater interest than did American men in farm and rural themes, the Laffals proposed a relationship between this trend and the large number of women memory painters whose art recalled pastoral childhoods and emphasized daily-living themes. Publishing updates of their studies in 1998 and 1999, the couple have reported similar patterns, but they have also noted a decline in the incidence of memory painting among women and men.[22]

As different in method and scope as these two types of studies are, they both intimately link women to autobiographical memory. What one emphasizes as an appreciation of communication, the other describes as visual creativity, yet they point to a similar thrust—sharing their impressions or knowledge of the past with others. The "small sketches" that comprise Moses' autobiography reveal how her life revolved around the family's ancestry, back to a great-grandfather's arrival in America in 1740, and the life cycles of her ten children and numerous grandchildren (fig. 8). Teaching the next generation and expressing one's life through family and other social bonds are central to the traditional maternal role that Moses fulfilled. It is hardly surprising that she called upon these gender-specific activities to navigate memory as the subject of her pictures and writing. Her children grown, she began painting in response to their encouragement, and they were the first recipients of her efforts. Once she identified narrative painting as an antidote to "things get lost," her desire to communicate a sense of the past provided comforting, even restorative, illustrations for a much wider audience challenged by enormous loss during the Depression and war years. Moses reminds us that the act of remembering cannot be separated from the act of communicating.

What we believe about ourselves is based on what we remember about ourselves. Yet memory, this powerful force for life, is also fragile. Too often we take it for granted until we lose it, usually because of the effects of the aging process. Spry, articulate, and active almost to the end, Moses seemed to defy this process by embracing art and writing late in life. Yet the intense and frequent need to draw upon autobiographical memories is a manifestation of her age, expressing the desire to recapture the people, places, and events that helped define her as a unique person. Ironically, Moses lived during a period in which reminiscence was considered an age-related pathology. Many professionals actively encouraged the elderly to avoid or abandon the past in the interest of diminishing depression. Current studies of the relationship between aging and memory have completely reversed this attitude, and research now indicates that older adults who reminisce are more likely to exhibit optimism and mental health than those who do not.[23]

We spend a lifetime creating our life's story and telling it to others and ourselves in the interest of keeping it (and us) alive. Writing autobiography and memoir provides the opportunity to live our lives twice, to move back and forth between the past and present in preparation for the future. Entering another person's life through his or her autobiography can be transformative because it often inspires self-reflection. At some point—not yet readily documented—entering our autobiography from the perspective of our own aging becomes a priority, another more poignant occasion to live our lives twice. What we create of our remaining life's story is based on a process that researchers have termed "life review."

This process uses reminiscence to help us come to terms with life, to finalize our sense of self, and even promote preparation for death.[24] By the time most of us reach old age, we have realized that memories can be deceptive or elusive, depending on the point in life at which we choose to view them. What often looms with the intensity of accuracy are the memories established and elaborated upon during late adolescence and early adulthood. This was the territory Moses mined most productively for her paintings. Like many older adults who engage in life review, she displayed a flair for telling stories, a cognitive function that age actually enhances. The telling fulfills a variety of needs, from maintaining a sense of usefulness and self-esteem to transmitting information across generations. Both were high priorities for Moses, who painted so that neither she nor the things and memories she valued would get lost.

What settles out after shaking the snow globe of assumptions about memory painting in these various ways? Memory has the capacity to recall things that are not present, rendering the past accessible. Memory mingles with imagination to translate experience into personal terms and to provide a shifting network of meanings. This accounts for the personal and collective purposes served by autobiographical memory as we gather knowledge and build our sense of identity. Our memories are uniquely our own, belonging to no one else. Yet our personal narrative must connect to a community of shared narratives, linking our own humanity to Humanity, our own history to History. Like Lewis Carroll's Red Queen in *Through the Looking Glass*, Moses understood that "it's a poor sort of memory that only works backwards." The ability to mesh her life story with our reservoir of life stories recommends valuing her paintings as a synthesis of knowledge, memory, and identity. ❦

NOTES

*   This essay is dedicated to my mother Frances Meek Roscoe, who struggles in her late eighties with debilitating memory loss. This sober autobiographical note might seem irrelevant to a discussion of Grandma Moses, an exemplar of elderly achievement. Yet the erosion of my mother's memory, knowledge, and identity has crystallized the interrelationship of these three elements for me, and provided the impetus for exploring memory painting by this constellation.

I would like to thank Estelle Friedman and Micaela Mendelsohn for the thorough research and patient support that they contributed to the preparation of this essay.

1.   My search for the first published use of the term "memory painting" continues. The earliest citation found thus far occurs in Herbert Waide Hemphill Jr. and Julia Weissman, *Twentieth-Century American Folk Art and Artists* (New York: E. P. Dutton, 1974), 10. Robert Bishop began using the term regularly in publications during the early 1980s. See his "Foreword," in Jay Johnson and William C. Ketchum Jr., *American Folk Art of the Twentieth Century* (New York: Rizzoli International, 1983), ix. Also Robert Bishop, *Folk Art Paintings, Sculpture, and Country Objects* (New York: Alfred A. Knopf, 1983), 10; and his introduction in Mattie Lou O'Kelley, *From the Hills of Georgia: An Autobiography in Paintings* (Boston and Toronto: Little, Brown, 1983) See also Florence Laffal and Julius Laffal, "Memory Painters: Folk Art Directory Tabulation," *Folk Art Finder* 4 (March–April 1983): 3.

2.   Grandma Moses, *My Life's History*, edited by Otto Kallir (New York: Harper and Row, 1952), 3.

3.   "Memory and Time," *Artweek* 25 (April 7, 1994): 18.

4.   Hubertus, Prince of Loewenstein, "Grandma Moses," in *Grandma Moses: New York Showing of an Exhibition of Paintings Presented in Europe during 1955–57*, exh. cat., Galerie St. Etienne, May 6–June 4, 1957 (New York: Galerie St. Etienne, 1957), 5.

5.   Michael Kammen, *Meadows of Memory: Images of Time and Tradition in American Art and Culture* (Austin: University of Texas Press, 1992), 41.

6.   Ibid., 43. Kammen identified the muralist as Wendell Jones, who published the observation in his article "Articles of Faith," *Magazine of Art* 33 (October 1940): 557–59.

7.   Moses, *My Life's History*, 138.

8.   Kammen, *Meadows of Memory*, 92. Washington Irving published this observation in 1836 in his book *Astoria, or Anecdotes of an Enterprise beyond the Rocky Mountains*.

9.   Moses, *My Life's History*, 3.

10.   Peter E. Morris, "Theories of Memory: An Historical Perspective," in Peter E. Morris and Michael Gruneberg (eds.), *Theoretical Aspects of Memory*, 2nd ed. (London and New York: Routledge, 1994), 15.

11.   The history of America's fascination with the concept of the self-taught individual dates back to the early nineteenth century. In 1832, after traveling in America, the English Mrs. Trollope wrote *Domestic Manners of the Americans*, in which she remarked on "the frequency with which I heard this phrase of self-taught used, not as an apology, but as positive praise." She reported that her American partner in conversation responded, "Well, madam, can there be higher praise? . . . Is it not attributing genius to the author, and what is teaching compared to that?" For a discussion of how "the 'original,' the character who seemed to spring wholly from his native environment without benefit of international polish, had become by the late 1850s, for better or for worse, a symbol of America," see Joshua C. Taylor, *America as Art* (Washington, D.C.: Smithsonian Institution Press, 1976), 39.

12. W. F. Brewer, "What is Recollective Memory?" in David C. Rubin (ed.),
    Remembering Our Past: Studies in Autobiographical Memory (Cambridge: Cambridge
    University Press), 60–61.

13. David C. Rubin, "Beginnings of a Theory of Autobiographical Remembering,"
    in Charles P. Thompson et al. (eds.), *Autobiographical Memory: Theoretical and Applied
    Perspectives* (Mahwah, N.J., and London: Lawrence Erlbaum Associates, 1998), 53.

14. S. J. Woolf, "Grandma Moses, Who Began to Paint at 78," *New York Times Magazine,*
    December 2, 1945, 167.

15. Mary Warnock, *Memory*, cited in James McConkey (ed.), *The Anatomy of Memory: An
    Anthology* (New York and Oxford: Oxford University Press, 1996), 124.

16. Ibid.

17. Louis Bromfield, introductory essay, in Otto Kallir (ed.), *Art and Life of Grandma
    Moses* (South Brunswick, N.J., and New York: A. S. Barnes, 1969), 9.

18. Jill Ker Conway, *When Memory Speaks: Exploring the Art of Autobiography* (New York:
    Vintage Books, 1999), 3.

19. Ibid., 6.

20. For an excellent discussion of the parent–child and gender-based dimensions of
    autobiographical memory, see Robyn Fivush and Elaine Reese, "The Social
    Construction of Autobiographical Memory," in Martin A. Conway et al. (eds.),
    Theoretical Perspectives on Autobiographical Memory (Dordecht, Boston, and London:
    Kluwer Academic Publishers, 1992), 115–32.

21. Jules Laffal and Florence Laffal, "Demographic Characteristics of Contemporary
    Self-Taught (Folk and Outsider) Artists," paper presented at the 92nd annual
    convention of the American Psychological Association, Toronto, August 1984. The
    Laffals published a version of their 1984 findings as "Demographic Perspectives on
    Twentieth-Century American Folk Art," in *Folk Art Finder* 15 (April–June 1994): 6.

22. Jules Laffal and Florence Laffal, "Some Facts about Women Folk Artists," *Folk Art Finder*
    19 (Jan.–March 1998): 2–3; and "Just the Facts, Ma'am: Statistics and Their
    Implications about Women Self-Taught Artists," *The Outsider* 3 (Winter 1999): 18–21.

23. For an excellent discussion of memory and age-related issues, see "Stories of
    Elders," in Daniel L. Schacter, *Searching for Memory: The Brain, the Mind, and the Past*
    (New York: Basic Books, 1996), 280–307.

24. Ibid., 297.

The Sense of Time and Place

Roger Cardinal

The fifteen hundred and more landscapes Grandma Moses painted over the four decades of her career represent not only an impressive artistic achievement but also a fascinating record of past events and situations, nearly all directly linked to both her personal life and that of the family and local community to which she remained so loyal.* Anna Mary Robertson Moses was born in 1860 on a farm about a mile outside the village of Greenwich in upstate New York. One of ten children, she spent her childhood and youth on various farms in south-ern Washington County, a terrain of wide valleys and rolling hills lying to the north of the Hoosic River as it runs west to join the Hudson.[1] Her marriage to Thomas Moses in 1887 led to an adventurous move south to Virginia, where the couple farmed for eighteen years in the Shenandoah Valley and raised a family (five of their ten children died in infancy). In 1905, the homesick Thomas Moses persuaded his wife to move back to New York State, whereupon the couple purchased a dairy farm near the Hoosic River and close to the hamlet of Eagle Bridge, where Anna had attended school as a child. The homestead lies just inside Washington County, and from here the main road runs south into Rensselaer County before veering east through the villages of North Hoosick (see note 1 for spelling) and Walloomsac to cross over into Bennington County, Vermont. This was to be a permanent return to a familiar countryside, for, during the remaining fifty-six years of her life, Grandma Moses scarcely ventured outside what she called her "home-land" (fig. 1).

The quite extensive home property (fig. 2) which her children dubbed Mount Nebo (nostalgically keeping the biblical nickname of the Virginia farmstead they had just left); the valleys, ridges, and hills of the northern Taconic Range, with peaks such as Willard Mountain, Fly Summit, and Goose Egg Hill, and the distant profiles of the Green Mountains over in Vermont; the local crop fields, the cattle and sheep pastures, the

Grandma Moses, *My Homeland*, detail of plate 34

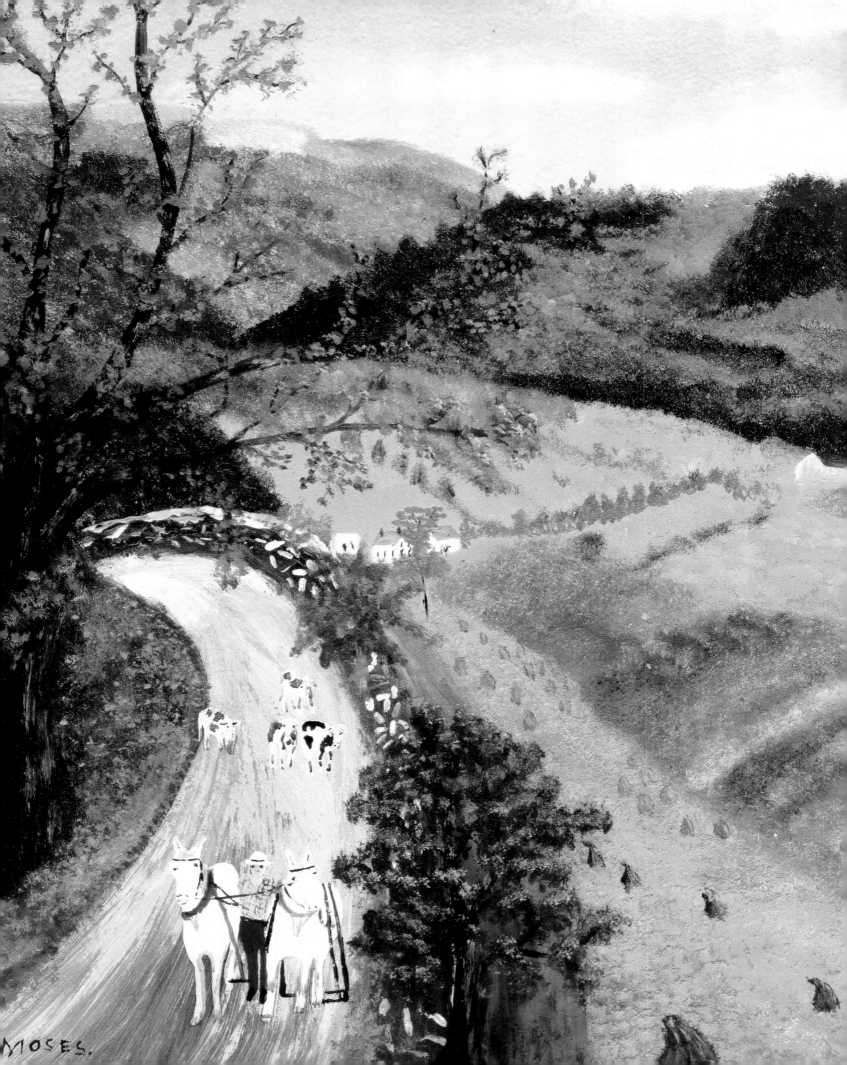

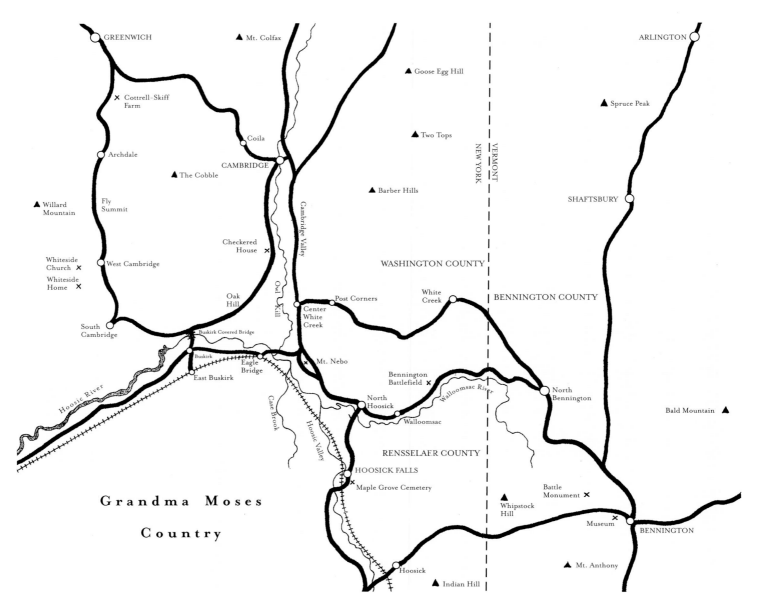

Grandma Moses Country

Fig. 1. Map of "Grandma Moses Country." Drawn by Roger Cardinal

pinewoods; the winding Hoosic and such tributaries as the Walloomsac, Little White Creek, and Owl Kill, with their many covered bridges; the Boston & Maine railway track that ran up from Hoosick Falls to follow the valley west and out to Troy upon the Hudson; and all the dozens of settlements, hamlets, farms, churches, mills, and hostelries scattered across this attractive locality—these are the multiple features of an elective domain within which Grandma Moses' creative imagination was to flourish. Many landmarks are treated again and again in the paintings—at times obsessively, always reverently—and the regularity and reliability of their recurrence establish an immutable frame of reference. What has been called "Grandma Moses Country" can be seen as an area of real countryside centered on Eagle Bridge; it co-exists with an internalized tapestry woven out of authentic topographical and anecdotal material and embroidered with colorful personal associations.

Moses, now acknowledged as the paradigmatic "memory painter," developed an exceptional lucidity of vision across a very wide span of time, although her work respects relatively narrow spatial bounds. By the 1920s, when she began painting on a regular basis, her experience of

Washington County and the Hoosic Valley was that of a sixty-year-old woman with a keen eye and a great appetite for reminiscence. By this time, she had resided in several different places in her native region, had regularly visited villages and farmsteads over a radius of several miles, and had made memorable trips by train to more distant destinations like Troy and Albany. In the early 1930s, she lived for some years in the town of Bennington, a few miles inside Vermont, and took care of two grandchildren there after the early death of her daughter Anna; she began making yarn pictures, and once she had returned to Mount Nebo in 1935 she embarked upon her artistic career proper. Then in her seventies, she visited a country fair in the region, putting her pictures up for sale alongside her homemade preserves. The exhibition of her work which led to her public recognition took place in 1938 in W. D. Thomas's pharmacy on the main street of Hoosick Falls, the small semi-industrial town upriver from her home which became a favorite topos in her art, and where—two decades later, at the age of 101—she would die and be buried.

"Memory is history recorded in our brain," the artist once wrote.[2] Her personal history was indeed preserved in the form of sharp memory traces, often anecdotal, in which details of the dress she wore or the children's games she played were treasured and retrieved during the act of painting. These private recollections were undoubtedly complemented by other people's oral accounts of past events and situations, so that Moses' individual renderings of what she called "old-timey things" were always embedded within the wider context of collective remembrance. Moreover, certain dominant historical events in the locality, such as the Battle of Bennington of 1777, having passed into regional folklore, became cornerstones of that project of structured commemoration to

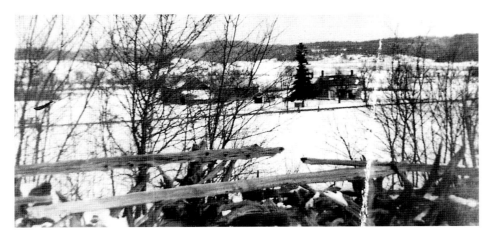

Fig. 2. Grandma Moses' farm. Photograph. Courtesy Carl and Shirley Moses

which her art seems essentially dedicated. In a sense, whether willfully or semiconsciously, Moses assumed the functions of local memorialist, accumulating a visual archive that preserves regional scenes that might otherwise have gotten lost. Insofar as it can be classified as "memory painting," her art highlights the typical—and sometimes the remarkable—moments in community life across time, tying social experience to a mapped and named topography.

Although one might expect a true "memory painter" to be alert to chronology and to possess a sense of history as shared experience, Moses was not altogether committed to the objective dating that her project might seem to entail. Her old woman's conception of the passage of time was more dependent upon an emotional calendar than one marked by precise sequential dates: for when she remembered something, it was not so much the month and year that mattered, nor the public context of large-scale political or social developments, but rather the intimate register of her own sensations and desires, whether as a child, an adolescent, a mother, or a grandmother.

Sometimes her memories appear admirably sharp and yet definitely positioned at a distance, tied to a time and place no longer present. This is certainly the effect of her verbal recollections, as witness this passage from her essay "My Life's History" (composed in her eighties at Otto Kallir's suggestion), where she recalls her time as a servant on the Whiteside Farm in the 1870s:

> when the Minster came and I could bring out the fine linen and the
> china tea set, and the heavy Silver, then with hot bisqwits home mad
> butter and Haney, with Home cured dryed beef, I was proud,
> But I some times now, think they came for eats more than to see Him,
> then mr whiteside died, and I drifted away from that neighborhood.[3]

But whereas this verbal evocation is set quite firmly in an irrecoverable past, Moses' visual records tend to carry a palpable sense that ancient scenes still linger on in the present: a strong impression of imaginative participation and the luminous particularity of her painterly style help to bridge the gap between *what once was* and *what still remains*.[4] Thus her visualizations of the past tend to play down the historian's concern with clear-cut dates and instead to engage with the vibrant immediacy of what is being summoned up. This displaces the temporal reference, transferring her scenes to another dimension, to a time outside history, glamorous and even utopian, the time of aesthetic timelessness, as it were.

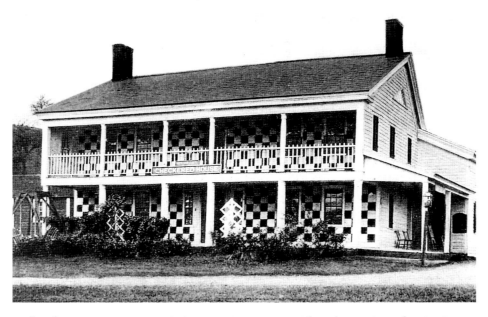

Fig. 3. The Checkered House, Cambridge, New York. Postcard. Courtesy Carl and Shirley Moses

In this connection, it is interesting to consider the series of paintings depicting the Checkered House: there are more than twenty recorded versions, produced over the period 1941–1959. The topos was patently one that attracted Moses because of its vivid historical associations. The Checkered House (fig. 3) was an old inn on the turnpike road a couple of miles south of the village of Cambridge, and not far from Eagle Bridge. Built in 1765, it achieved notoriety during the Revolutionary War, when it was taken over as the headquarters of the British forces in August 1777; a few days later it was used as a hospital after General Baum's troops succumbed at the Battle of Bennington.

In 1812, the inn served as a bivouac for volunteers marching to the Lake Champlain battlefields, and Lafayette was entertained there in 1824. Subsequently, it became a regular staging post, and horse races were held on a track nearby. With its distinctive façade of fourteen-inch square checkers in bright red and white, the house remained an unmistakable landmark for over a century, and it must have been very well known to the young Anna in the Washington County of the 1870s. Nevertheless, it is important to note that the building was destroyed by fire in 1907, so that by the time she came to depict it, it was no longer possible to revisit it in actuality. (Only a small stone marker records the location today.) Almost certainly she consulted picture postcards to refresh her idea of the subject, so that while there is no disputing the accuracy of her representation, the process of reconstitution itself is qualified by indirectness and a long time-lapse (see *The Old Checkered House*, 1944, plate 40). Curiously enough, the titles of several pictures in the cycle tie them to an explicit point in time: those executed during the 1940s invoke such diverse dates as 1850, 1853, 1860, and 1862. One of the last to be completed, a *Checkered House* produced in 1959, is inscribed by the artist "in the year 1841." It is noticeable that none of these dates corresponds to the "famous" dates mentioned above. (The year 1853, it happens, is the date when the house was repainted; 1860 is the date of Moses' birth.) One painting, done in 1949, is titled *The Checkered House in 1717*, an obvious anachronism since the house was not even built until 1765! One explanation may be that Moses' dating is altogether arbitrary, its purpose simply being to articulate the concept "long ago." Beyond this, it can be said that the flickering vividness of the checkered design transmutes the house into something unreal or, rather, mythical, as if the documentary impulse were ceding to poetic fancy. And although the painted scenes reflect seasonal changes—many show high summer, while others present the landscape under deep snow—they invariably repeat the same routine situation of travelers coming and going, whether by horse-drawn sleigh or by carriage, making scarcely any allusion to the unique events that mark the house's history. (Admittedly, some of the travelers are in uniform.) We may infer that, whereas within folk memory the Checkered House continued to be "historic" in the sense of being connected to momentous real events in the collective past, within Moses' creative mind the motif had forfeited its referential function to become a kind of abstract icon of the Memorable. Indeed, we could even speak of it as, more precisely, a symbol of *forgetting*, insofar as its historical import has been superseded by an aura of nostalgic vagueness.

May 10, 1862, is an exact date in regional history—it refers us to the great fire that enveloped the city of Troy on that day. The conflagration started in a high wind when a spark from a locomotive flew onto the roof of the rail and road bridge crossing the Hudson; the wooden structure was consumed in a few seconds, and embers were blown across to the city, torching hundreds of buildings. In the year 1939, a bank placed an advertisement in the local Troy newspaper to invoke the event of seventy-seven years before, under the claim that "this bank is proud to have played a part in rebuilding the stricken city." Grandma Moses' eye was caught by this item in the paper, and she cut it out. Her imagination converted its small oval image into her most dramatic theme, giving rise to another cycle of paintings between 1939 and 1959. The variant treatments of the Troy fire are testimony to Moses' inventiveness, for the comparatively feeble black and white illustration is marvelously transfigured in her color version, in which silhouetted firefighters with water buckets dash into an inferno of scarlet flames and black smoke (see *The Burning of Troy*, ca. 1939, plate 11 and *The Burning of Troy in 1862*, 1943, plate 12). In later versions, the town of Troy (elided in the newspaper image) is added to the background, its white houses looking vulnerable though as yet intact. Such an image represents a most successful conversion of a true fragment of history into an enduring public image.

As with the Checkered House, there are other series where the selfsame identifiable locale is linked to discrepant dates. Thus there are two paintings entitled *Home of Hezekiah King in 1776*, produced in 1942 and 1943, as well as a version done in 1943 entitled *Home of Hezekiah King in 1800 (No. 4)*. We know that the scene pays tribute to the onetime home of the artist's great-grandfather, who had enlisted in the Albany County Militia and in 1777 fought against the British at Ticonderoga. Moses' essay "My Life's History" indicates that King cleared land and built his home only in about 1786, so it might be argued that, whereas the latter title is plausible, the first-mentioned must be wrong. Yet the fact that Moses made two pictures with the same anomalous date can hardly be a simple lapse of concentration. Might it be that, for Moses, this is an emotional rather than a literal date, the glorious Revolutionary War being invoked in the formula "1776" as a reminder of the heroism of her ancestor? Pride in her personal connection with the past may have been a stronger motivation than the aspiration to historical accuracy.

As a child, Moses would naturally have learned all about the Battle of Bennington (probably during lessons in that same schoolhouse which, nowadays, has been relocated to the regional museum in Bennington town). This was an undoubtedly momentous happening from the same heroic period and another instance of a real event entering regional folklore. The Battle of Bennington—which in fact took place just inside New York State, some five miles outside the town—occurred when General Baum's troops (mostly German mercenaries, as it happened) approached Bennington in the hope of capturing horses and supplies, and clashed with the Green Mountain militia under General John Stark. The latter surrounded and almost annihilated Baum's troops on August 16, 1777, a decisive victory which cleared the way for the surrender of the British at Saratoga two months later. The battle site itself is nowadays a memorial park, set close to the Walloomsac River on the road from Bennington to Eagle Bridge. Moses knew all this, and, having lived in

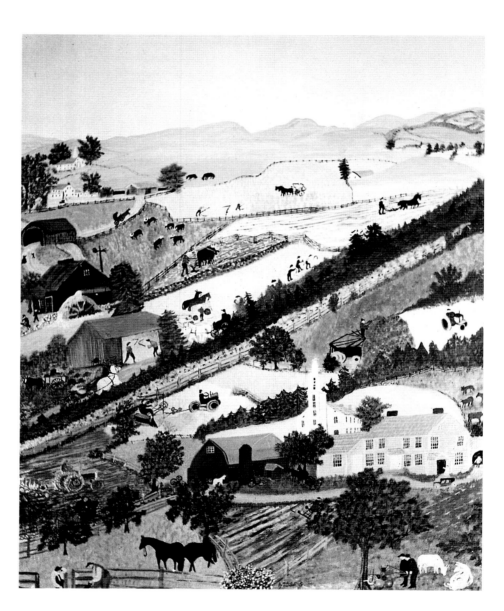

Fig. 4. Grandma Moses, *Year 1860, Year 1940,* 1949. Oil on Masonite, 26 x 21 inches (66 x 53.3 cm). Kallir 847. Private collection. Courtesy Galerie St. Etienne, New York

Bennington itself, she was well acquainted with the striking Bennington Battle Monument, a tall white spire erected in the late nineteenth century to commemorate the victory.[5]

It is said that the artist, having been invited to produce a history picture by the National Society of the Daughters of the American Revolution, pored over a number of reference works before commencing, principally in order to dig out authentic details of battle dress. Thanks to a curious error of conception, Moses depicted the historical scene of battle with its flags, cannon, and troops dressed in old-fashioned uniforms and firing muskets, but she couldn't stop herself from adding a clear representation of the distinctive white monument in the background (see *The Battle of Bennington*, 1953, plate 41). Once the incongruity was pointed out, she made shift in a subsequent version to omit it, seemingly embarrassed by the anachronism.

However, I would see this conflation of *then* and *now* not so much as an intellectual error as a manifestation of an emotional truth: namely, that Moses' predilection to remember was so strong that past events resonated in her mind to the point of seeming simultaneously recent *and* long-gone. The interpolation of an object from the late nineteenth century into a portrayal of a scene dated 1777 could be construed as an effective device to signal the persistence of memory, the monument and the painting enacting a double commemoration. And although it appears that Moses probably did not have access to any contemporary document on which to base her version of the battle and was in all likelihood fabricating an impression thereof, it might not follow that her image is "wrong"—only that its impetus is to invoke a radiant myth rather than to record unimpeachable facts.

A unique work which very obviously foregrounds the contrast between *then* and *now*—and thereby shifts ineluctably into the elegiac mode—is the programmatic painting *Year 1860, Year 1940* (1949, fig. 4). The picture constitutes a coherent landscape, but this is emphatically divided into two time zones by a stone wall running diagonally from bottom left to top right: the left-hand zone represents 1860 and the right-hand one 1940. It is harvest time on both sides of the diagonal, yet the viewer is clearly meant to notice that farm work proceeds on the left by way of handheld scythes or horse-drawn plows, while on the right the workers are driving great tractors and mechanical harvesters. The overt message is obvious enough: the old farming practices of yesteryear have been overtaken by new technologies. No doubt there is also a covert message, which we can fairly infer from the general context of Moses' celebrations of the old farming life: that the new machines, for all their efficiency, mark a transition to a new lifestyle which places traditional rural values at risk. The painting draws no explicit moral, yet its paradoxical structure—two eras contracted within a single space—surely alerts us to the possibility of a choice, an emotional engagement with either one or the other of the two eras. To the right is what we have, to the left is what we have lost. The contrast can hardly be seen as a very original one on Moses' part, yet her quiet treatment may secrete a secondary shock wave.

Other images celebrate "first time" moments in regional history. The appearance of the first automobile on the Cambridge Pike implicitly

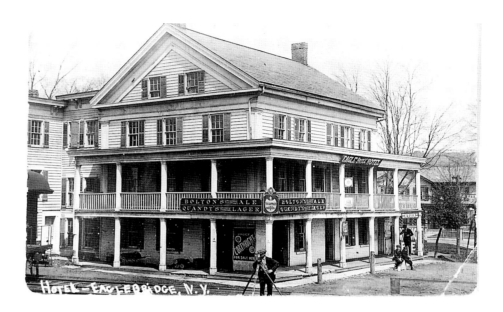

foreshadowed the demise of the horse-drawn vehicle. Moses, who had
seen her first automobile in 1896 at a fair at Gypsy Hill Park in Virginia,
painted her first automobile in 1939 or earlier in the form of a large
black monster (see *The First Automobile*, plate 13). A more humorous image
painted in 1944, called *The Old Automobile* (plate 14), places a contraption
dating from around 1900 at a country crossroads in a near collision with
a horse-and-trap: perhaps Moses was amused at the thought that both
designs had become equally obsolete.

Many of Moses' images record places that no longer survive, as in the
various evocations of her birthplace and childhood home, the Cottrell–
Skiff Farm near Greenwich, which had long since vanished in reality
(see *Grandma's Birthplace*, 1959, plate 79). Yet, despite the vicissitudes of
history, there are many examples of sites or buildings that did still exist
at the time she painted them. Equally, it is true that a majority of these
already dated back a considerable number of years, so that her renderings are typically premised upon the longevity of constructions which,
because they have survived so long, appear extremely vulnerable and
in urgent need of being recorded. One of Moses' most characteristic
concerns was the covered bridge, of which there were dozens to be found
in the locality. "Bridges were landmarks in olden times," she wrote in
her autobiography.[6] Although she sometimes identified them by name,
isolating the structure as if in a portrait (as in *The Old Hoosick Bridge*, a
motif she addressed no less than five times in the year 1947), her more
common practice was to use the covered bridge as a *passe-partout* device

which she could drop at will into any landscape where there was a river. The covered bridge thereby becomes a mobile sign, its archaic design implying the quality of "pastness" without the artist having to make an attempt to pinpoint any actual structure by date or location.

Some paintings do tackle specific buildings, such as the *Eagle Bridge Hotel*, which Moses carefully rendered in a picture dated 1959 (plate 78). Here the hotel with its white wood balconies and columns seems to have been copied from an old postcard (fig. 5), while the train station and smoke-belching locomotive in the background look like spontaneous inventions. Otto Kallir has pointed out that the house in the painting *Apple Butter Making* (1947, plate 29) is "lifted" from an old photograph of the Dudley Place near Staunton in Virginia, one of five places where the Moses family had farmed during their time in the Shenandoah Valley.[7] Moses transliterates the photographic image in painstaking detail, down to the white lyre pattern to either side of the portico and the white rocking horse half-hidden just inside the door. Here is an example of fidelity to appearances coinciding with gross disregard of spatial logic.

At the age of twelve, Moses began work as a domestic in the household of the wealthy Whiteside family, and she loved to remember the crowded Sunday gatherings in the Whiteside Church, built at the beginning of the nineteenth century on a wooded slope above the stream of Fly Brook. Beside the church, which still stands, there is a cemetery, largely occu-pied by descendants of the Whitesides. Moses' *Whiteside Church* of 1945 (plate 36), with its plain presentation of a white building and white gravestones, is a good example of an unadorned documentary record—though one suspects some emotional investment in the preponderant color *white*.

Moses' views of local towns are usually executed with panache and an air of authenticity. Assuredly, the dozen or so pictures labeled "Hoosick Falls" ask to be seen as faithful renderings of the real Hoosick Falls: the river, the rail track, the roads and bridges, the factories and their chim-neys, the churches and the rows of houses—all these seem to be disposed in a fair semblance of actuality, albeit there are discrepancies of scale and several fluctuations of detail between the images (see plates 44 and 45). A large aerial view of the town, published as a lithograph, survives among the artist's papers and may, together with local photographs, have been a key consultation document. Her renderings of the hamlet of Eagle Bridge, with its rail station, local Methodist church with white steeple, flax mill, two prominent hotels, and covered bridge complete with painted eagle at one end[8] correspond likewise to a layout still recognizable to today's visitor to Washington County, and may be seen as convincing reconstructions of a site fixed in memory from her early days there as a schoolgirl and later as a servant in Mrs. Abraham Vandenberg's house.[9] In later life, it was from the station at Eagle Bridge that Moses regularly took the train to Hoosick Falls to attend the Episcopalian church, and it was here that she was fêted by crowds of proud local residents on her arrival home in 1949, after her momentous trip to Washington to meet President Truman. One might almost see a kind of spatial necessity at work, as if certain magnetic sites, frequently invoked and depicted, were invested with a special capacity to recur in her biography and to embody a mythic continuity. To a degree, Grandma Moses reconstructed Grandma Moses Country, yet at the same time she managed to reside within it in a literal way and to savor its objective coherence.

Unlike the Hoosick Falls cycle, other depictions that at first might have appeared to be "local" turned out to be more or less imaginary. For instance, there is a story that the municipality of Williamstown, Massachusetts, hearing of the existence of a picture called *Williamstown*, took steps to purchase it and then backed off when nobody could recognize any of the buildings. Indeed, the three or four versions of this subject (e.g., plate 46) suggest a miscellany of independent architectural motifs, each almost certainly copied from irrelevant sources in her image bank. Similarly, the Troy that Moses places in the background of later versions of the *Burning of Troy*, a Troy *not* shown in the original press clipping, is entirely fabricated.

The inevitable question thus needs to be posed as to the authenticity of Moses' portrayals of places. Just how reliable was her memory? Is this how those places really looked? What liberties did she take with the visual facts? Can we be sure we are really seeing what we are told we are seeing?

In certain respects, Moses does seem to have aspired to be a reliable and accurate copyist. An early work made before 1940 and entitled *On the Road to Greenwich* (fig. 6) is annotated very scrupulously in a hand-written text drawn up in 1946 for Otto Kallir's book *Grandma Moses: American Primitive*:

> *This is a north west vew of my Fathers Russell King Robertson Farm, on Oak Hill,*
> *Looking south east you can see van Ness Hill, and Battle field Park.*
> *the Owl Kill, and the state road, runing from Troy to Glens Falls.*
> *some call this a pretty valley. But give me the Shandoah valley, every time,*[10]

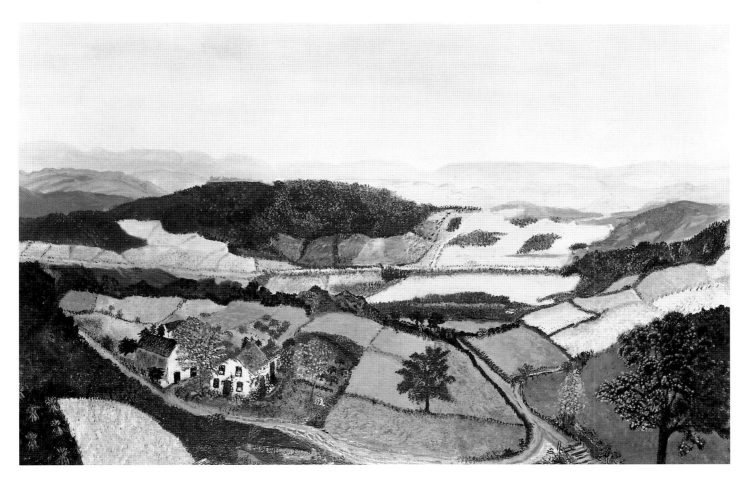

Fig. 6. Grandma Moses, *On the Road to Greenwich*, 1940 or earlier. Oil on cardboard, 14 x 22 inches (35.6 x 55.9 cm). Kallir 26. Private collection. Courtesy Galerie St. Etienne, New York

At first glance, this caption advertises the artist's confidence, authority, and scruple, for its successive names point to the topography on the page opposite, moving from the near-to farm to more distant landmarks, as if annotating a pictorial map. (We may recall that Moses was an avid map-maker as a schoolgirl.) Once we reflect on the matter, though, we realize that the picture was prepared many years after Moses had last seen the farm, and her apparently faithful details turn out to be a little askew. If the farm is indeed sited at Oak Hill—lying on higher ground about a mile north of the Hoosic after it has begun to flow westward from Eagle Bridge—then one might be prepared to concede that it is possible to glimpse Bennington Battlefield Park five miles away to the southeast. Yet Moses does not mention her own farm, lying only two miles off in a similar direction, nor does she indicate that the rooftops of Eagle Bridge might crop up within the same prospect. True, there does exist a stream known as Owl Kill which runs from north to south across this prospect, flowing into the Hoosic at Eagle Bridge: and indeed the painting features a stretch of water in the middle distance. Yet the highway that runs clear across the picture cannot possibly be the state road from Troy to Glens Falls: to see that, we would need to look in the opposite direction (i.e., toward the northwest), and even then it would be impossible to make out the road following the floor of the Hudson Valley some nine miles away from Oak Hill. Of course, the artist could have made an innocent mistake, misidentifying what is in fact another state road which comes north out of Hoosick Falls and then runs parallel to the Owl Kill up to Cambridge and Salem. I daresay that these minutiae are trivial in themselves, yet—given that this is such a rare and punctilious effort on Moses' part to justify her painted image—they do seem symptomatic of a tendency to relinquish objectivity in favor of another standard of truth. As it is, the reference to the beauty of the Shenandoah Valley may betray the fact that her mind's eye was being seduced by other visual memories, encouraging her to enhance her view of a stretch of New York State in the light of the more inspiring landscape of Virginia.

Let us turn to the farm outside Eagle Bridge where Moses spent most of her life. Of the Mount Nebo homestead there are many portrayals, beginning with one of her first yarn pictures, known as *Mt. Nebo on the Hill* (1940 or earlier, plate 3). The layout of the farm is always simple yet distinctive: a white-painted wooden farmhouse with a prominent portico stands to the right of a driveway advancing from the road, while darker outbuildings, including one massive barn, stand to the left. This disposition, invariably shown "head-on" and roughly from the west, can be found in all the paintings with explicit titles like *Mt. Nebo* (plates 47 and 48) or *Grandma Moses' Home*. Elsewhere, similar (though never quite identical) farms lend a square-cut emphasis to her favorite snowscapes or else appear as incidentals in narrative or genre scenes where no precise locale is signaled. By now we are not surprised to note a loosening of specificity in the general topography of the painted version of Grandma Moses Country.

Moses finally left this house in 1951, when she moved across the road to live with her daughter in a new and smaller home set just above a steep slope down to the Hoosic River, at a point where it enters upon a long curve, just after Case Brook has flowed into it. It was this little panorama that, in the space of a few days in 1952, Moses reproduced in two of her most striking local views, *Hoosick River, Summer* and *Hoosick River, Winter* (plates 49 and 50). These are both dated March 7, 1952. Since it is known that Moses often recorded her paintings in batches, we can be sure that the two scenes were contemporary though not necessarily worked up simultaneously. Nonetheless, it is obvious that the two are a closely associated pair, representing the same scene at two different seasons, and using the selfsame compositional schema with the river swagging below the viewer and around a flat promontory with wooded hills in the background. In the summer scene, the landscape is packed with narrative detail: on this side of the river (i.e., on Moses' family property), children are climbing a tree to pick blossoms, while a farmer with a white horse (somewhat resembling the plowman in Brueghel's *Fall of Icarus*) is halfway through plowing a fenced-off field. Across the river, a man and another white animal are standing by a farmhouse and a red barn. Beyond this, another farm nestles on a slope below trees; two separate zones of woodland cover the two hilltops, with a band of pastureland in between. To the right, one or two white houses amid the trees hint at the location of Eagle Bridge. A bold upright rising insistently nearby could represent a tall pole. Most significantly, running clear across the middle distance is a railway track with a long goods-train drawn by a jaunty black locomotive: this accords perfectly with the fact that the Boston & Maine line still operated through this spot in the 1950s. Pictorially, the composition relies on a rhythmic disposition of soft tones, with dabs of red—the coal fender and conductor's van of the train, the walls of the barns, the dresses of the two girls playing on the left—creating a visual interplay of near and far objects that makes for a strong sense of buoyancy and animation.

Once juxtaposed with this florid image, the companion piece entitled *Hoosick River, Winter* reveals itself as a fascinating mixture of fidelity and deviance. The basic compositional schema is retained, albeit with some slight variations in the outline of the river and the undulations of the wooded skyline, which at the very least demonstrate that Moses did not transpose her design mechanically. It is notable that she has now inserted a couple of flood ponds on the low-lying bank to the right. Indeed, everything else about the view has changed. The warmth conveyed by the presence of farmsteads has evaporated: Moses has deleted all signs of habitation across the water, apart from some minimal rooftops to the far right, again at the point where Eagle Bridge is situated. The enigmatic pole has been shifted forward to the trees at the far riverbank: painted even taller, it now looks like a warning finger as it crosses the skyline of distant hills (one of which might be thought to be Willard Mountain). Moses has decided to insist upon the fact of wintriness and to exaggerate the atmosphere of deathly silence by not only removing the warm reds of the barns but also excising all reference to the railway. This is quite

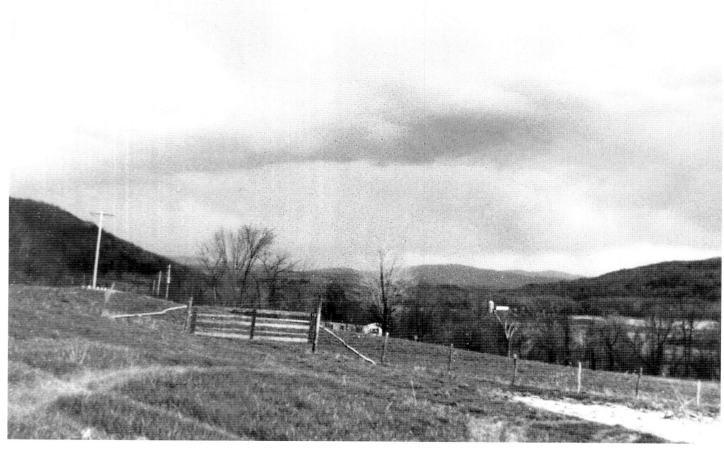

Fig. 7. View along Hoosic Valley from Mt. Nebo, 1982. Photograph by Hildegard Bachert. Courtesy Galerie St. Etienne, New York

remarkable, since passing trains were objectively a prominent feature of the view and might have been expected to stand out even more than usual under snowy conditions. In this regard, the image stands in mournful contrast to the classic snowscape treatments of Hoosick Falls: *Hoosick Falls in Winter* (1944) in the Abby Aldrich Rockefeller Folk Art Collection, Williamsburg, Virginia and *Hoosick Falls in Winter* (1944, plate 45) in the Phillips Collection, Washington, D.C. In these Falls paintings, the ebullient locomotive and train are an indispensable embodiment of animation and conviviality. Practically the only moving objects indicated in *Hoosick River, Winter* are the brace of pheasants flapping their wings in the right-hand corner. We also see a hunter with a gun taking aim in the center foreground, as well as other figures at the left, and two red-costumed horsemen just across the river. Yet the fundamental impact of the image is one of stasis: the morbid beauty of bare trunks and dun-colored foliage, the tingling whiteness of ribbons of snow, and the exquisite equilibrium of zones of palest blue—ponds, river, sky, far hills—gripped in frozen inanimateness. (Another Brueghel echo would be the great snowscape of *The Hunters in the Snow*, which also plays on a contrast between the magical stillness of a vast frozen landscape and small, isolated pockets of human activity.) The implication of this deviant, and emotionally quite shattering, version of the view from below Moses' new house is that the painter was ready to eradicate real-life features, in this case the railway line, if her artistic instinct so dictated. The comparison forces us to recognize that the winter scene aims not to replicate an actual view but to evoke an atmosphere. It most successfully captures the impression of extreme wintriness, while renouncing the corroborative references that would anchor the scene to a specific place in real space.

It has become obvious that we must adjust our sense of the relation between Grandma Moses' paintings and the real-life terrain she inhabited. We are beginning to see that, despite the recourse to regional photographs, there is after all a strong tendency to neglect strict realism. Did Moses ever make sketches on her travels or set to work directly in front of her subject matter? The signs are that she was never a *plein air* painter, despite the color photograph taken in the 1950s in which the artist has been studiously posed, sitting in a field and dabbing with a brush at a painting of a river, a church, and forested hills.[11] Nevertheless, we do know that Moses was an attentive observer of the effects of color and light out of doors: "When I paint, I study and study the outside lots of times," she stated in her autobiography, going on to discuss the nuances of green to be found in the natural world and refuting the suggestion that snow in shadow gives off any hint of blue.[12]

Despite her inclination to execute her work indoors, relying on memory and visual prompts, there is firm evidence that Moses did work directly in front of at least one motif: for we know that her bedroom doubled as her studio, on the upper floor of the Mount Nebo house, with a window facing roughly southeast up the Hoosic Valley.[13] But let us first consider what was the likely tract of landscape visible to her from such a viewpoint. Shot on a wintry day in 1982 when all the leaves had fallen, a photograph taken at ground level from near the house (fig. 7) indicates the fundamentals of the prospect: first comes the sloping pastureland of the farm, with a wooden gate and fencing, telegraph poles and wiring, a neighboring house, and several single trees; then thicker woodland in the middle distance half masking a stretch of the river, with a silo and one or two other farm buildings; to either side of the river stand two local hills, rounded and wooded and rising to about 250 feet;

and finally there is a series of more distant ridges and peaks receding to the horizon (possibly these include Indian Hill and Whipstock Hill, which both rise over 1,000 feet, to the west of Bennington at the southern end of the Green Mountain range).

When compared with this photograph, *Hoosick Valley (From the Window)*, dated 1946 (plate 42)—a justly celebrated image and one of the artist's personal favorites—reveals the liberties which Moses could take with strict visual fact. Even if we allow that the painter's vantage point was some twenty feet higher up than that of the photographer on the ground, it is at once obvious that the painted prospect has been considerably doctored. Moses is painting not what she sees, but what she knows is there, soaring up in her imagination to an aerial viewpoint a hundred feet and more above the house. The pictorial landscape makes the photograph look wretchedly uninformative, for it offers such a generous supply of supplementary details: not only a bold red barn and a significant scattering of local homesteads, none of them masked by trees, but also the bold, bright band of the river, a wooded ridge in mid-distance, some hint of a township beyond the right-hand hill (this may be Hoosick Falls), and finally a stretch of green pasture leading up to rounded blue hills at the skyline, with at least one sharp peak to the left (perhaps Bald Mountain, to the northeast of Bennington). The image is made paradoxical, and magical, by the further addition of a willfully, though delicately, daubed imitation of a dotted curtain and a window frame around the rim of the image. By telling us so unequivocally that this really is the view from her window, Moses demands our acquiescence to what is in reality a fabrication. The view is preposterous, it is plainly at variance with physical fact: and yet somehow we can believe in it. In some sense, this is what Moses saw when she gazed out of her bedroom window up the valley.

All the same, what does it mean to say that she so clearly "saw" what in actuality was hidden? Perhaps the answer is that another mode of perception comes into play once a gifted artist has absorbed an intimately loved landscape. There is a shift to a fresh outlook in which inner vision, nourished by memory and imagination alike, feels entitled to treat perception simply as a pretext, a springboard to a loftier viewpoint. Indeed, we may add, it would be a rare human being whose idea of an environment was uniquely based on the data of the senses, independent of feeling, reverie, or hearsay. In the time it took for Moses fully to develop her painterly fluency and aesthetic sense, her apprehension of the forms and phenomena that made up her "homeland" had been transfigured, regulated by a whole range of internalized perspectives indebted as much to intuition and invention as to observation. One might even say that the gesture of attributing names and dates to her imagery had become an emblematic act—no longer an index of literal truth and more like a magical invocation.

Similar versions of the same Mount Nebo prospect include *From My Window* of 1942/1950, as well as three superb renderings of *Hoosick Valley* produced in 1942, 1943, and 1946, which inject a further thrill by adopting an even loftier viewpoint. Now we are looking out and up the valley as if from an airplane, and the widening panorama turns into a breathtaking sequence of recessions softening from green to blue. In the 1942 painting, Mount Nebo, complete with farmhouse and outbuildings, is quoted as a tiny vignette popped into the bottom left-hand corner of the image, like a marginal detail in a medieval Book of Hours. It is neat as a doll's house, a plaything set there at whim; it is like a little signature addressed to the select few who will catch the reference.

Undoubtedly there are other, unnamed views that could be invoked as belonging to this same series. While she never again used the device of the curtain and window frame, Moses' postwar style typically pursues the same softening of the landscape, exploiting a looser brushstroke to draw together areas of pale pasture and dark woodland, as if deliberately to install a restful, homely, comforting surface without shadow or roughness. In their combination of slightly irregular zones of varied hue, her typical landscapes can readily be compared to a patchwork quilt, with its connotations of softness, warmth, comfort, and homeliness. Thus it is that Grandma Moses Country—by which I now mean that intimate homeland reconstituted in her art—may be said to have been shunted off the regulated track of historical and geographical referentiality and into an unmeasured dimension exempt from interruption and change.

I have mentioned the existence of a major visual resource which acted as a distinct alternative to the resources of personal observation, private memory, and public history or folklore. As Jane Kallir has shown, not only did Moses often base her scenes on Currier & Ives prints, such as the rural compositions of a George Henry Durrie or a Fanny Palmer, she also exploited popular imagery in the form of local postcards, calendars, Christmas cards, and greeting cards, as well as cuttings from newspapers and magazines such as *LIFE*, *Saturday Evening Post*, and *National Geographic*. Her extensive image bank has been preserved by the Galerie St. Etienne, where its items have been sorted under a variety

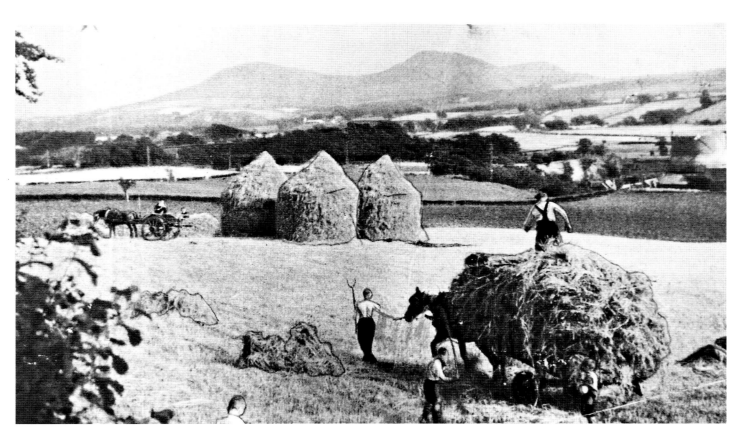

Fig. 8. Field with haystacks. Magazine clipping with pencil notations by Grandma Moses. Courtesy Galerie St. Etienne, New York

of headings, with idyllic narrative scenes of sugaring, haymaking, plowing, dancing, picnicking, or skating, and depictions of fields, hills, villages, farms, churches, mills, bridges, wagons, sleighs, automobiles, locomotives, and so forth.

This treasure trove of printed vignettes is irrefutable proof that Moses exploited readymade imagery, for it appears likely that few works were composed without some recourse to these templates. It seems that the artist's practice was to lay down a basic "arena" in the form of an uninhabited white space and then to position her various clippings on the surface, moving them around until they harmonized. Finally, using pencil and carbon paper, she would firmly transpose her motifs onto the board and then complete them in paint.

Among many examples of landscapes preserved in the resource box is a kodachrome print taken from the April 1941 issue of *National Geographic*. Its caption is entirely apposite: "Fields of Ripening Crops Cover a Rolling Maryland Countryside Like a Giant Patchwork Quilt." Though ostensibly a landscape that Moses never visited, the view seems perfectly consistent with the patchwork effect typical of her poeticized domain.

(It is noticeable that this particular magazine page has been carefully lined off in rectangular segments, as if to facilitate transposition, though this was not her normal practice.) Elsewhere, colored landscapes have been snipped out from magazines and marked in bold pencil—the curves of a road, the outlines of haystacks and farmworkers, the profile of distant hills—all these lines are sure evidence of the practice of transposing through the use of carbon paper (see fig. 8). We are bound to suppose that any landscapes constructed by this method must be at odds with the reality of Eagle Bridge and environs. This means that if she ever did make use of that image of Maryland "like a giant patchwork quilt," then any claim of regional authenticity in regard to the resulting work would collapse.

Ultimately, there is no point in judging Grandma Moses' work on the criterion of fidelity to literal fact, when the evidence is that she never really pursued this ideal. Rather, we are beginning to see that Moses' painterly world is governed by a principle of creative orchestration whereby different elements—some real, some imagined; some authentic, some made-up—are integrated within an overall pattern of topographical allusion and cross-connection. Personal recollection, local postcards, popular imagery of arbitrary provenance, and folkloric associations, combine with her more and more assertive aesthetic sensibility to establish a perfectly consistent and recognizable "world." It is one in which it is still possible to trace actual topographical and temporal references, suggestive of authenticity while not being slavishly accurate: these painted representations are, as it were, "appropriate fictions." Hence, in its disparate amalgamations, Grandma Moses' pictorial world tends finally to be more a matter of imaginative reconfiguration in an ahistorical or poetic mode. If the popularity of her art rests on its air of documentary scruple, it is a fact that the vast majority of her pictures are fabricated and generalized, pointing less to an actual time and space than to a utopian calendar and realm, marked by such ritualized social events as Sugaring-Off, Harvesting, and Thanksgiving, as well as by equally ritualized or talismanic references to a Mount Nebo, a Hoosic River, and a Cambridge Valley which have by now modulated into autonomous artistic properties.

One final example may serve to round off what has become an attempt to determine the balance between replication and invention in Moses' landscape art. It is, I think, a masterpiece which Otto Kallir saw as pivotal to her output. Now known as *Black Horses* (plate 17), it was produced in the autumn of the wonderfully prolific year of 1942. First cited in Moses' own Record Book as *Lower Cambridge Valley*, it was subsequently retitled and then discussed by the artist in a commentary written a few years later.[14]

Undoubtedly, then, this image began as a prospect of the lower Cambridge Valley and is thus consonant with the view I discussed above, namely *On the Road to Greenwich* (fig. 6). We do indeed find the same neat farmstead in the left foreground, previously identified as the Robertson Farm on Oak Hill. This time, however, the farm is portrayed as a tiny miniature (exactly as happens to Mount Nebo in *Hoosick Valley* of 1942). There are also discrepancies in the maplike rendering of the lines of the Owl Kill stream and of the various roads running straight or in long curves about the countryside. Further, the background of *Black Horses* is inconsistent with the outlook to the southeast, which the earlier picture had claimed to treat: the hills have now closed in, with no outlook through them, so that the view could be construed as an east or northeast prospect toward the Vermont border, with the Green Mountains in the distance. Moreover, the outlined fields have multiplied, creating a tighter, almost gridlike mosaic. Strangely too, as viewers, we are now both higher up, looking down on the tiny farm, and lower down, unable to peer as far over the blue-tinged horizon as we could in the pre-1940 painting. In fact, the foreground of *Black Horses* constitutes something rather more stable and credible, for the implied viewer is no longer suspended above the valley but stands on a thickly grassed piece of level ground, a kind of viewing ledge reaching across the forefront of the outlook. Moses has framed the prospect with a stand of white birch trees and another single tree, their boughs stretching upward toward the skyline and thus, through a well-known device of landscape art, persuading us to connect foreground to distance. To the left, two children dressed in white are riding a single black horse, while to the right the two magnificent black horses of the title gallop freely and with noticeable wildness.

While she omits to say whether these are living children and related to her, Moses' commentary makes it plain that she identifies the paired black horses with her remote family history. In 1777, her great-grandfather Archibald Robertson had been plowing one day in a field and had spotted the approaching British army. He promptly rode one of the horses down through Coila toward Bennington, meeting the Bennington Boys on his way; he was then involved in the ensuing battle near Walloomsac, which led to the death of that horse, and to its subsequent near-sanctification in Moses' reminiscence. I would suggest that, in her work, the black horse becomes a multivalent symbol. On one level, it functions as a recognizable and authentic element of country life

in the early decades of the twentieth century; on another, it represents
a private sign of family pride and nostalgia for a distant moment of
colorful history. By extension, it connotes the progressive demise of that
happy ruralism which had flourished up until the twentieth century.
Looking back at the programmatic *Year 1860, Year 1940* (1949; fig. 4),
we see several pairs of black horses actively participating in scenes of
plowing and harvesting in the archaic section of the image, whereas a
single surviving pair of black horses has been left to graze idly in a
small field in the modern section, their labor value superseded by the
mechanical horsepower of tractors and gasoline. (A glance through the
Moses catalogue shows a predilection for paired horses pulling carriages,
sleighs, or farming vehicles, although principles of visual variety seem
to dictate that these are not invariably twinned black horses, but are
often a black next to a white horse, or a black next to a brown horse.)

My conclusion must be that Moses did aspire to render her locality in the
light of reminiscence and that she remained loyal to topographical fact
in a certain percentage of her paintings. Yet she set no premium upon
pedantic realism and was quite prepared to rearrange her scenes in
accordance with an aesthetic of visual cohesion and emotional coziness,
often careless of spatial logic. Similarly, her grasp of history proper—
rather weak—relied more on family anecdote and regional tradition than
on anything approaching erudite study. Significantly, the chronological
references she cherished tend to cluster around the heroic date of 1777,
while more recent dates have a diminished aura. It is an obvious point
to make that such major events as the two World Wars occurred in Moses'
lifetime, yet they left not the slightest trace upon her artistic expression.
We must recognize that this old woman's sense of time and place was
often flagrantly at odds with the world she literally inhabited.

   At the same time, I think it clear that fidelity to objective fact is no
longer a self-evident value in our culture and that artistic license can
often facilitate a positive rerouting of the impulse to represent the outer
world, giving rise to heightened versions of the real. Sometimes such
enhancement involves emphatic stylization, and it can even embrace
hyperbole and distortion. The point to remember is that an artist who
neglects the discipline of direct observation may invest in the alternative
discipline of subjective vision and attend to the illuminations which are
fashioned within the mysterious workshop of memory and then perfected
in the work of painterly transposition and orchestration. In a way,
I think Moses was perfectly aware of what Washington County "really"

looked like, but equally she understood that there was nothing to be gained by turning out a series of pedantic pictorial maps. Instead, she became the attentive surveyor of a topography of the heart, splendidly impervious to any charge of anachronism or perspectival inconsistency. The virtue of her work must finally be located in its emotional integrity, its intuitive coherence as a poetic archive. And while some viewers may find that this art of elegiac remembrance smacks of sentimentality, a pointless harking back to a doomed ruralism, others may discern in its implicit drama of difference—Year 1777 versus Year 2001, as it were— a quite spirited defense of elemental values that may still have a bearing upon the lifestyles and ethical options of our social future. ❧ ❁ ❧

NOTES

*   I am grateful to the Galerie St. Etienne for having allowed me access to the Moses image bank, and to Hildegard Bachert for her illuminating comments. I wish also to record my thanks to Jane Kallir for helping me test the topographical hypothesis by driving me around Grandma Moses Country with tireless enthusiasm; and to Carl and Shirley Moses for their hospitality and help with documentation.

1.   This river is a key reference in the creative topography I am examining here. I refer to it as the "Hoosic River" in accordance with present-day mapping convention, though Grandma Moses always spells it "Hoosick," which indeed remains the standard spelling in place-names like Hoosick Falls and North Hoosick.

2.   Grandma Moses, *My Life's History*, edited by Otto Kallir (New York: Harper and Row, 1952), 3.

3.   Grandma Moses, "My Life's History," in Otto Kallir (ed.), *Grandma Moses: American Primitive* (New York: Dryden Press, 1946; 2nd ed., Garden City, N.Y.: Doubleday, 1947), 44.

4.   Here one might invoke Marcel Proust's distinction between the more or less shallow and mechanical act of *réminiscence* and the overwhelming experience of *reviviscence*, wherein sensations generated by involuntary memory bring about an illusion of total immersion in a past experience.

5.   It happens that today's Bennington Museum, close to the monument, houses not only Moses' former schoolhouse, but also an old scale-model of the battleground, showing the confluence of the Hoosic and the Walloomsac. Moses' 1953 painting of the battle hangs in the museum's Grandma Moses Gallery.

6.   Moses, *My Life's History*, 101.

7.   See Otto Kallir, *Grandma Moses* (New York: Harry N. Abrams, 1973), 229.

8.   Moses, *My Life's History*, 101.

9.   Ibid., 40.

10.   Uncorrected hand-written commentary (facsimile) by the artist, accompanying plate 12, titled *Cambridge Valley* instead of *On the Road to Greenwich*, in Otto Kallir (ed.), *Grandma Moses: American Primitive*.

11.   In effect a publicity still, the photograph was reproduced on the cover of the Gallery of Modern Art's exhibition in New York in 1969. The painting Moses is supposedly completing is nameless and undated, and cited simply as *River Landscape* in the unnumbered appendix to the catalogue in Otto Kallir's *Grandma Moses* (1973), p. 325. It shows a very wide river stretching to a distant lake and is clearly a larger-than-life fantasy rather than a portrayal of any actual local scene. (If there are any real-life memories informing the work, they are more likely to be of the Shenandoah Valley or of the Hudson and Lake Champlain.)

12.   Moses, *My Life's History*, 134.

13.   Other ways of viewing the outer world were known to Moses and contributed to her painterly style. In a 1952 interview, she speaks of having been impressed by the reflection upon the shiny hubcap of an automobile which arrived in the yard one day, a distorted yet perfect little image which she later replicated when she found a window on her porch which also bore a reflection and which she could frame at will by moving the window slightly, this way or that. See Gregory Clark, "'I Just Follow Nature' Says Grandma Moses," in *Weekend Picture Magazine*, February 16, 1952. I think the anecdote is suggestive, pointing to a typical facet of her style, namely the tendency to miniaturize and compress her scenes into neatly delineated ensembles.

14.   See the uncorrected hand-written commentary (facsimile) by the artist, accompanying plate 13, *Black Horses*, in Otto Kallir (ed.), *Grandma Moses: American Primitive*.

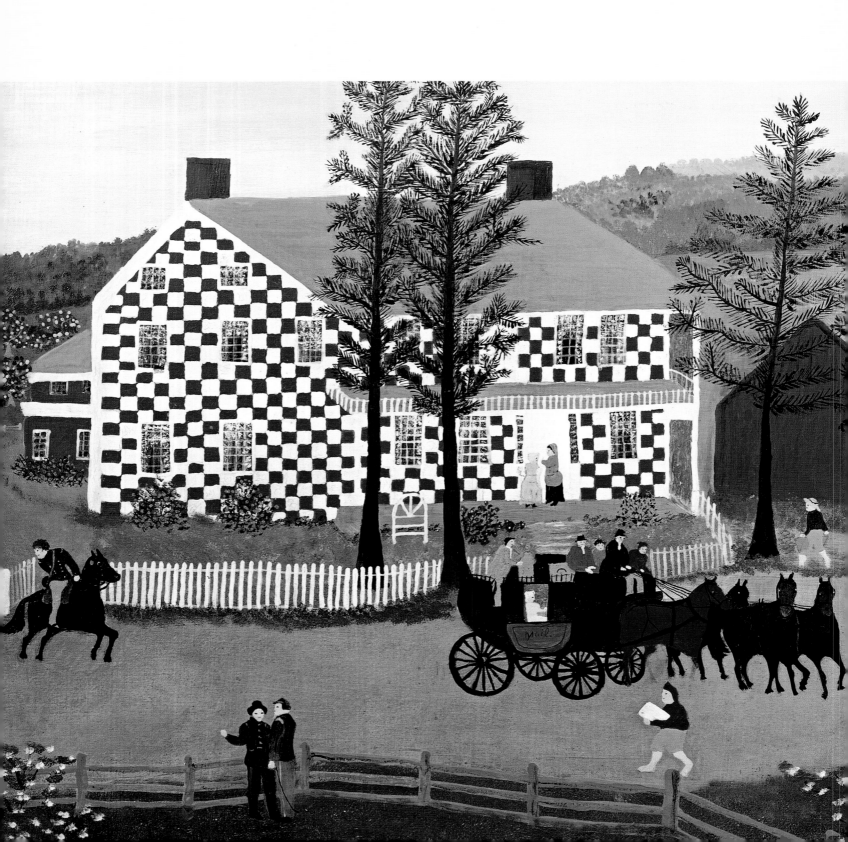

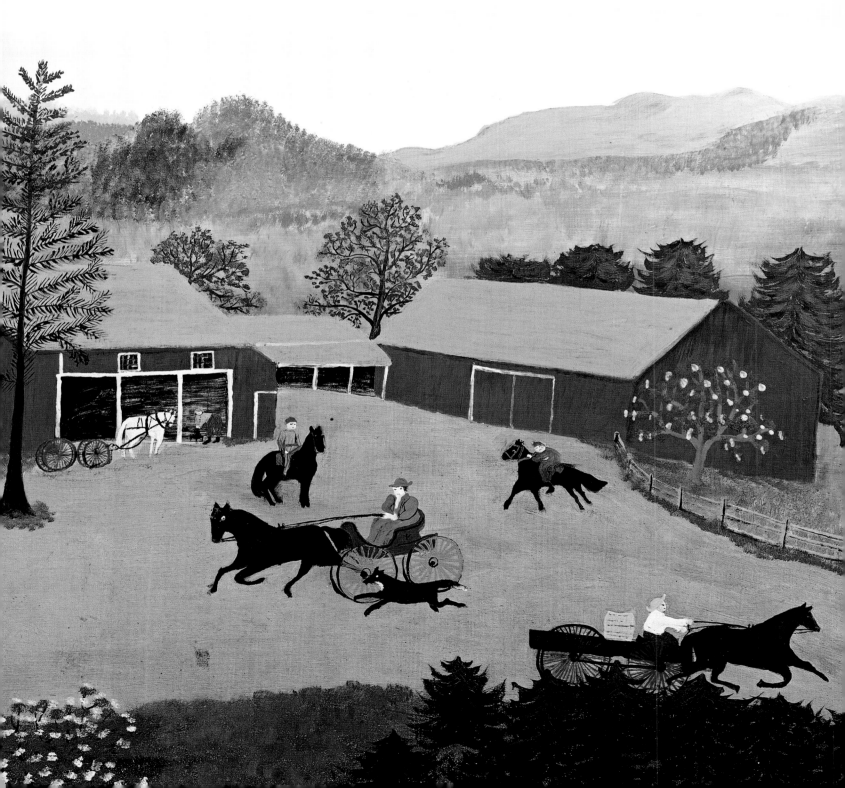

Catalogue

Notes to the Reader

Most of the quotes in the Catalogue are derived from the books *Grandma Moses: American Primitive* and *My Life's History*. In accordance with the artist's wishes, her idiosyncratic spellings and grammatical quirks have been modified to conform to standard usage, although an attempt has been made to retain the flavor of her original locutions.

Dimensions, height before width, are given in inches with centimeters following in parentheses.

The spelling of "Hoosic/Hoosick" varies according to its referent. On present-day maps, the river and the valley are spelled "Hoosic"; the towns, "Hoosick." Grandma Moses always used "Hoosick" in the titles of her paintings.

The Kallir number in the captions is the identifying number assigned to the works of Grandma Moses by Otto Kallir in his authoritative catalogue raisonné, published in 1973.

Early Work and Development

Many people wrongly believe that folk artists never show signs of stylistic development. This misconception is fueled by the fact that self-taught artists' oeuvres are often ill documented, fragmented, and hard or impossible to date—thus impeding the reconstruction of a developmental trajectory. Then, too, it is true that some self-taught artists *do* seem to hit their strides with their first works and just stay there. In some cases (for example, that of John Kane or Morris Hirshfield), this is because a late-life career allows scant time for change. In other cases, the artist in question does not have a great deal of intellectual curiosity about the creative process, does not consciously engage in his or her mission as an artist. There are also a number of self-taught artists who simply hit upon a marketable style and intentionally stick to it. And, finally, because many partisans of self-taught art like to cultivate the myth that such artists emerge stylistically full-blown, like Athena from the head of Zeus, scholars seldom study their development systematically. Obviously, what one does not look for is not likely to be found.

There is no intrinsic reason, however, why a self-taught artist should not develop just as a trained one does. Painting is an evolutionary process, and a talented artist should logically examine his or her work in progress, learning from both successes and failures. Grandma Moses, perhaps above and beyond all other self-taught artists, displayed an exceptional ability to learn from her work. And since, unlike many other folk artists of her era, she lived a remarkably long life, she had a chance to explore her artistic potential to its fullest.

Another common myth has it that folk artists are uninfluenced, though this, again, defies logic. After all, what visually sensitive person would ignore available pictorial stimuli? The difference between trained and self-taught artists is that the latter group does not learn to emulate an accepted style in school, but rather patches together a homemade style from an array of ad hoc influences. In the case of Grandma Moses, the most pervasive early influences were domestic arts such as embroidery, nineteenth-century chromolithographs, and popular illustration.

From these various sources, Moses gradually formulated a wholly original folk style. Rote copying was gradually supplemented by personal observation of the landscape, until finally the copied sources were subsumed within the artist's overriding vision. The study of Grandma Moses' development is facilitated by the fact that her oeuvre is fairly thoroughly catalogued, and with few exceptions, all her work is dated. In addition, much of her source material has been preserved.

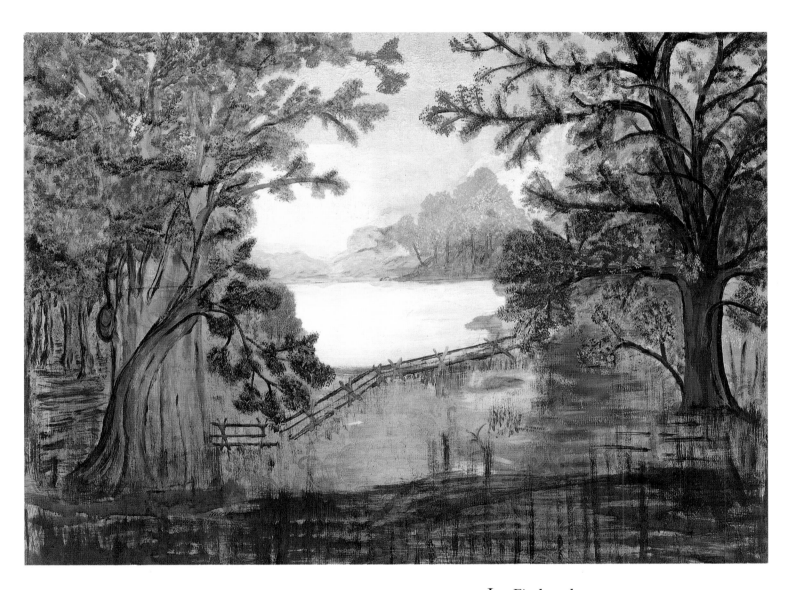

I **Fireboard**
1918. Oil on pressed wood
32 ¹/₄ x 38 ³/₄ inches
(82 x 98.4 cm)
Kallir I. Private collection

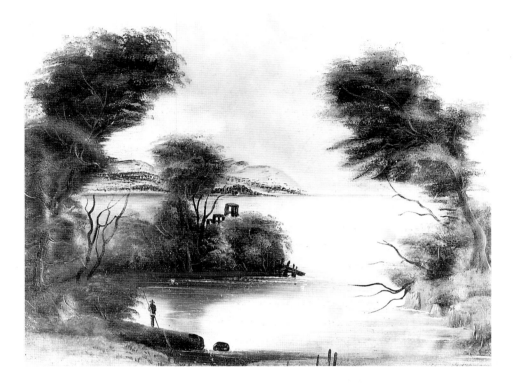

In her autobiography, Grandma Moses remembered that as a child
she loved to draw "lambscapes" but that she soon had to put aside such
unproductive pursuits in favor of serious domestic work. Accomplished
in all the practical tasks germane to a woman's realm on the farm, Moses
nevertheless always tried to find time to make her home beautiful.

Moses' earliest known painting dates to 1918 (plate 1). She had run
out of wallpaper while repapering the parlor, so she decided to paint
her own landscape on the board that is customarily used to seal off the
fireplace in summertime. Grandma Moses' *Fireboard* recalls the work of
such nineteenth-century folk painters as the itinerant Rufus Porter, and
it is tempting to speculate that she may have seen his murals as a child.
In a more general sense, the *Fireboard* landscape, with its loosely brushed
foliage and relatively somber palette, vaguely resembles the paintings
of the Hudson River School, whose influence would have been felt
throughout New York State when Moses was growing up. Her father,
Russell King Robertson, painted similar landscapes (fig. 1).

2   The Covered Bridge, 1818

1940 or earlier
Embroidery yarn on fabric
7 $^{1}/_{2}$ x 9 $^{1}/_{2}$ inches
(19 x 24.1 cm)
Kallir 13W. Private collection

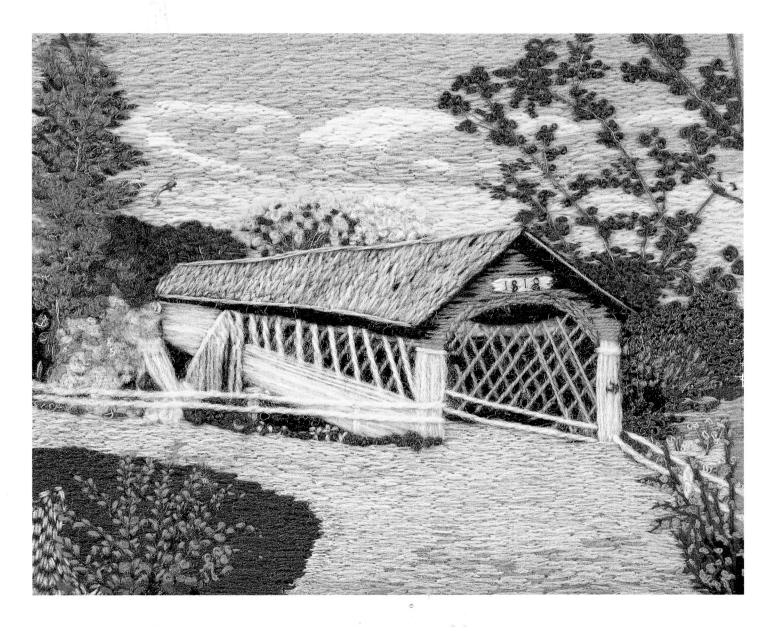

Grandma Moses' earliest sustained encounter with image-making
involved not paint, but worsted yarn. Sewing and embroidery were
an integral part of every girl's education when Anna Mary was a child.
Unlike painting, which seemed frivolous, embroidery had a practical
aspect.

Grandma Moses first began making embroidered pictures in the
1930s, when she moved temporarily to the nearby town of Bennington
to look after her daughter Anna, who suffered from tuberculosis.

3 **Mt. Nebo on the Hill**
1940 or earlier
Embroidery yarn on fabric
10 x 14 inches
(25.4 x 35.5 cm)
Signed, lower right
Kallir 34W. Private collection
Courtesy Galerie St. Etienne,
New York

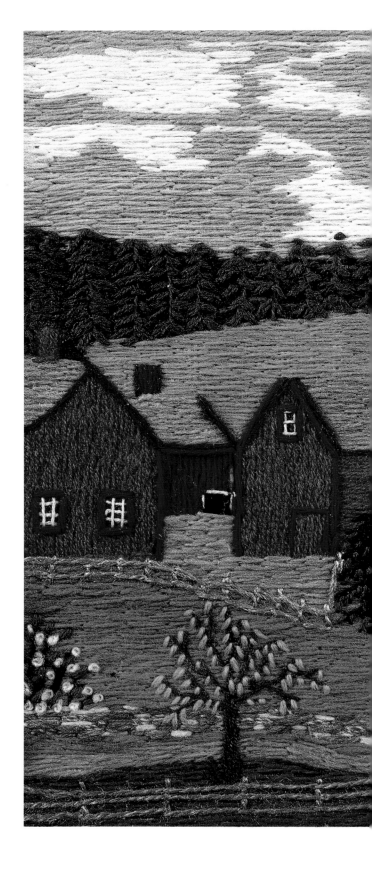

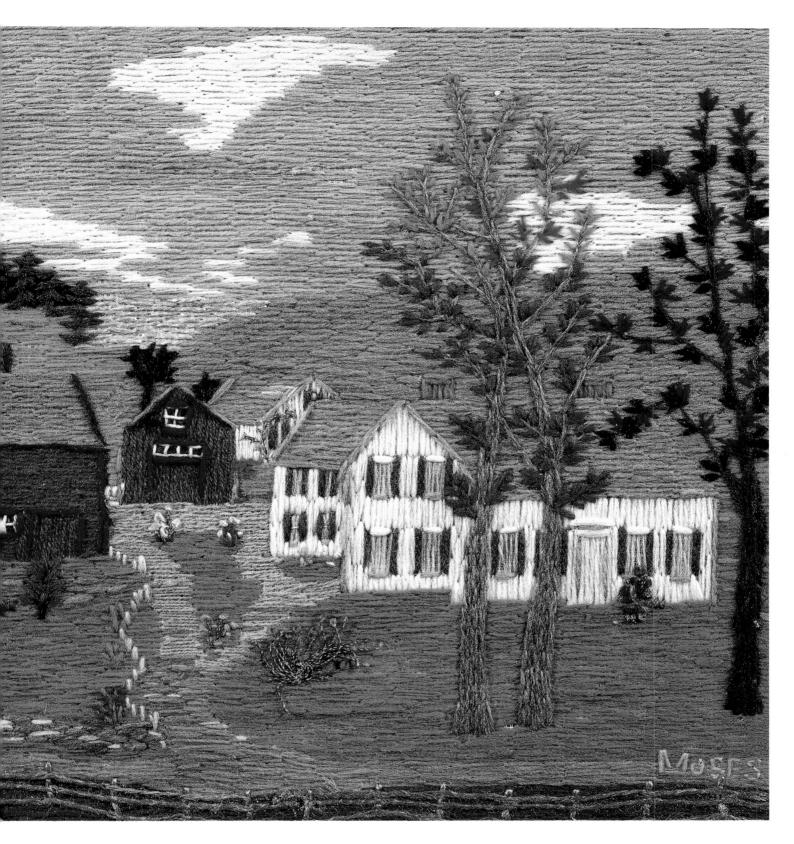

Moses created her first "worsted picture" as a gift for Anna's child Zoeanne, and when the picture was well received, Grandma produced more and gave them away to friends and family. However, arthritis made it difficult for Moses to wield a needle, and so, at the suggestion of her sister Celestia, she gradually switched to painting.

4 In the Berkshire Hills, Massachusetts

Before 1938
Chromolithograph by
Andrew Melrose
with modifications in oil by
Grandma Moses
22 x 36 inches
(55.9 x 91.4 cm)
Private collection

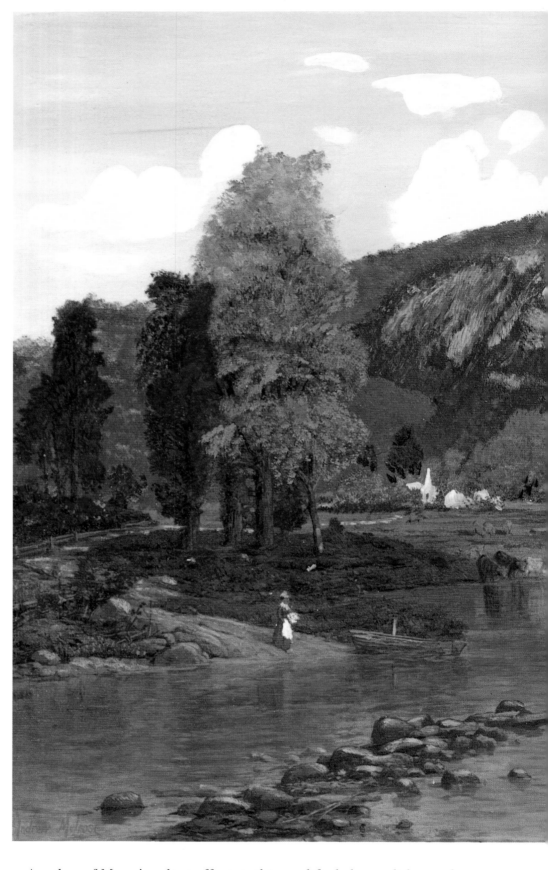

Another of Moses' earliest efforts is this modified chromolithograph.
The artist saw fit to "improve" the picture, either because she found fault
with the original or possibly because it was damaged. The dusky palette of
this work—typical of late-nineteenth-century landscape prints—recurs in
many of Moses' initial pictures.

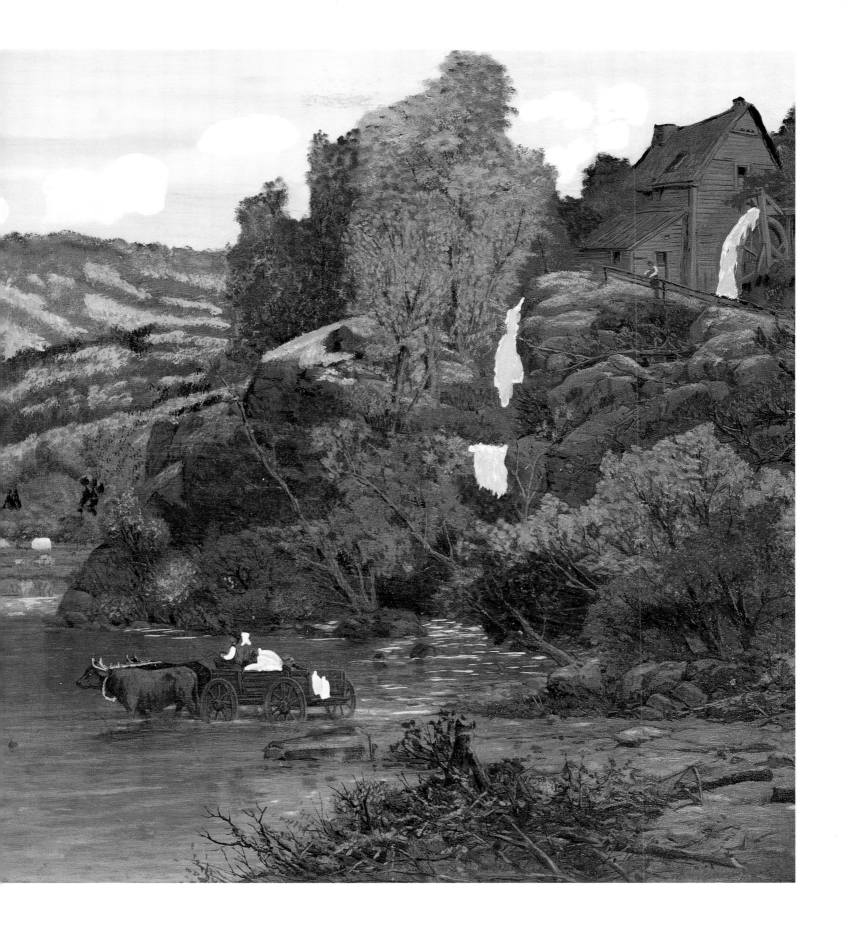

5 Autumn in the Berkshires

Before 1938. Oil on canvas
8 x 14 ¼ inches
(20.3 x 36.2 cm)
Kallir 8. Private collection

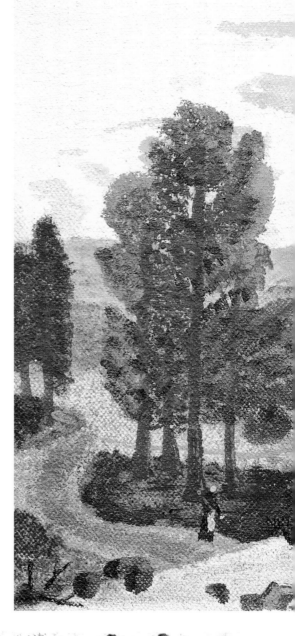

Autumn in the Berkshires was one of Moses' first independent attempts to copy and adapt a common nineteenth-century chromolithograph subject (compare plate 4). The painting is executed on a scrap of canvas that was left over after making a new cover for the threshing machine on the Moses farm. Difficult to date precisely, *Autumn in the Berkshires* may have been done as early as the 1920s, prior to the embroidered version of the same subject (fig. 2). Comparing the painting with the embroidery reveals how the artist translated needlework techniques into paint: instead of blending pigments in the conventional manner, Moses placed colors side by side, much as one would strands of different-hued wool. This pseudo-Impressionistic method accounts for the richness and subtlety of her landscape effects.

Fig. 2. Grandma Moses, *Autumn in the Berkshires,* 1940 or earlier. Embroidery on fabric, 9 x 21 ¾ inches (22.9 x 55.2 cm). Kallir 1W. Private collection

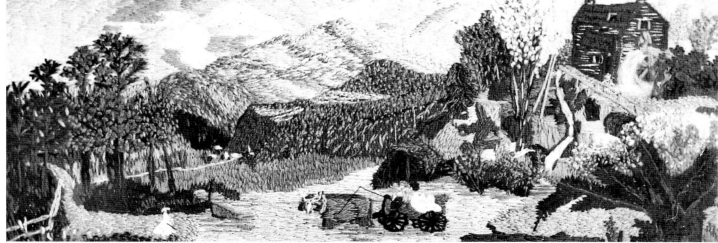

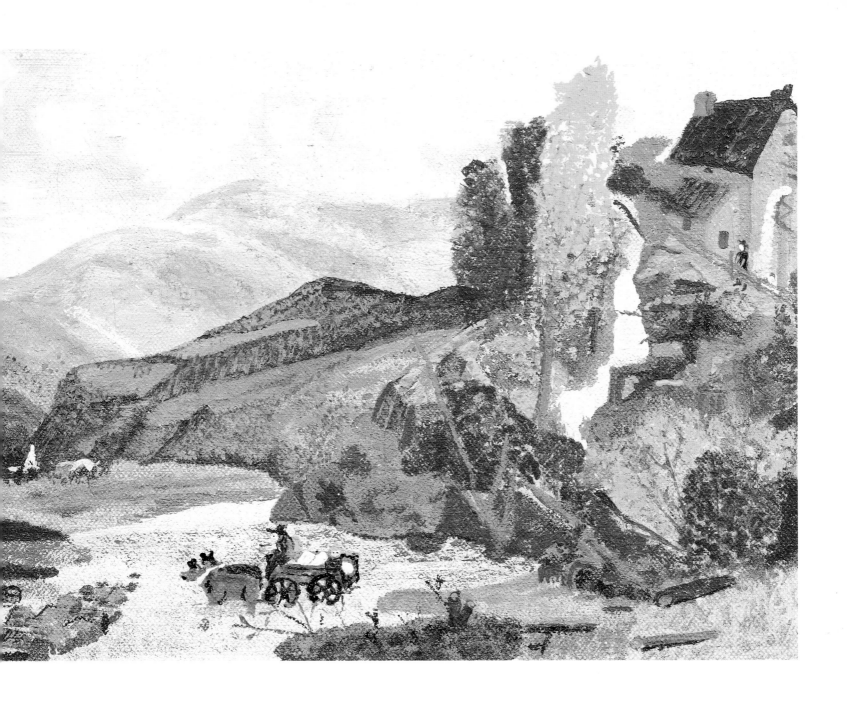

Shenandoah Valley, South Branch

Circa 1938. Oil on oilcloth
19 ³/₄ x 14 inches
(50.2 x 35.5 cm)
Signed, lower left
Kallir 51. Private collection

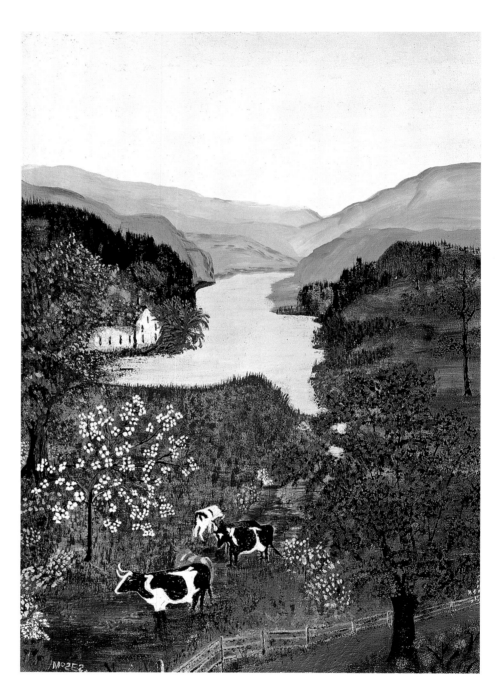

An oft-repeated story has it that when Louis Caldor first visited the Moses farmstead, Grandma was out. So he asked her daughter-in-law, Dorothy, how many paintings she thought the artist had on hand and said he'd come back the next day to see them. Moses, returning home, was appalled to learn that Dorothy had offered Caldor ten works, since

**Shenandoah Valley, 1861
(News of the Battle)**
Circa 1938. Oil on oilcloth
20 ¹/₂ x 16 ¹/₄ inches
(52 x 41.3 cm)
Signed, lower right
Kallir 52. Private collection

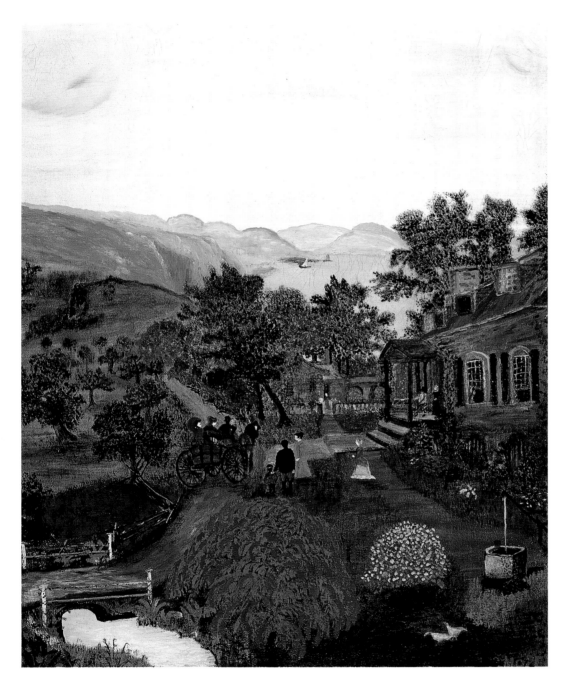

she had only nine. After fretting through the night, Grandma cut one
of her larger pictures in half, thereby fulfilling Dorothy's promise.
Since the two surviving halves do not match up exactly, it is apparent
that Moses excised a portion in the center, either for compositional
reasons or to fit the frames she had on hand.

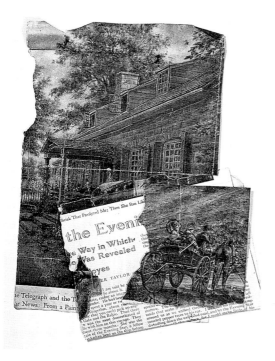

Fig. 3. Four-color magazine
illustration with Moses' pencil
outlining

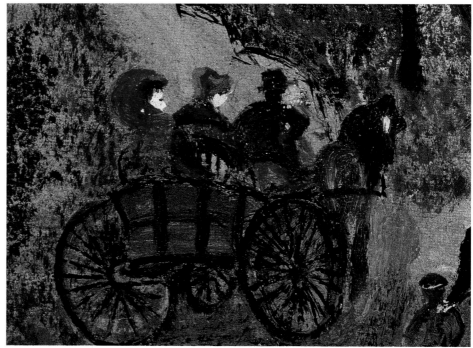

Fig. 4. *Shenandoah Valley, 1861 (News of the Battle),*
detail of plate 7

Both Shenandoah paintings (plates 6 and 7) evidence the subdued
tonalities, derived from nineteenth-century prints, so typical of Moses'
early work. Although the composition as a whole (inspired by the artist's
memories of the South) is entirely original, portions were taken from
an old magazine illustration (fig. 3). Cutting up clippings and reconfig-
uring them was to become a staple of Moses' method; however, hers
were never rote copies, but rather abstractions of the initial sources that
eliminated much basic illustrative detail (fig. 4). At first, lacking professional artist's supplies, Moses used ad hoc tools such as matches and pins
to render fine details, resulting in a certain crudeness of appearance.

8 **Back Yard at Home**
1940 or earlier. Oil on cardboard
12 x 16 ½ inches
(30.5 x 42 cm)
Signed, lower left
Kallir 7. Private collection

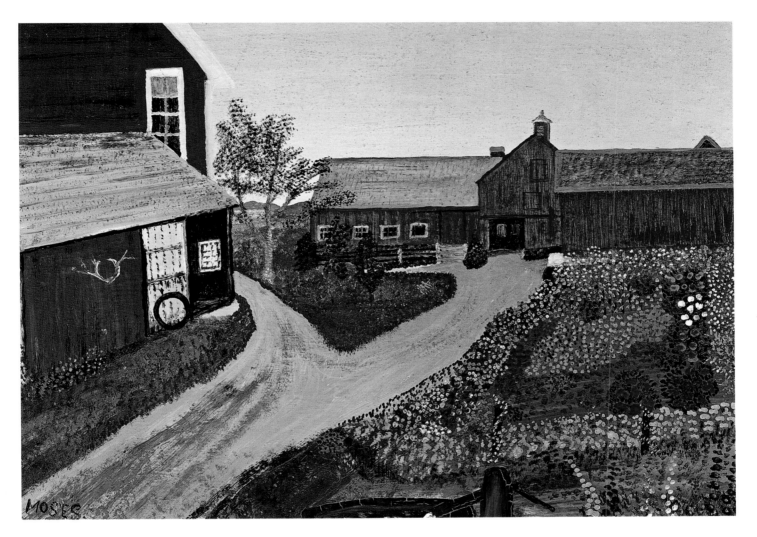

Back Yard at Home, *A Fire in the Woods* (plate 9), and *Where the Muddy Missouri Rolls* (plate 10) were all included in Moses' first one-woman show (as were plates 3, 6, 7, 11, and 13). These three works encapsulate the artistic issues confronting Moses at the start of her career: the shifting balance between close-up and panoramic views, and between copied subjects versus observed reality. All three pictures are painted on cardboard, and their scope is limited by their relatively small size. *Back Yard at Home* is a literal depiction of the subject referenced in the title: the artist's own farm as seen from its driveway. Although the perspective is slightly askew, the buildings nevertheless have a fairly conventional relationship to one another and to the surrounding landscape: the barn in the foreground is larger than the house at the back, and both effectively block out the loamy hills beyond.

9 A Fire in the Woods

1940 or earlier. Oil on cardboard
10 $\frac{1}{4}$ x 15 inches
(26 x 38 cm)
Kallir 22. Private collection

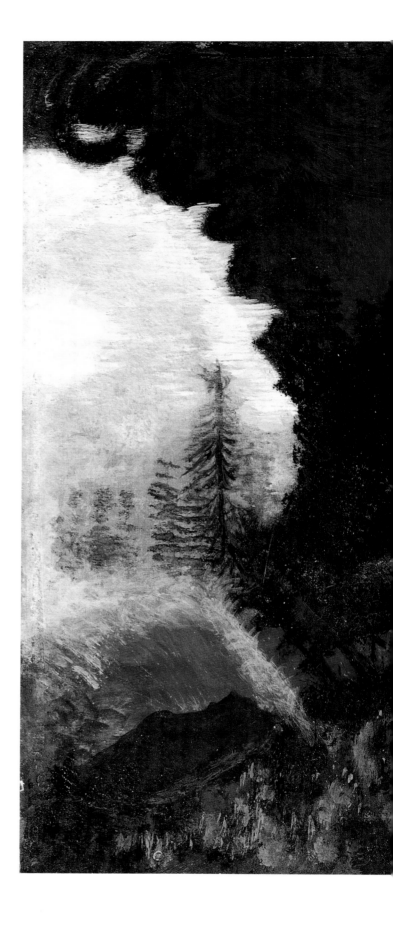

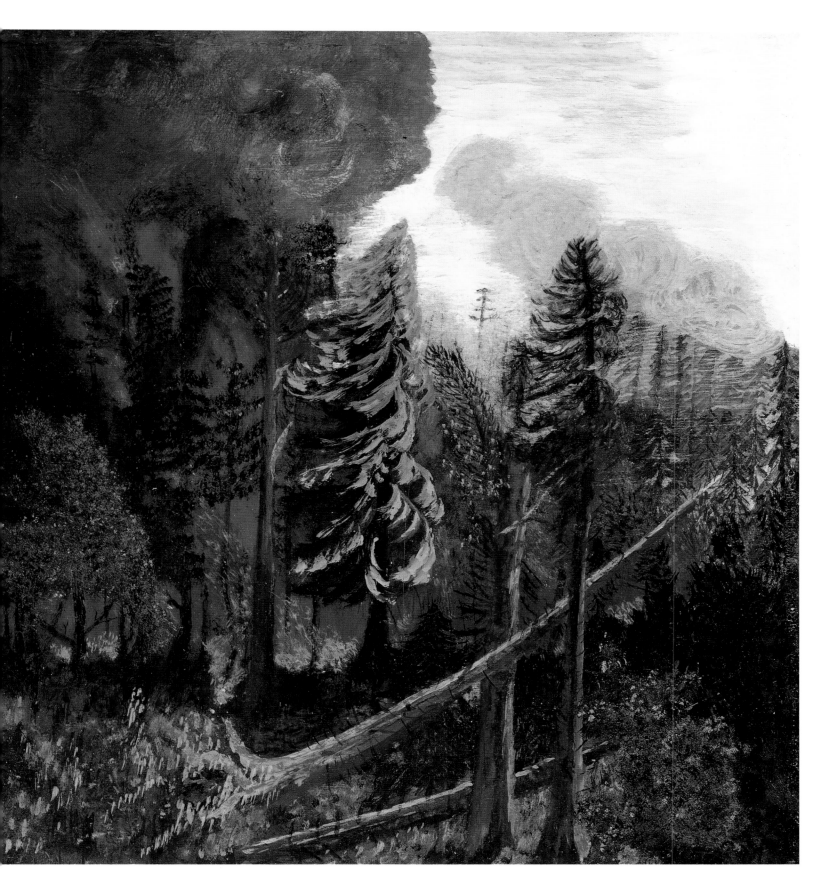

A Fire in the Woods, would seem to clearly derive from a print, even though the specific source has not been identified. The colors once more suggest nineteenth-century chromolithographs (see plates 1 and 4–7), and the subject is one that, while undoubtedly familiar to Moses, could not readily have been rendered from direct observation.

10 Where the Muddy Missouri Rolls

1940 or earlier. Oil on cardboard
12 x 16 inches
(30.5 x 40.7 cm)
Signed, lower right;
inscribed on verso with poem
Kallir 47. Private collection

Moses presents a panoramic vista in *Where the Muddy Missouri Rolls*, a landscape not obscured by man-made structures. The painting was inspired by a poem, which the artist pasted onto the back of the picture: "Where the Muddy Missouri Roll[s] on to the sea/Where a man is a man, if he is willing to toil,/And the humble may gather the fruit of the soil." Although Moses was undoubtedly not the author of this ditty, and she had probably never seen the Missouri River, the composition appears to be original. The landscape shows a striking resemblance to the New England area where Moses lived.

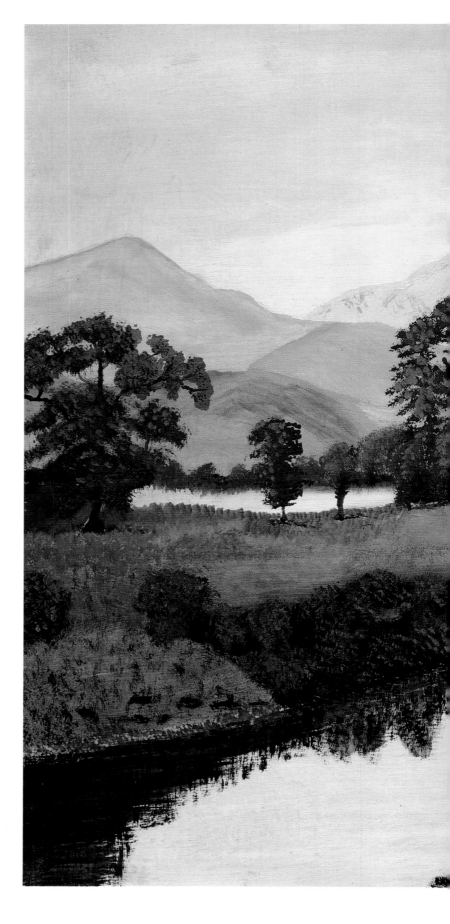

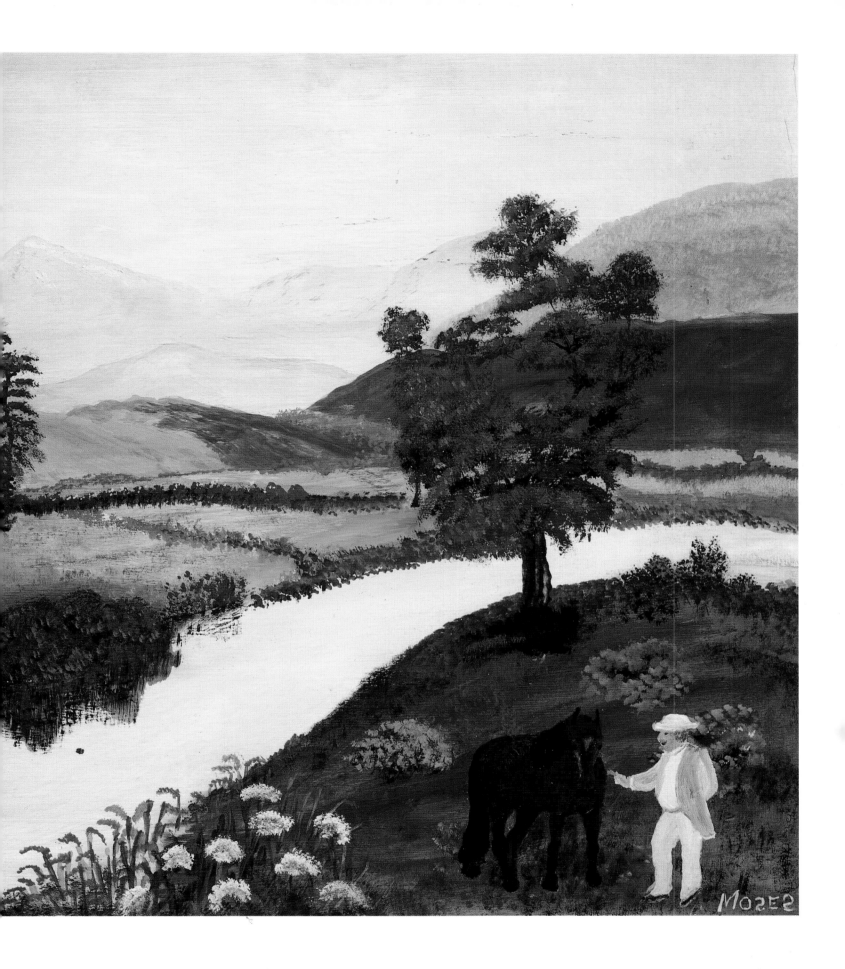

II The Burning of Troy

Circa 1939. Oil on cardboard
9 x 11 ¼ inches
(22.8 x 28.5 cm)
Kallir 62. Private collection

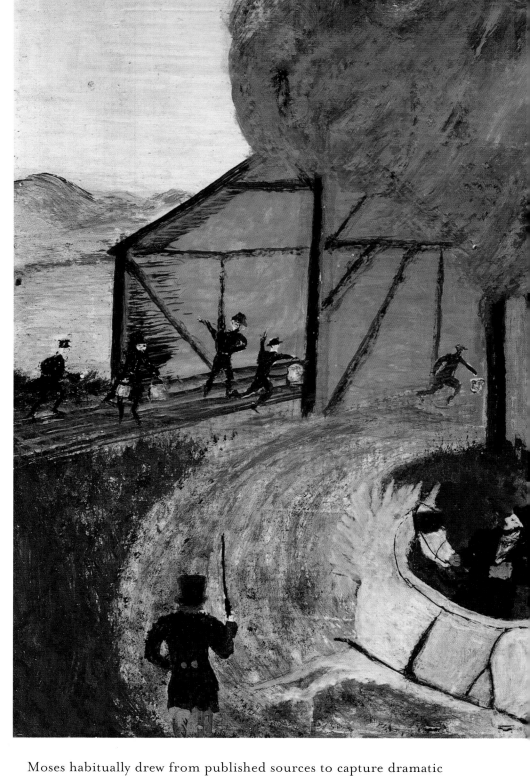

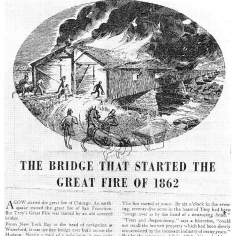

Fig. 5. "The Bridge That Started the Great
Fire of 1892." Newspaper clipping with
Grandma Moses' pencil notations, circa 1939

Moses habitually drew from published sources to capture dramatic
experiences that could not be depicted based on memory and observation alone. The burning of Troy, a city some twenty-five miles south
of Eagle Bridge, when the artist was two years old, was a matter of local
legend. The artist's initial depiction of the subject was clearly copied

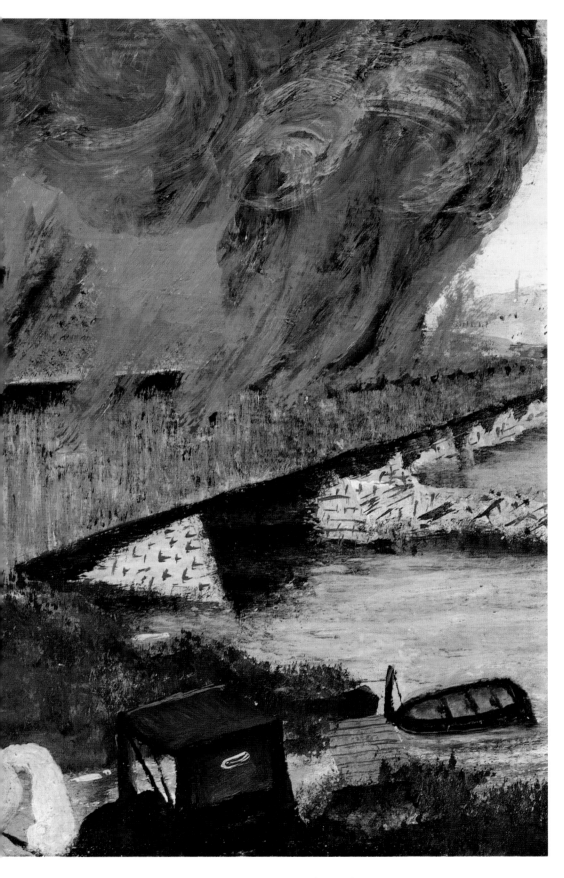

from a news clipping, published in 1939 (fig. 5). Pencil
notations on the clipping indicate how Moses proposed to expand
the vignette, transforming the original oval into a rectangle. Her
painting, with its jarring colors, is far more dramatic than the original
illustration, even though the compositional modifications are slight.

12 The Burning of Troy in 1862

1943. Oil on pressed wood
18 15/16 x 29 15/16 inches
(47.7 x 75.8 cm)
Kallir 298. Seiji Togo Memorial,
Yasuda Kasai Museum of Art,
Tokyo

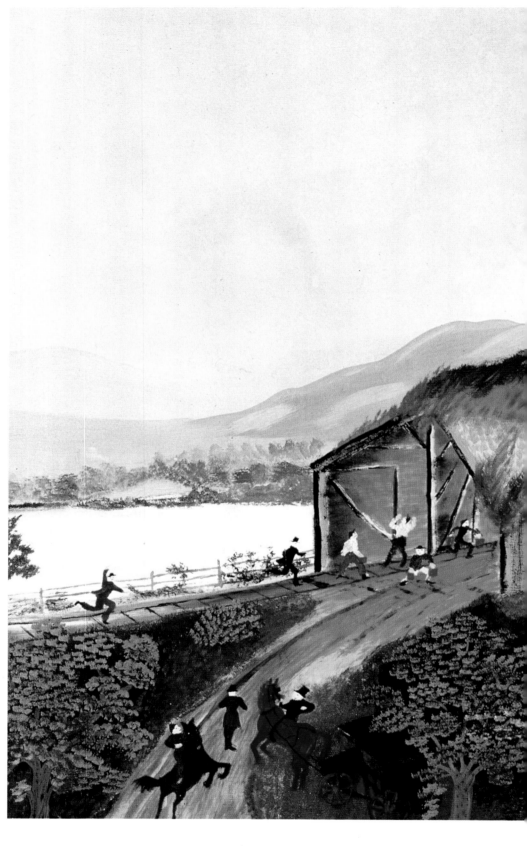

A later depiction of the Troy fire (compare plate 11) demonstrates Moses' artistic growth in the intervening four years. Now the burning bridge is more firmly positioned in its specific locale: the shorelines on both sides of the river are shown in much greater detail, as is the river

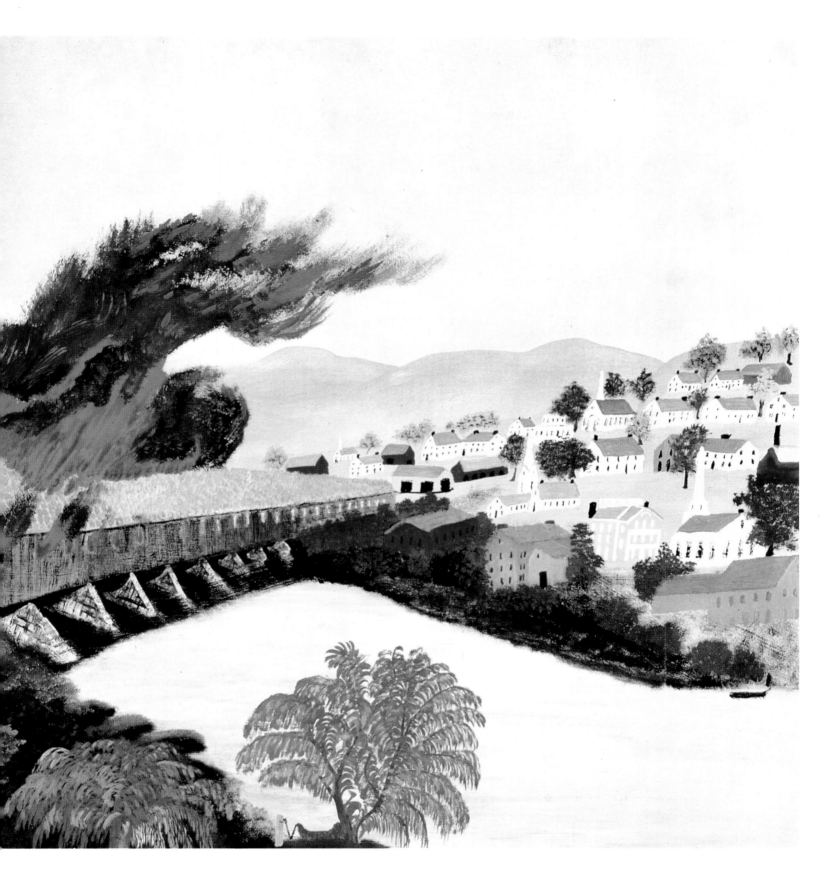

itself. The effect is not only to situate the event in place, but also in time: the scene is both literally and metaphorically apprehended from a greater distance, so that historical perspective is gained and dramatic immediacy lessened.

13 The First Automobile

1939 or earlier
Oil on cardboard
9 3/4 x 11 1/2 inches
(24.8 x 29.2 cm)
Signed, lower left
Kallir 6. Private collection
Courtesy Galerie St. Etienne,
New York

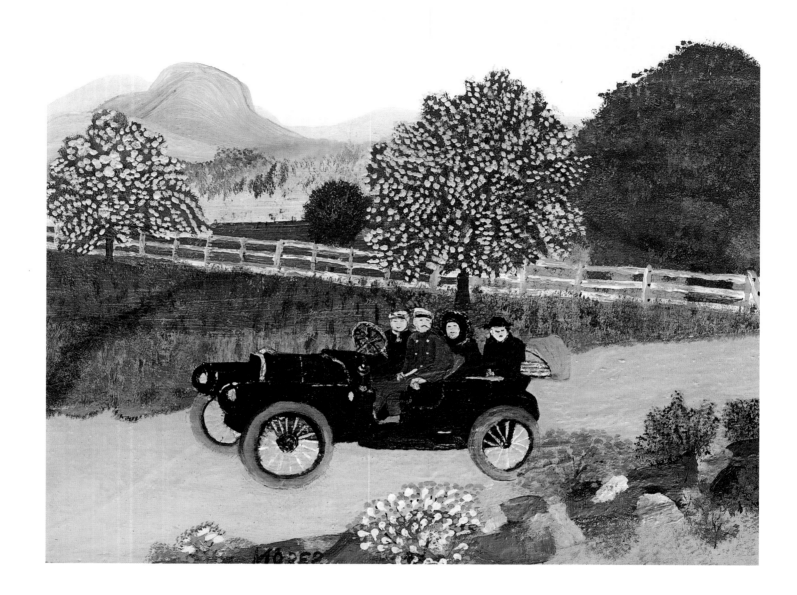

So long as Moses worked on a relatively small scale and oriented her approach to conventional landscape illustration, her compositional options remained limited. Traditionally, landscapists have tended to concentrate on either foreground or background but seldom both at once. When the focus is on anecdotal detail, as in *The First Automobile*, the surrounding landscape is reduced to little more than a backdrop. However, Moses had a pressing need to give equal weight to both foreground *and* background: it was from this need that the famous "Grandma Moses style" derived.

14 **The Old Automobile**
1944. Oil on pressed wood
18 3/4 x 21 1/2 inches
(47.7 x 54.7 cm)
Signed, lower right
Kallir 442. Private collection
Courtesy Galerie St. Etienne,
New York

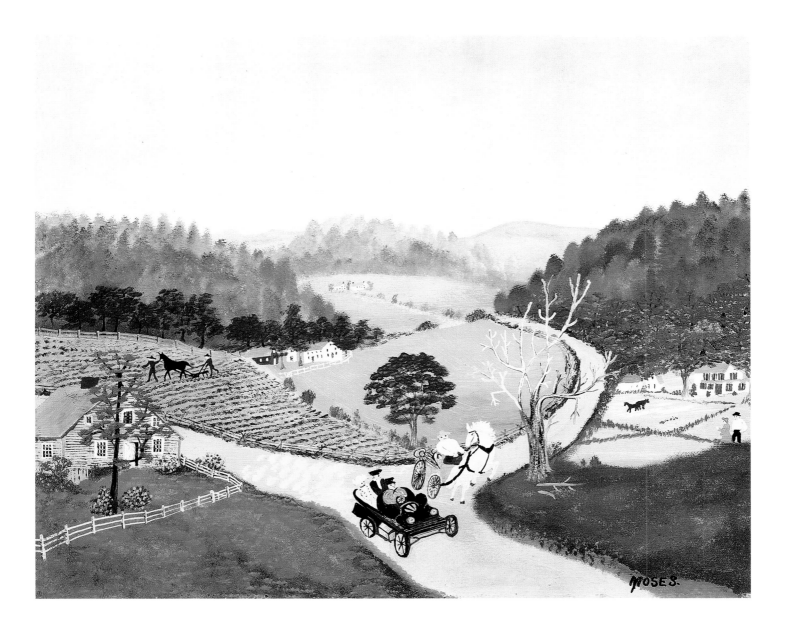

By 1944, when she painted *The Old Automobile*, Moses had hit her stride artistically. By adopting a larger support and stretching the composition to accommodate more detail than could possibly be viewed from a single vantage point, Moses managed to incorporate both a wealth of anecdotal material (not just the automobile itself, but houses and horses and men plowing the fields) and a sweeping rural panorama.

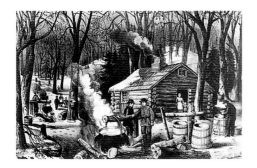

Fig. 6. *Maple Sugaring—Early Spring in the Northern Woods*, 1872. Lithograph published by Currier & Ives, New York

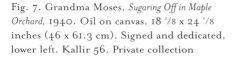

Fig. 7. Grandma Moses, *Sugaring Off in Maple Orchard*, 1940. Oil on canvas, 18 ¹/8 x 24 ¹/8 inches (46 x 61.3 cm). Signed and dedicated, lower left. Kallir 56. Private collection

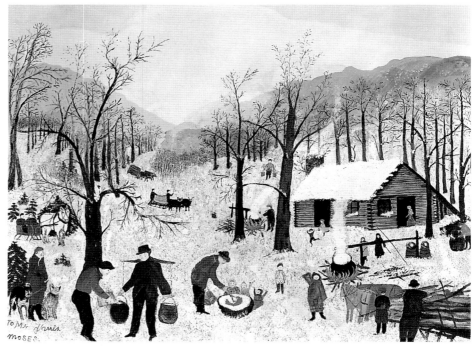

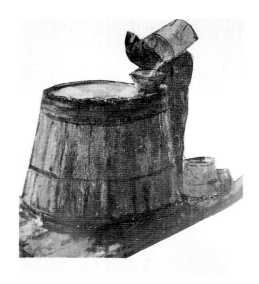

Fig. 8. Four-color magazine illustration with Moses' pencil outlining

Of all Moses' favorite subjects, "sugaring off" was the one she returned to most frequently (see plates 15, 18, and 82). And like other recurring motifs, it combined lived experience with a venerable pictorial tradition. The process of tapping the maple trees in early spring to release the sap in order to make maple syrup and candy was familiar to the artist from earliest childhood. "Sugaring off" was also the subject of a well-known Currier & Ives lithograph (fig. 6).

While Moses never executed a verbatim copy of the Currier & Ives print, it did significantly influence her initial versions of the subject (fig. 7). But, even at this early stage, Moses chafed at established landscape conventions. In order to open up her compositional options, she began collecting magazine and newspaper clippings, and by the time she died she had hundreds of little cutout images depicting such stock items as houses, barns, farm animals, and people.

Fig. 9. Two-color magazine illustration with
Moses' pencil outlining

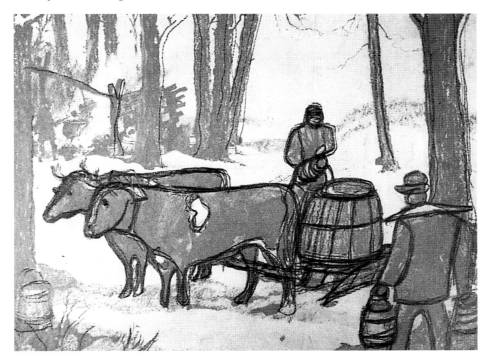

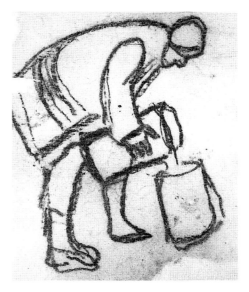

Fig. 10. Grandma Moses, *Man Bending Over with
Buckets*, detail. Pencil on tracing paper, 3 x 3
inches (7.6 x 7.6 cm). Courtesy Grandma
Moses Properties Co., New York

Moses found the clippings inspirational. Leafing through them, she
would begin to get ideas for paintings. Then, after selecting the clippings that were appropriate to her chosen subject, she would move them
around until she had a pleasing arrangement. She had several methods
for transferring the images to the pressed wood panel that was her preferred support: some clippings were cut out, so that they could be used
like stencils (fig. 8), but in most cases the artist employed carbon paper
to trace over the salient outlines. Many of the clippings retain pencil
marks indicating the features being transferred (fig. 9). On rare occasions, Moses traced an image onto a separate piece of paper, which then
served as a template (fig. 10). These drawings are quite scarce, but significant, as they closely resemble the drawings underlying all the artists'
paintings, which are generally visible only as pentimenti.

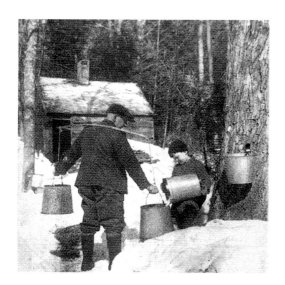

Fig. 11. Black-and-white magazine illustration

Sugaring Off epitomizes the classic Grandma Moses landscape. Although a number of clippings served as sources, the composition is entirely original. To the extent that vignettes from the Currier & Ives print (fig. 6) have been retained, they are barely identifiable. The artist has copied only the outlines of her source material, in the process losing all illustrative detail. This transformation is completed through the application of paint, which turns the figures into evocative abstractions (compare figs. 11 and 12). Rather than alluding to a specific past, these symbols of rural life become generic types with whom everyone can identify.

By 1943, Moses had made artistic progress in a number of salient ways. The palette of *Sugaring Off* is bright and cheery. Rather than timidly aping the dusky hues of nineteenth-century prints, she had learned to create images that were true to her own experiences. A comparison of a detail from this painting with one from an earlier "sugaring" (figs. 13 and 14) demonstrates how Moses' command of her medium had improved, in part owing to better materials. The crisp details of the later painting heighten the effectiveness of the abstract figural vignettes. Together with the squarish format and its concomitant expansive, stretched-out vista, these abstract vignettes are the hallmarks of the style that cemented Grandma Moses' reputation in the mid-1940s.

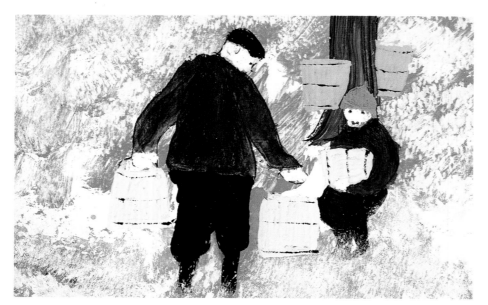

Fig. 12. *Sugaring Off*, detail of plate 15

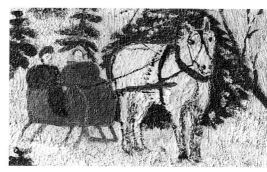

Fig. 13. *Sugaring Off in Maple Orchard*, detail of figure 7

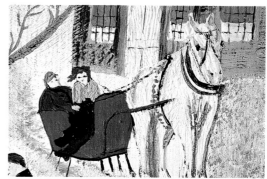

Fig. 14. *Sugaring Off*, detail of plate 15

15 **Sugaring Off**

1943. Oil on pressed wood
23 x 27 inches
(58.3 x 68.5 cm)
Signed, lower right
Kallir 276. Private collection
Courtesy Galerie St. Etienne,
New York

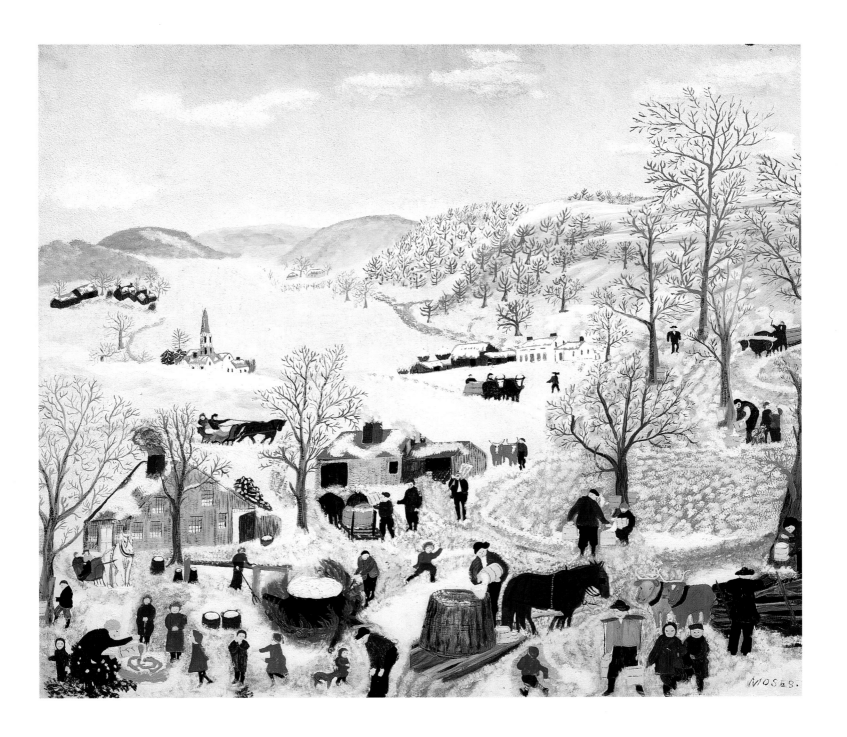

16 Cambridge Valley

1942. Oil on pressed wood
23 1/2 x 27 inches
(59.6 x 68.9 cm)
Signed, lower right
Kallir 164. Private collection
Courtesy Galerie St. Etienne,
New York

If a more inventive use of printed sources provided one key to the development of the "Grandma Moses style," the other key may be found in the hilly landscape of upstate New York, where the artist lived. Nature gave life to her abstract little vignettes, and for a number of years she struggled to find a means to combine these anecdotal details with the sweeping panoramas she loved. According to the artist, she discovered the solution to her problem in the hubcap of a car. In the convex, mirrored surface common to hubcaps in the 1940s, Moses saw the entire valley below her farm spread out and enlarged, as in a "fish-eye" camera lens. This revelation prompted her to adopt a deeper, almost square, format for her pictures. *Cambridge Valley* and *Black Horses* (plate 17) both depict the local landscape as a kind of patchwork quilt, granting equal attention to the background, middleground, and foreground. Exquisitely sensitive to the shifting hues of nature, each painting is an accurate evocation of the season as well as of place.

Compared to the small, constrained landscapes of Moses' early years (see plates 5, 8, 9, 10, 11 and 13), these new paintings demonstrated a remarkable freedom of pictorial invention as well as a sure command of color (fig. 15). It was *Black Horses* that convinced Otto Kallir of Moses' artistic genius and prompted him to solidify their professional relationship.

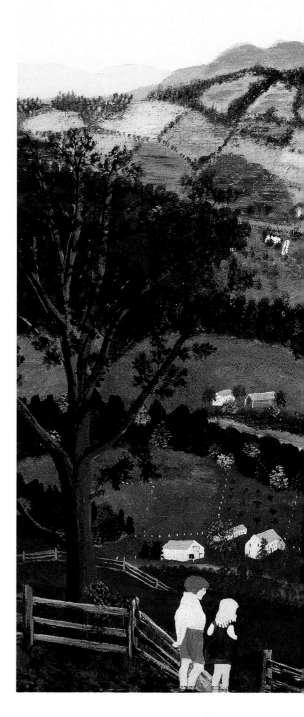

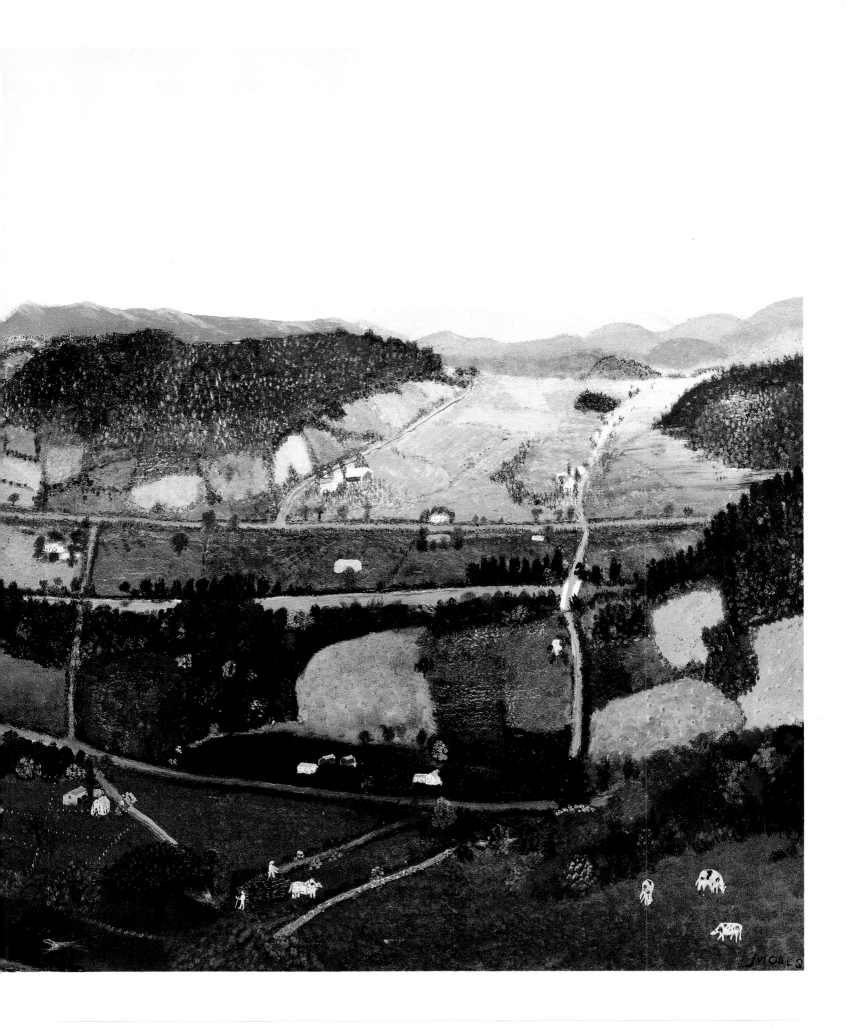

17 Black Horses

1942. Oil on pressed wood
20 x 24 inches
(50.8 x 60.9 cm)
Signed, lower left
Kallir 181. Private collection
Courtesy Galerie St. Etienne,
New York

Fig. 15. *Black Horses*, detail of plate 17

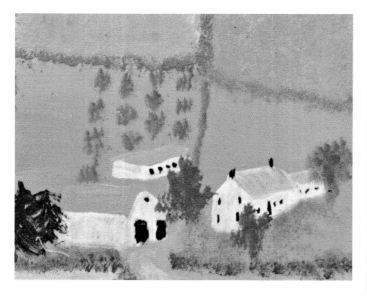

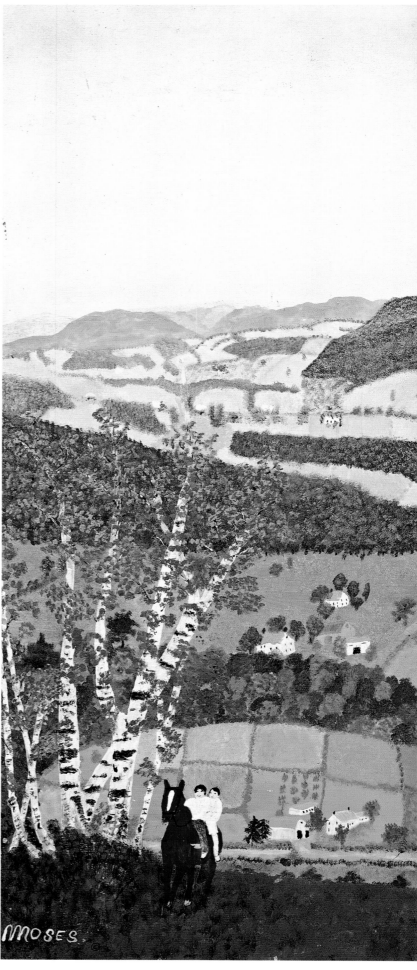

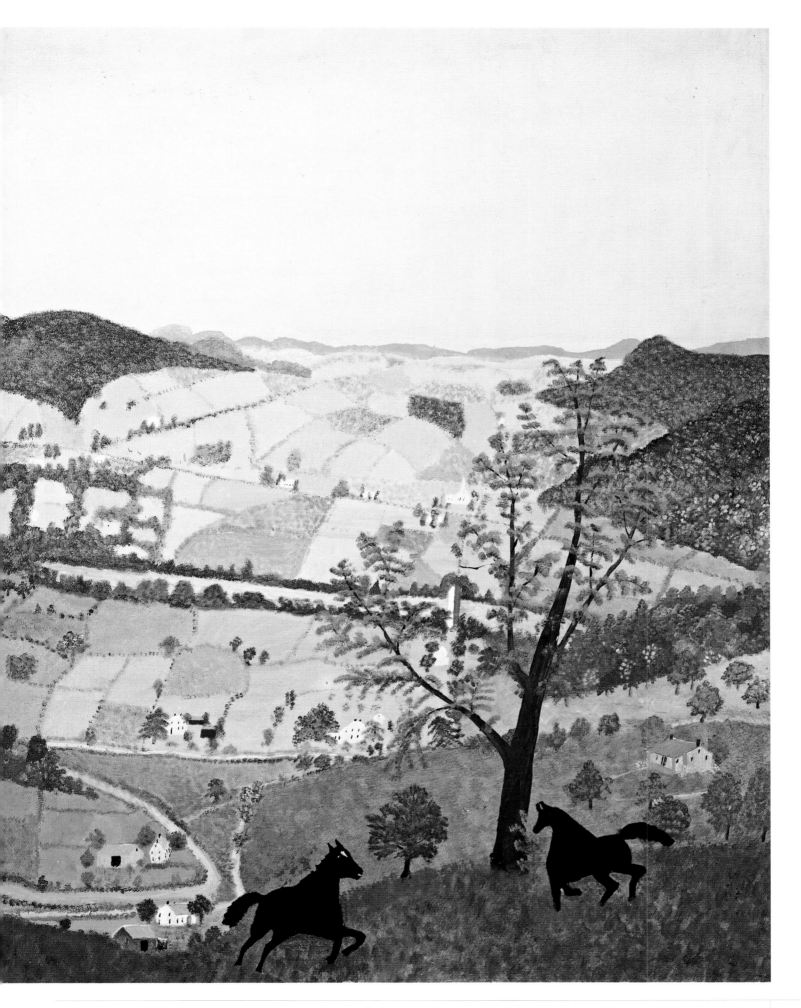

Work and Happiness

Looking back on her life on the occasion of her 95th birthday, Moses summed up her philosophy in an essay titled "Work and Happiness." "Work of any description adds to one's happiness," she wrote:

> *If anybody is occupied all the time, and they keep their mind on their work, they have no time to think of their worries. And I believe with children, the sooner you can teach them to commence to do things, the happier they are, the prouder they are. When I was a child, I would always help Mother with different things in the house. She might be cutting out some material and she might say: "Anna Mary, you can have all those giblets for your dolls' clothes." How I would work for it, to get all those pieces. Maybe the work that she would want me to do would be to fill the wood box, or fill the reservoir in the back of the stove. It would hold six pails of water. We had to bring the water upstairs from the well in the cellar; to bring it up was quite a chore.*

> *I have kept busy all my life. It seems foolish to sleep when there is so much to do all over. There is always something to do and to work for, you must never give up.*

> A Tribute to Grandma Moses, 1955

Moses' entire life was ruled by a strong work ethic, and her values are enshrined both in her paintings and in her autobiography, *My Life's History*. Many have marveled that the autobiography devotes scant space to the artist's spectacular late-life career. Nor does Moses provide much in the way of emotional color, even when she is recounting the deaths of her siblings and children. Rather, her memoir is a vivid documentation of life on a farm at the turn of the last century: the interweaving of countless mundane tasks and the profound satisfaction they yield. Many of Moses' paintings are similarly autobiographical, depicting familiar farm activities or memories of bygone rural rituals. These paintings express the belief that all members of society—men, women, and children alike—have their particular roles, and that productive work places each in harmony with his or her surroundings, thus ensuring happiness.

Work and play were intimately connected in Moses' world view, but seldom were the two as closely combined as in her memories of "sugaring off" (see also plates 15 and 82). The artist's written account and depictions of this annual ritual stress the integration of children into the working life of the farm, whereby they learn early on to share in both its burdens and pleasures.

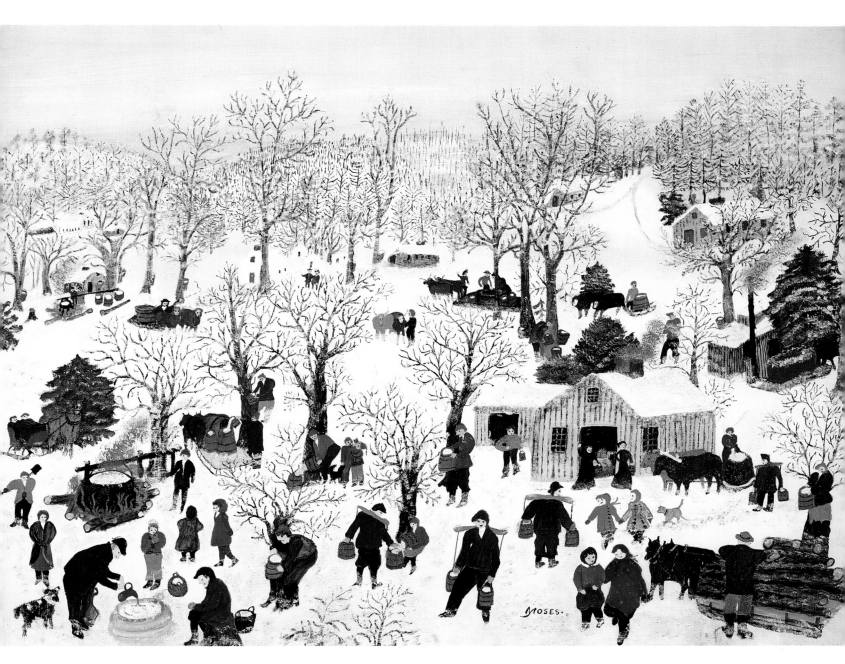

18 Sugaring Off

1955. Oil on pressed wood
18 x 24 inches
(45.7 x 60.9 cm)
Signed, lower right
Kallir 1166. Private collection

The rural work routine was governed by gender, age, and by the calendar. As Moses noted in *My Life's History*, "on a farm . . . nothing changes but the seasons," and her schedule of chores was set according to the day of the week and the time of year. "Monday washday, Tuesday ironing and mending, Wednesday baking and cleaning, Thursday sewing, Friday sewing and odd jobs, such as working in the garden or with flowers," she wrote. In addition, there were seasonal tasks, such as sugaring off, spring-cleaning, and fruit picking. "In between, the housework must be kept up," the artist noted. "All this is supposed to be cared for by the women and children."

Moses' casual acceptance of "woman's work" may be jarring to contemporary feminists, though it is also true that the artist had an independent and egalitarian view of femininity. Her role as wife and mother was different from her husband's, but it was not lesser in anyone's eyes.

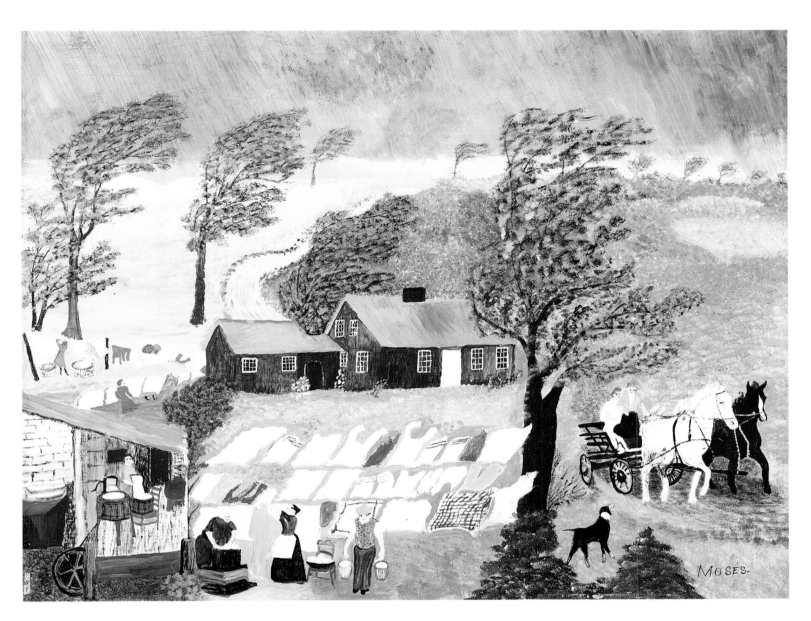

19 Taking in Laundry

1951. Oil on pressed wood
17 x 21 3/4 inches
(43.18 x 55.2 cm)
Signed, lower right
Kallir 967. Private collection
Courtesy Galerie St. Etienne,
New York

20 Baking Bread

1955. Oil on pressed wood
12 x 16 inches
(30.5 x 40.7 cm)
Kallir 1182. Al M. Nakamura

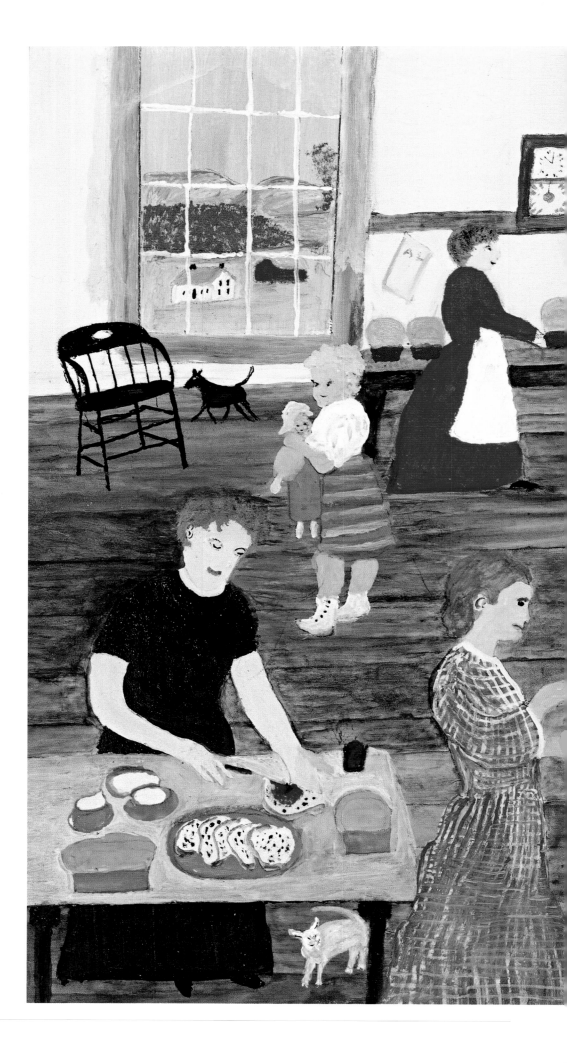

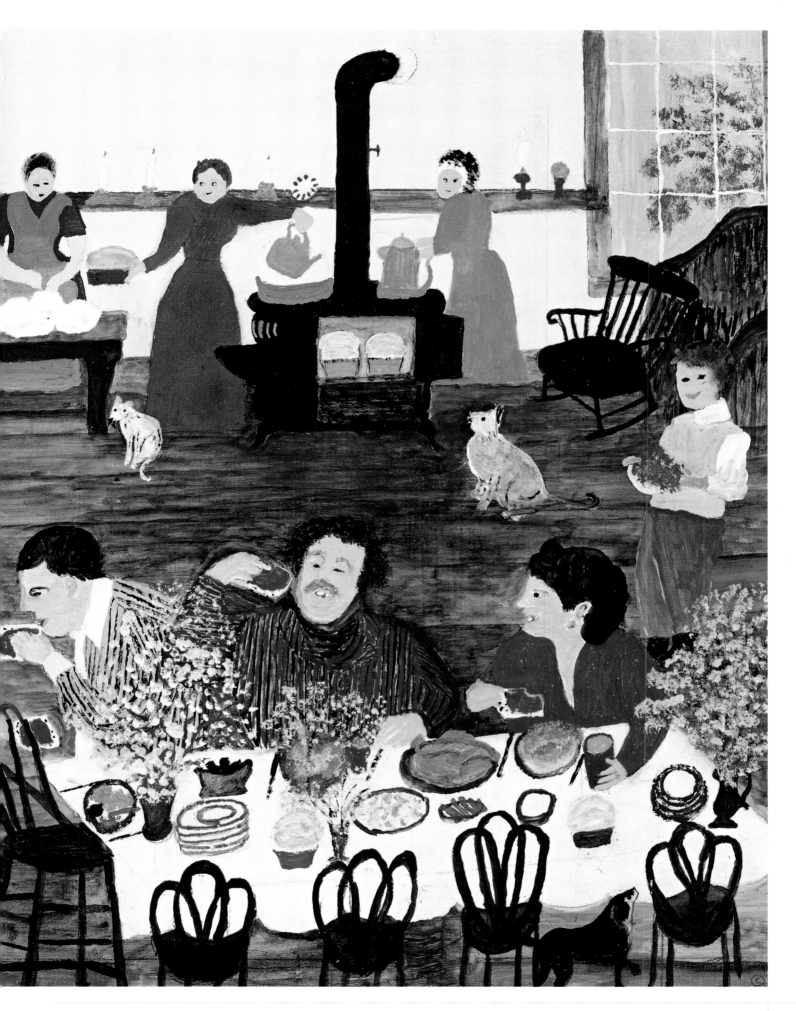

21 **May: Making Soap,
Washing Sheep**
1945. Oil on pressed wood
17 ¹/₄ x 24 ¹/₄ inches
(43.8 x 61.6 cm)
Signed, lower right
Kallir 509. Miss Porter's School,
Farmington, Connecticut
Gift of Mrs. Raymond F. Evans

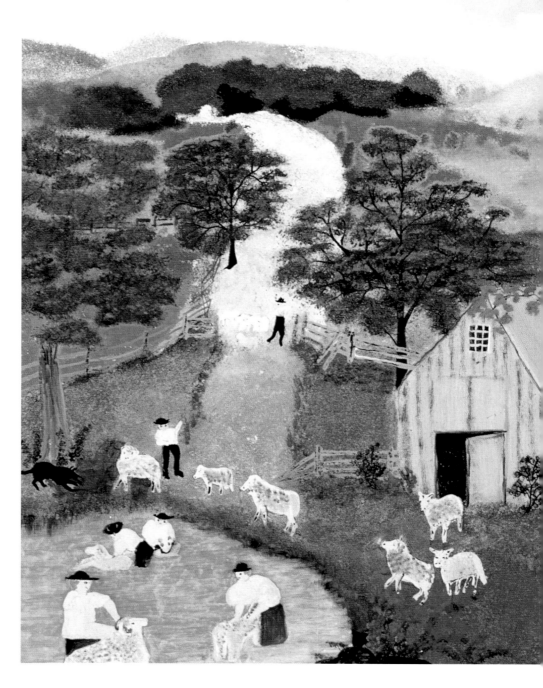

Soap-making and sheep-washing were springtime activities, the former attended to by women, the latter by men. "The farmers would always wash the sheep after a few hot days before shearing," Moses recalled, "and the

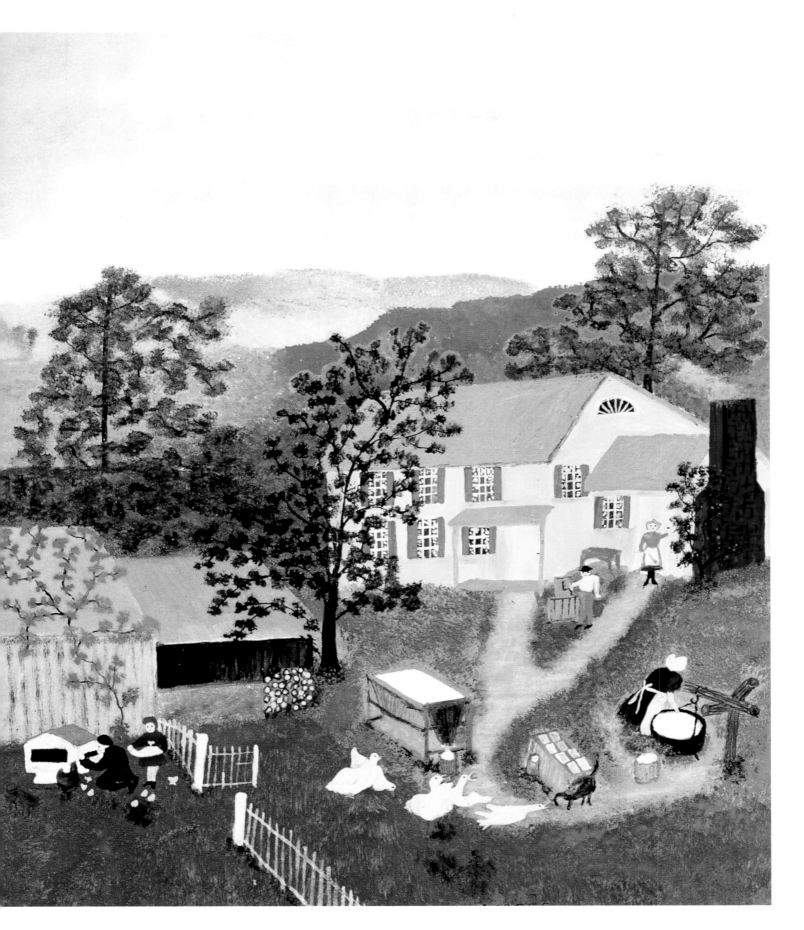

wives would make up the year's supply of hard and soft soap, which would
be a barrel or more. This was used on wash day and [for] housecleaning.
We were thrifty in those days. Nothing wasted, nothing lost."

22 Barn Roofing

1951. Oil on pressed wood
17 15/16 x 24 1/16 inches
(45.6 x 61 cm)
Signed, lower right
Kallir 986. Seiji Togo Memorial,
Yasuda Kasai Museum of Art, Tokyo

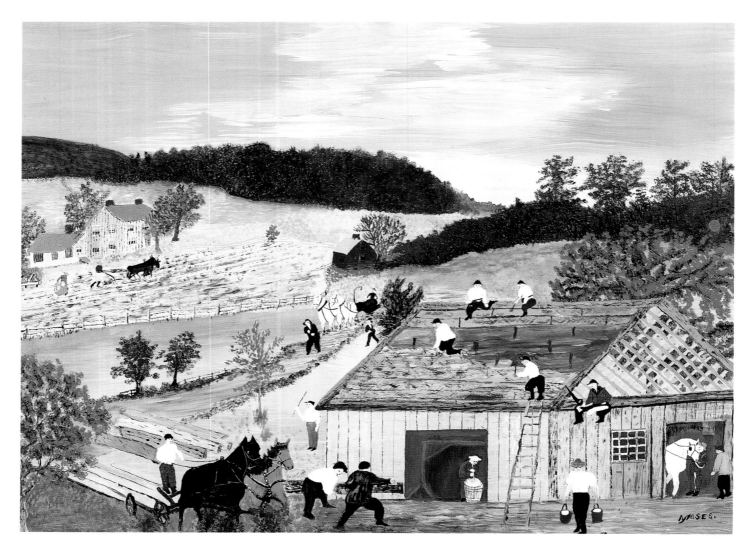

Not surprisingly, Moses' autobiography goes into far less detail about men's work than it does about the activities that she herself participated in or supervised. Nevertheless, her paintings provide a good overview of such masculine pursuits as carpentry and blacksmithing. These necessary occupations take their place in Moses' well-ordered rural universe. The male world, while considerably less playful than that ruled by women and children, is nevertheless clearly a happy one. There is no hint that the men's labor is ever tiresome or unpleasant; rather, all the workers seem to take pride in their productivity, and to exist in harmony with the natural environment.

23 **Horseshoeing**

1960. Oil on pressed wood
16 x 24 inches
(40.7 x 60.9 cm)
Signed, lower left
Kallir 1471. Roy W. Moses and
Harry L. Moses

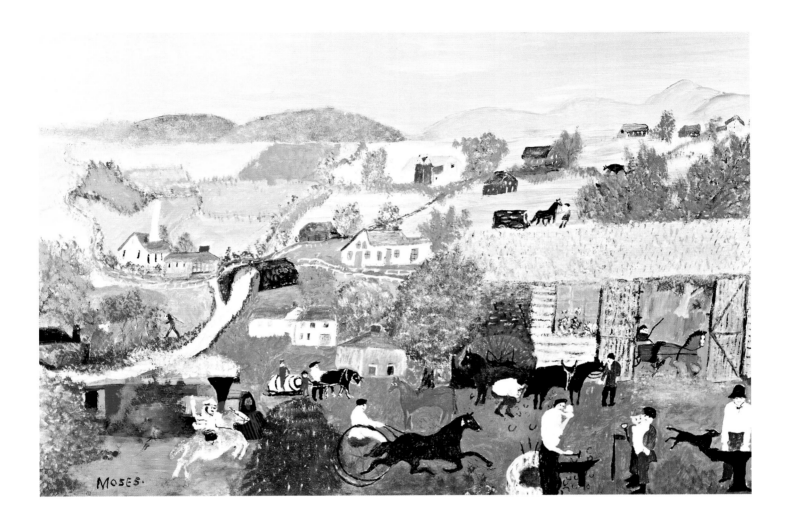

24 Plow Boy

1950. Oil on board
12 x 16 inches
(30.5 x 40.7 cm)
Kallir 929. Bruce and
Alice Ivy Weiss

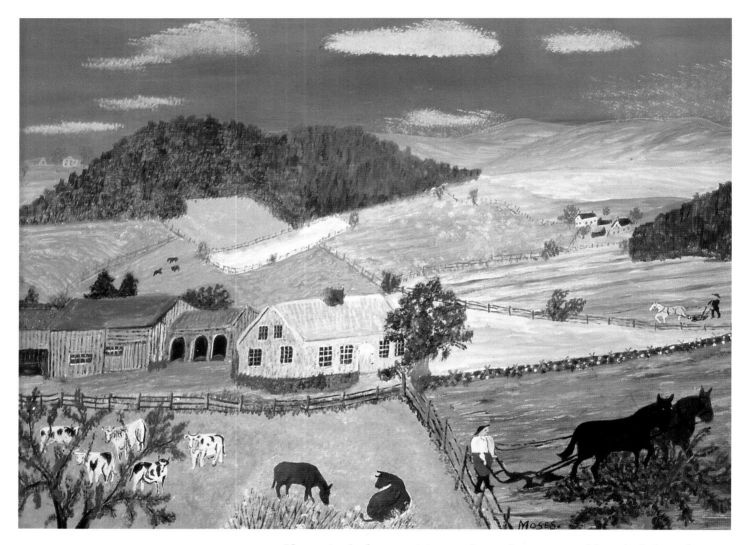

If any single farm activity can be said to sum up Moses' philosophy, it is the process of sowing and harvesting, the annual pay-off for productive labor. What little schooling Anna Mary received as a girl stressed rote learning, and even as an old woman she could recall a number of memorized poems and ditties. Of harvesting, she wrote:

> They were sowing the seed of noble deed,
> With a sleepless watch and an earnest heed,
> With a ceaseless hand o'er the earth they sow,
> And the fields are whitening where'er they go.
> Rich will the harvest be,
> Sown in darkness or sown in light,
> Sown in weakness or sown in might,
> Sown in meekness or sown in wrath,
> Sure will the harvest be.

25 **Haying Time**
1945. Oil on pressed wood
24 x 30 inches
(60.9 x 76.2 cm)
Signed, lower left
Kallir 485. Private collection

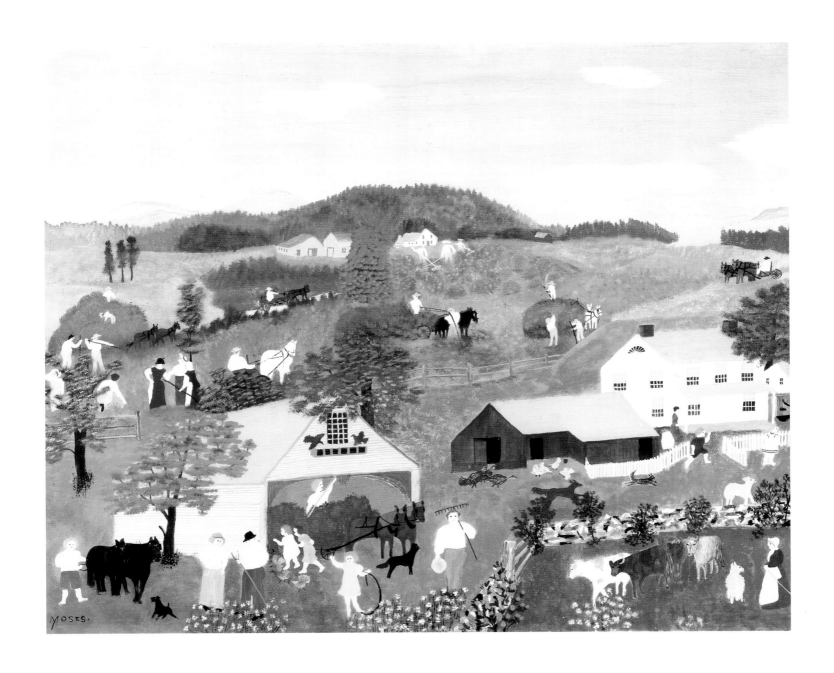

26 In Harvest Time

1945. Oil on pressed wood
18 x 28 inches
(45.7 x 71.1 cm)
Signed, lower left
Kallir 537. Private collection
Courtesy Galerie St. Etienne,
New York

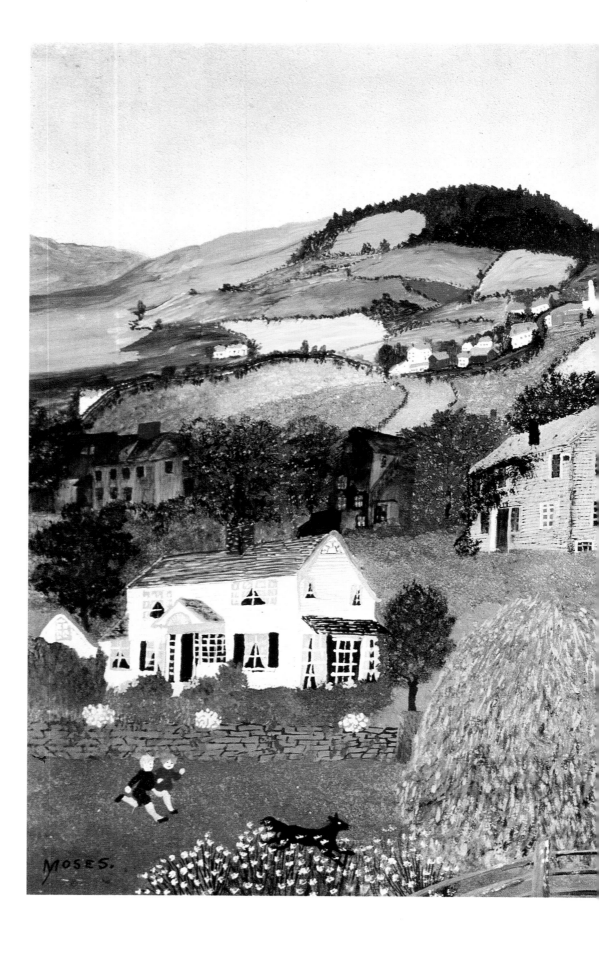

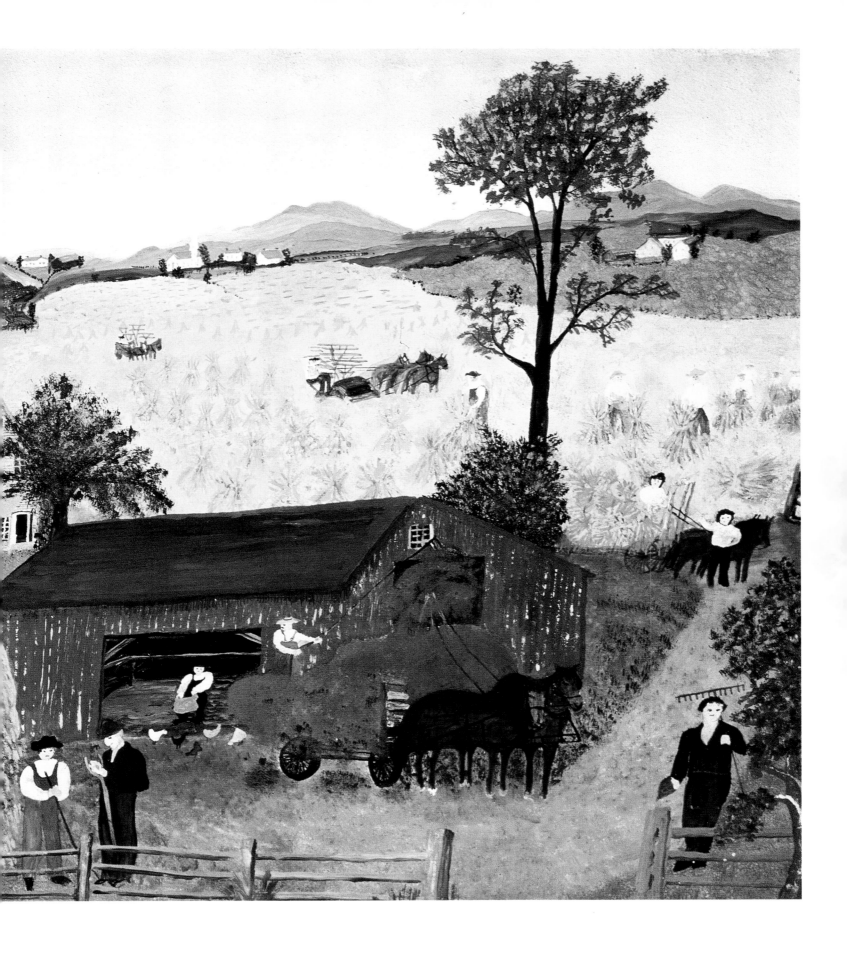

27 Auction, Number 2

1961. Oil on pressed wood
16 x 24 inches
(40.7 x 60.9 cm)
Signed, lower left
Kallir 1508. Private collection

Though we associate Grandma Moses' paintings with a sort of stability that is seemingly long lost, in fact the Moses family moved a great many times, from farm to farm in Virginia, and finally back north, to Eagle Bridge, New York. Each move involved a great upheaval. Sometimes a move was preceded by an auction, at which everything the family could or would not take along was sold. And then came the adventure of packing up the rest and transporting it. For the move to Eagle Bridge, Moses recalled, they actually had to charter a railroad car.

By taking a car, we could bring lots of produce, apples, meat—we butchered a hog—a cow, hens and stock. With the car, if there was livestock in it, we had to have a man to take care of it. So Thomas went with the car, but he smuggled in the two little boys, Forrest and Loyd, besides himself. . . . In one corner was the cow tied up with the feed and the fork for manure. In another corner was the chicken coop and in the other was the produce. The apples made the whole car smell. And the little black and tan dog went with them, too. So now, that was a family. . . .

Hugh, Anna and Ona went with me on the train. We should have gone out from Staunton at 12 o'clock, but we didn't leave till 6 o'clock next morning. All the way up to New York, it was a muggy, rainy day. . . . We got into New York that night, and we stayed overnight, but I don't know now where. From New York we took the train up to Eagle Bridge, and we came through Albany, had to stay there overnight, and came here next morning. . . . So we got home, and it was two days before the car came in with the other bunch.

My Life's History, pp. 95–97

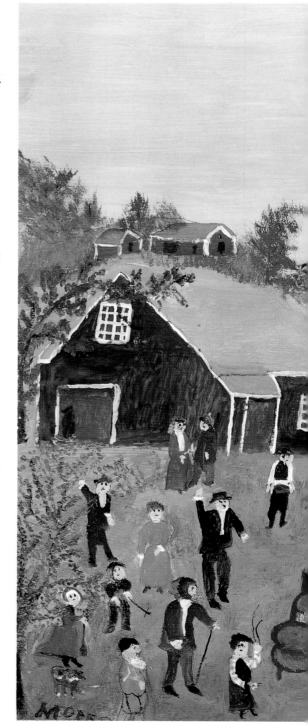

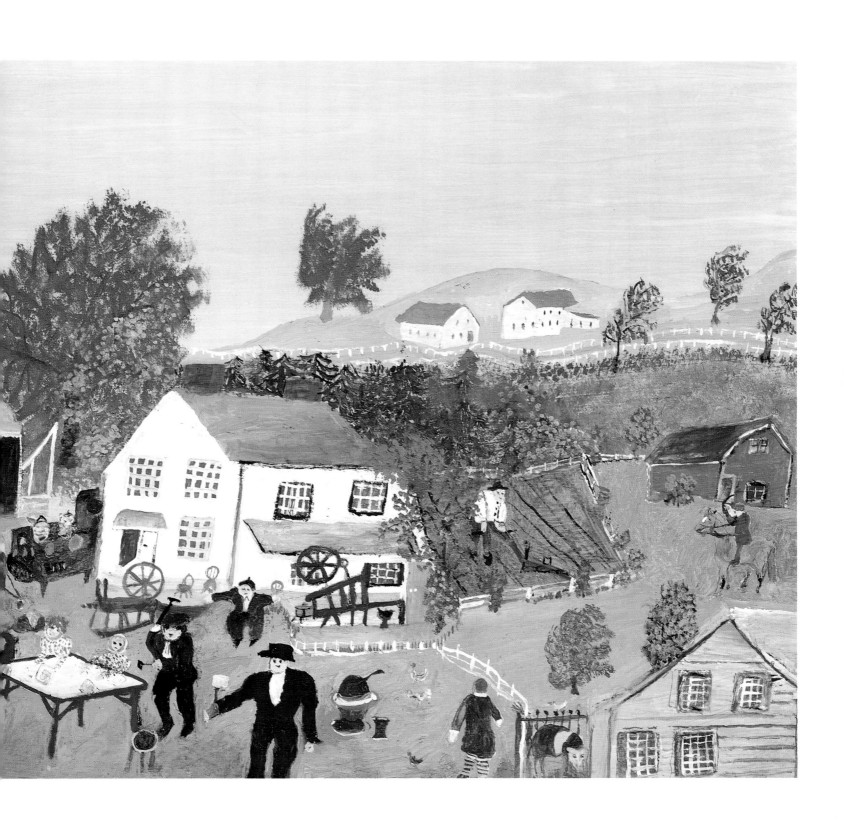

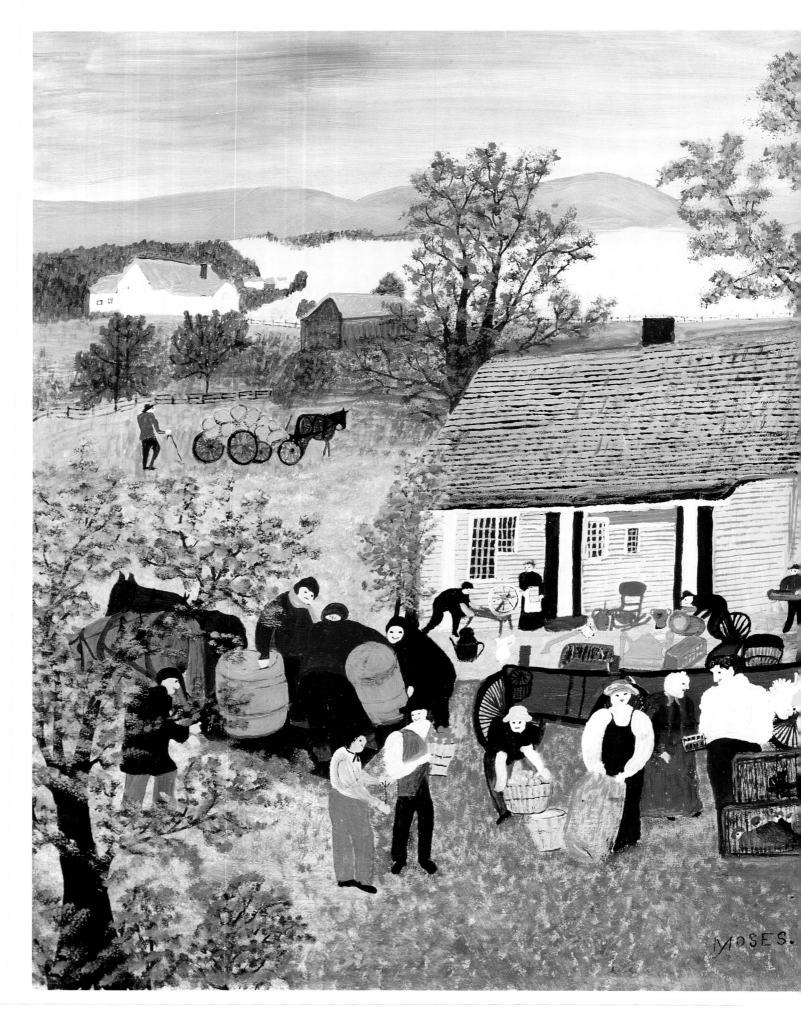

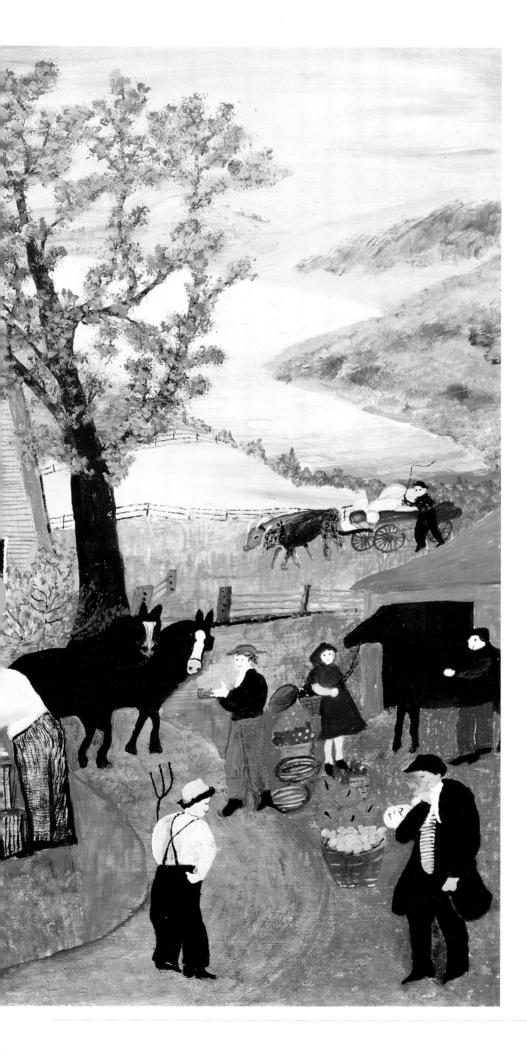

28 **Moving Day on the Farm**
1951. Oil on pressed wood
17 x 22 inches
(43.2 x 55.9 cm)
Signed, lower center
Kallir 965. Private collection
Courtesy Galerie St. Etienne,
New York

29 Apple Butter Making

1947. Oil on pressed wood
19 ¼ x 23 ¼ inches
(48.9 x 59.1 cm)
Signed, lower right
Kallir 654. Private collection
Courtesy Galerie St. Etienne,
New York

"Late summer was the time for apple butter making," Moses wrote in her autobiography. "The apple butter was considered a necessity."

To make apple butter, you take two barrels of sweet cider (you grind the apples and make sweet cider first), then you put them on in a big brass kettle over a fire out in the orchard and start it to boiling. You want three barrels of quartered apples, or snits, as they called them, with cores taken out, and then you commence to feed those in, and stirring and keeping that stirrer going. . . . Women folks would keep that going, feeding in all the apples until evening. Then the young folks would come in to start stirring. They'd have two—a boy and a girl—to take hold of the handle. They'd have a regular frolic all night out in the orchard.

My Life's History, p. 73

Once again, work for Moses is accompanied by play.

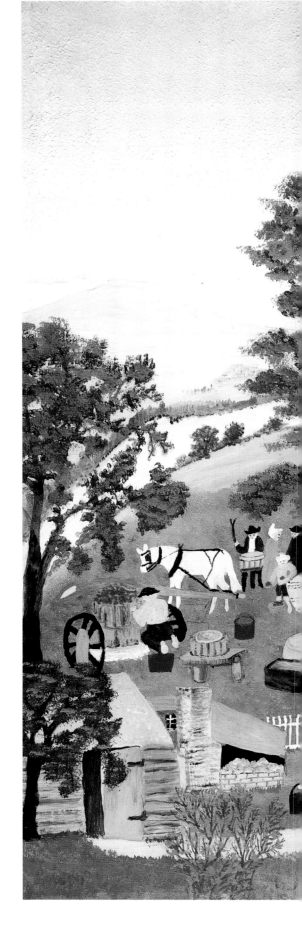

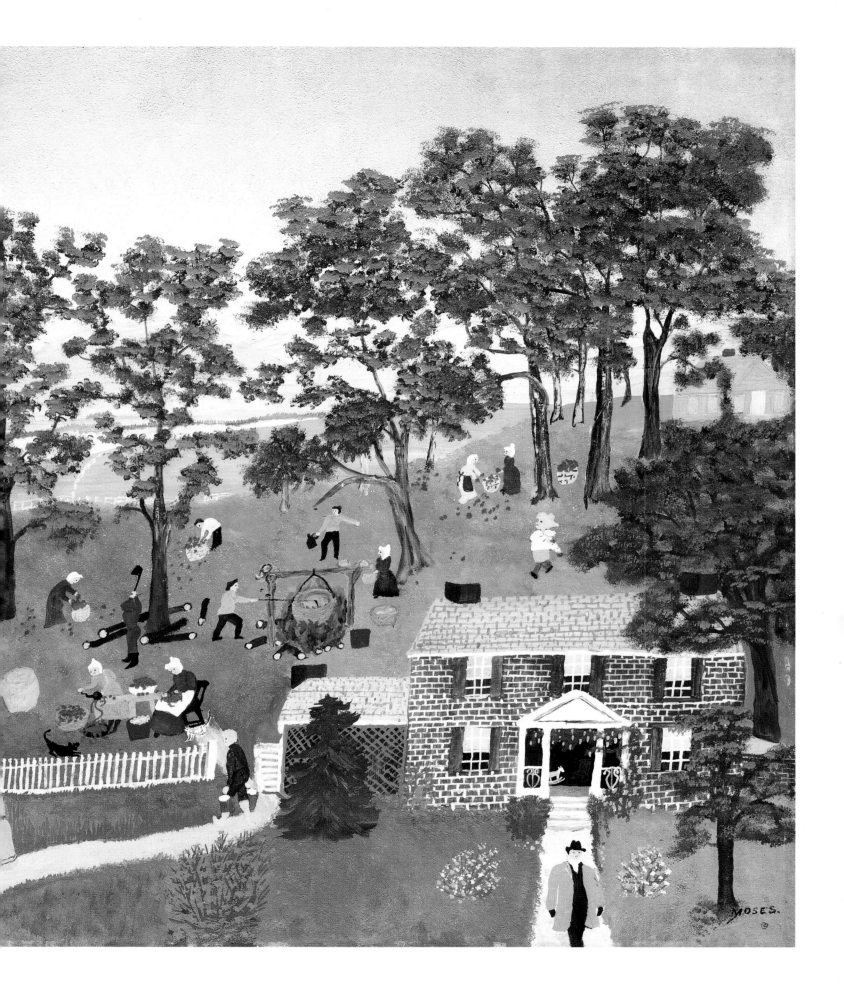

30 Pumpkins

1959. Oil on pressed wood
16 x 24 inches
(40.7 x 60.9 cm)
Signed, lower right
Kallir 1380. Private collection
Courtesy Galerie St. Etienne,
New York

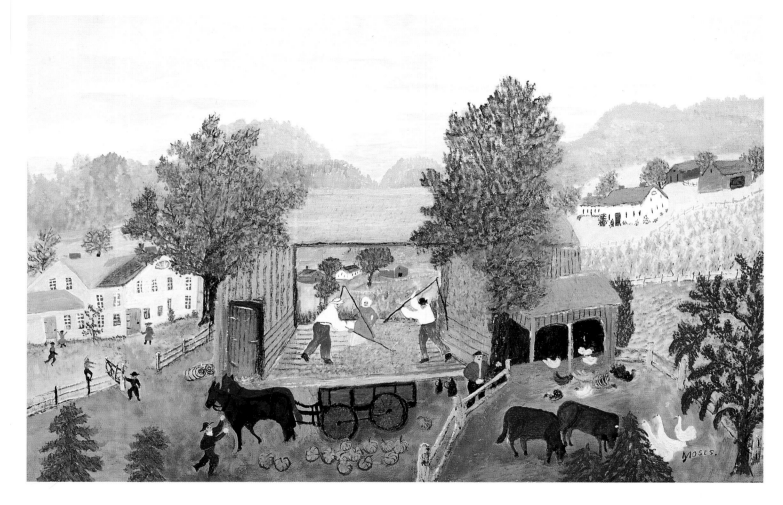

Once the drama of the harvest was over, autumn was spent attending to odd jobs and preparing for winter. Moses listed the tasks as follows:

Feed to be stored away for the coming cold weather.
The ground to be plowed for rye and other crops before it's frozen hard.
Ditches to dig.
Poultry to cull and house.

My Life's History, p. 50

31 Candle Dip Day in 1800

1950. Oil on pressed wood
9 x 9 1/4 inches
(22.9 x 23.5 cm)
Signed, lower right
Kallir 941. Private collection

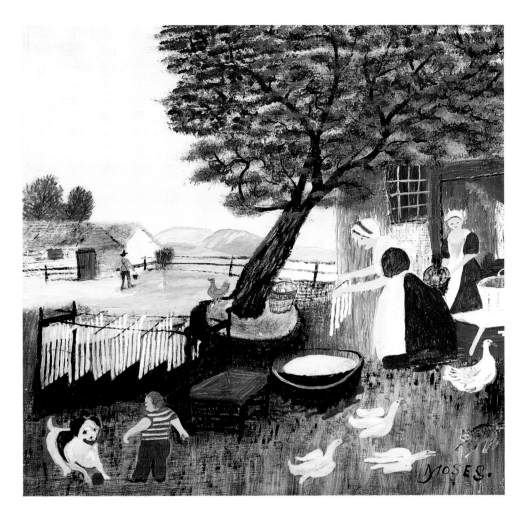

Candle-making was women's work, done in winter to speed hardening. "We always butchered one beef a winter," Moses remembered,

> and the fat from the beef is called tallow. . . . The tallow is dried out and saved to make candles with. The minute it come around cool weather, we commence to make candles for the following year. We thread the candle molds with candle wicking and then melt up some of the tallow and pour it from the top into the candle mold, so it runs down into the mold. Then we set it outdoors for it to harden. Generally, we would fill the mold twice a day, morning and evening, depending on how many molds we had. That would produce from one dozen to three dozen candles, depending on the size of the molds. When they were perfectly cold, then we would cut off the wicks and pull out the candles. Then you pack them in a box and set them away for the next summer. The children and the hired girl and the lady of the house, everybody had a chance in it, depending on who was the most idle. . . .

My Life's History, pp. 31–32

32 Logging

1957. Oil on pressed wood
15 7/8 x 24 inches
(40.3 x 60.9 cm)
Signed, lower left
Kallir 1265. Private collection

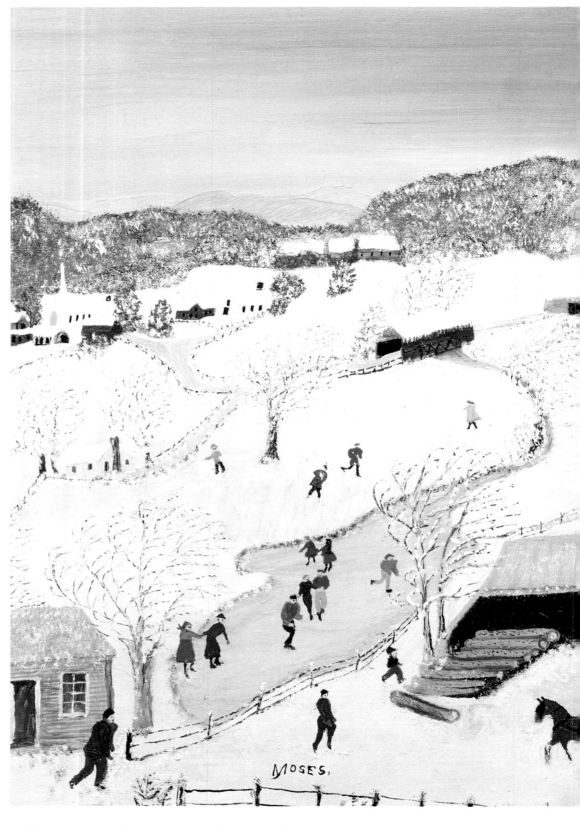

Wintertime work was very much curtailed by the snow. In upstate New York, where Moses lived, there was usually snow by Thanksgiving. With the fields fallow and frozen, logging was one of the few farming industries that thrived. In addition, the farm animals had to be fed, the cows milked. Hunting and trapping also helped to supplement the family's income.

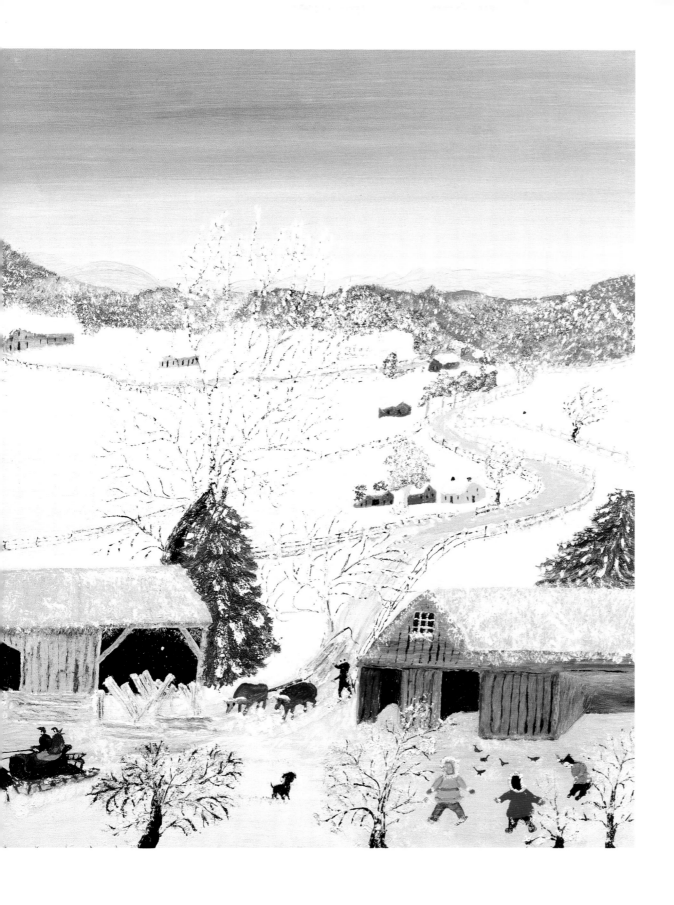

Place and Nature

Moses' art was firmly grounded in the artist's sense of place. She often memorialized precise spots in the local landscape as well as historical events that had had an impact either on her personally or on the region as a whole. In addition to this very specific grounding, Moses was also highly attuned to the more general indicators of time and place provided by nature's changing palette. Her paintings are always animated by an astute awareness of the nuances of season and weather.

However, as Roger Cardinal discusses elsewhere herein, Moses' depictions of local landmarks are not entirely accurate. Combining memory, printed sources, and her own idiosyncratic sense of color and composition, Moses created composites that reflected the landscape as it existed in her mind's eye, rather than as it looked in reality. The architectural elements were abstractions, based on clippings that sometimes had nothing to do with the subject at hand and that were configured according to aesthetic rather than reportorial considerations. Whereas specific buildings, such as the artist's home (plates 47 and 48) or *The Whiteside Church* (plate 36), are rendered fairly precisely, one is hard pressed to identify individual structures in many of the townscapes (plates 44–46).

If Moses took liberties when it came to the verisimilitude of her compositions, she was nonetheless scrupulously attentive to natural details. Her precise evocations of the rural environment literally breathe life into her abstract vignettes and account for her paintings' enduring appeal. Rather than serving merely as nostalgic reminders of a lost past, or as personal records of Moses' life, her landscapes occupy an eternal present. Reminding us that nature's pleasures—the smell of new-mown grass or the glitter of sun on fresh snow—do not fade, her landscapes celebrate lasting values and, in the process, seem to secure the future.

❧ ✣ ❧

My Forefathers' Mill, with its English architecture, was probably based on a print. Nevertheless, the title makes the subject Moses' own and illustrates how she was able to appropriate pre-existing imagery and turn it to her particular purposes. The artist's father, Russell King Robertson, had a flax mill near Greenwich, New York, and it is undoubtedly his mill Moses intended to depict in the painting. She was proud that her family had numbered among the early settlers in what is now Washington County. Thus personal history, regional history, and the artist's observations of the local landscape were integrally connected.

33 My Forefathers' Mill
1940 or earlier
Oil on pressed wood
14 x 12 inches
(35.7 x 30.5 cm)
Signed, lower right; inscribed
on verso "My forefathers"
Kallir 44. Private collection

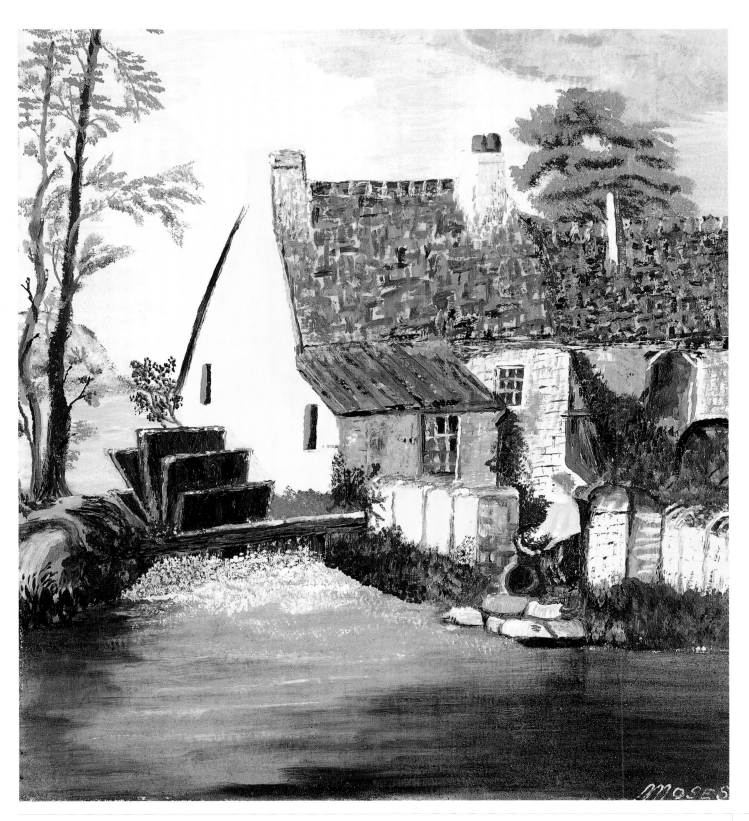

1945. Oil on pressed wood
16 x 20 inches
(40.7 x 50.8 cm)
Signed, lower left
Kallir 510. Private collection

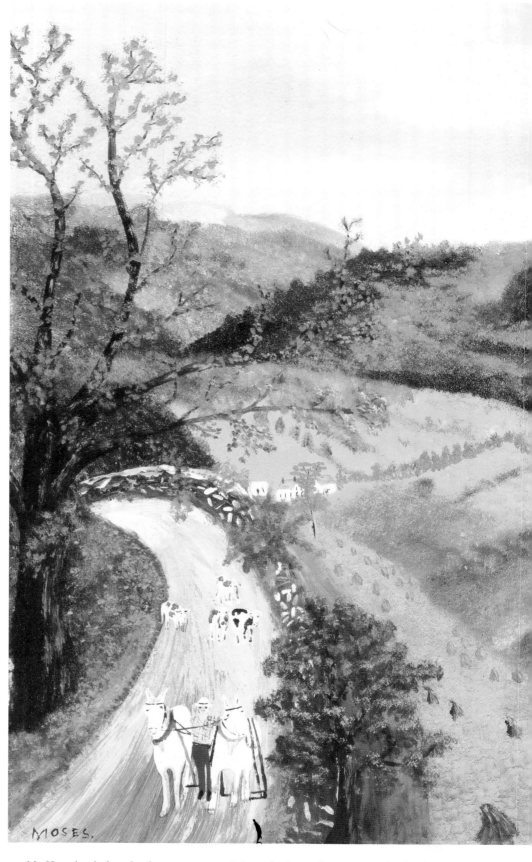

My Homeland clearly demonstrates Moses' identification with the land, which she rendered with a precision borne of deep affection. The painting depicts the hills and valleys of upstate New York in a moment of repose: the harvest is in, and the autumn palette creates a tapestry of rich yellow hay, green and red foliage, and dusky brown earth.

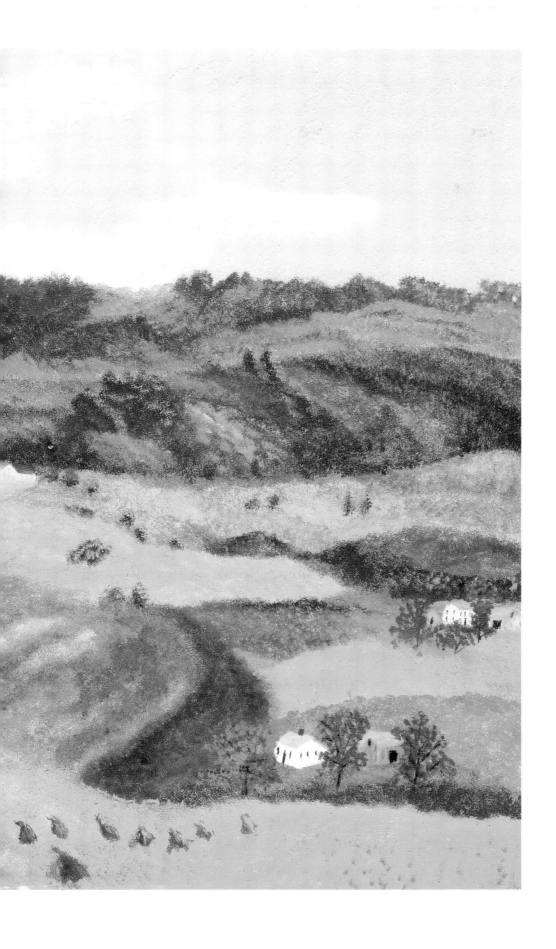

35 Down the Road

1950. Oil on pressed wood
19 x 24 inches
(48.3 x 60.9 cm)
Signed, lower right
Kallir 914. Private collection
in honor of Mr. J. B. Olstein

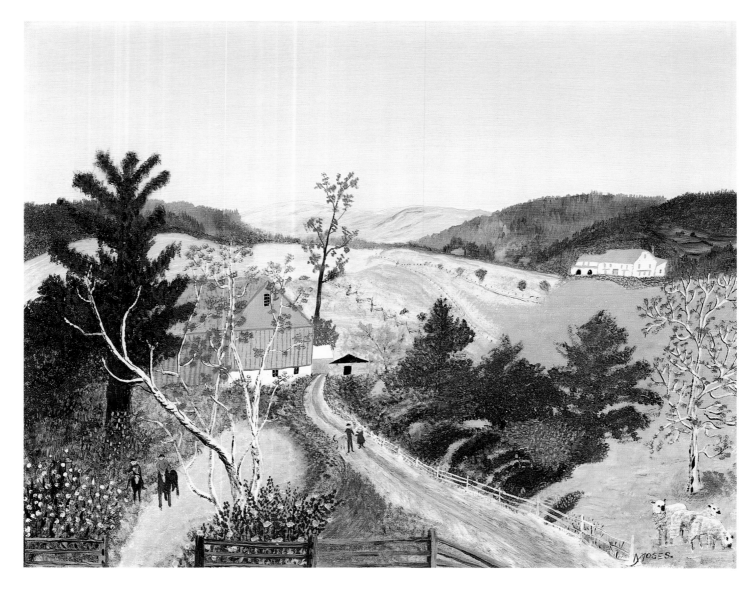

Down the Road is a comparatively generic depiction of Moses' environment. Although the title suggests that the road in question is Moses'
own, it could in fact be any rural thoroughfare. It this manner, the
artist managed to share her homeland with everyone.

36 **The Whiteside Church**
1945. Oil on pressed wood
9 3/4 x 17 inches
(24.8 x 43.2 cm)
Signed, lower center
Kallir 543. Private collection

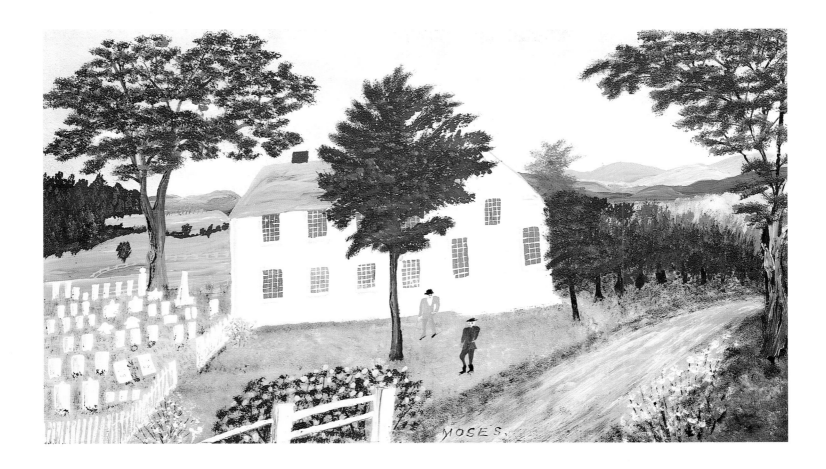

When Anna Mary was twelve years old, she hired out as a household
helper to the Whiteside family, who were distant relations. The
Whiteside Church had been built around 1800 by the family's ancestors,
and it served as a weekly gathering place for several denominations.
Members of the community (including some of the artist's relatives)
were buried in its small graveyard. A relatively accurate representation,
The Whiteside Church was important to Moses not only because of its place in
her own life's story, but chiefly as a symbol of community engagement.
In the days before telephones, Sunday services performed a social as well
as a spiritual function. "Going to church on Sunday, this was a pleasure
in olden times," Moses wrote. "Here they can exchange the news of the
week, hear from the sick and the well, and spend the day in prayer,
thanksgiving and song, a day of pleasure and rest from drudgery."

Like many of Moses' early subjects, the *Old Oaken Bucket* combines local lore and personal experience. In 1877, young Anna Mary worked as a hired girl for an elderly woman, Mrs. David Burch. Mrs. Burch told Anna Mary that the well on her farm was the original well that had inspired the famous song, "The Old Oaken Bucket." Mrs. Burch then recounted the following story:

Back in the 18th century, [Mrs. Burch's] great-grandfather lived in this place. He had an older brother who in his boyhood days fell in love with one of his neighbor's daughters. But her parents did not want her to go with Paul Dennis, as he and his people were poor folks. Well, that made trouble, and the young folks would write letters to each other, and they used one of the apple trees for a post office, and would sly out at night and exchange mail. Then Paul went off for three years as a sailor, in those days one had to sign up for three years, and Paul was young and got very homesick, and wrote up the verses of the "Old Oaken Bucket." Then, when the three years were up, he came back to Boston and gave them to Woodworth, who set them to music, and therefore claimed them.

My Life's History, p. 48

"The Old Oaken Bucket" was one of Grandma Moses' best-loved subjects. After she was awarded the New York State Prize for her first rendition of the theme (Kallir 94) in 1941, she received many requests to repeat the work. Always ready to oblige, she honored these requests, though no two versions of the painting are the same.

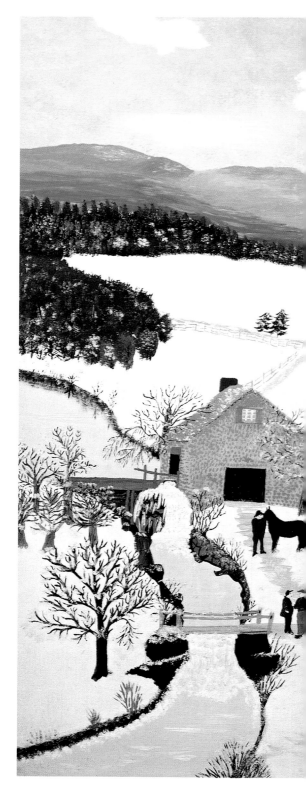

37 **The Old Oaken Bucket of 1760 in Winter**
1944. Oil on pressed wood
24 1/16 x 34 inches
(61 x 86.4 cm)
Signed, lower right
Kallir 376. Seiji Togo Memorial,
Yasuda Kasai Museum of Art, Tokyo

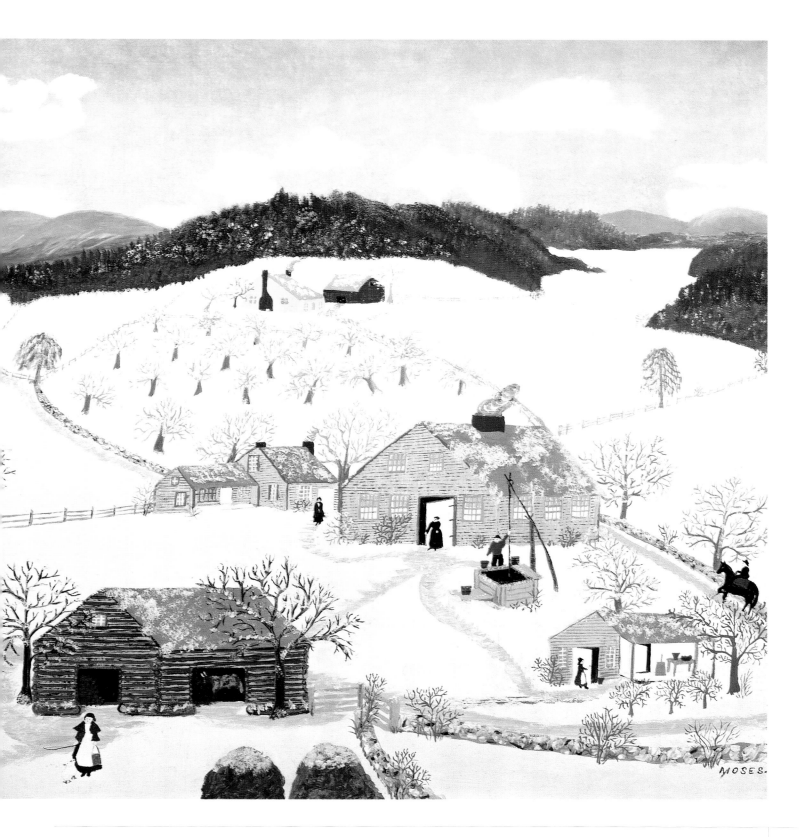

38 Old Oaken Bucket in Winter

1952. Oil on pressed wood
18 x 24 inches
(45.7 x 60.9 cm)
Signed, lower right
Kallir 1061. Private collection

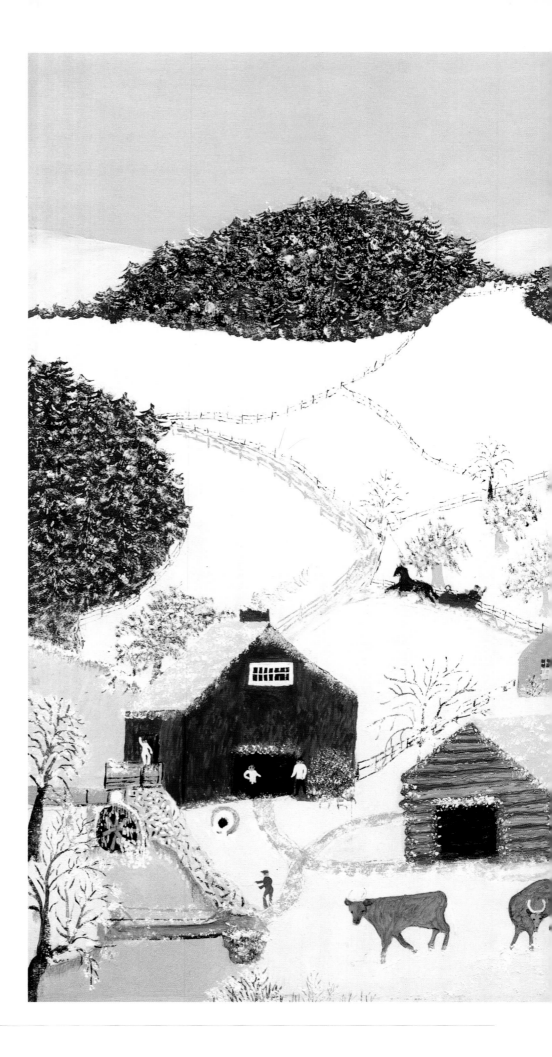

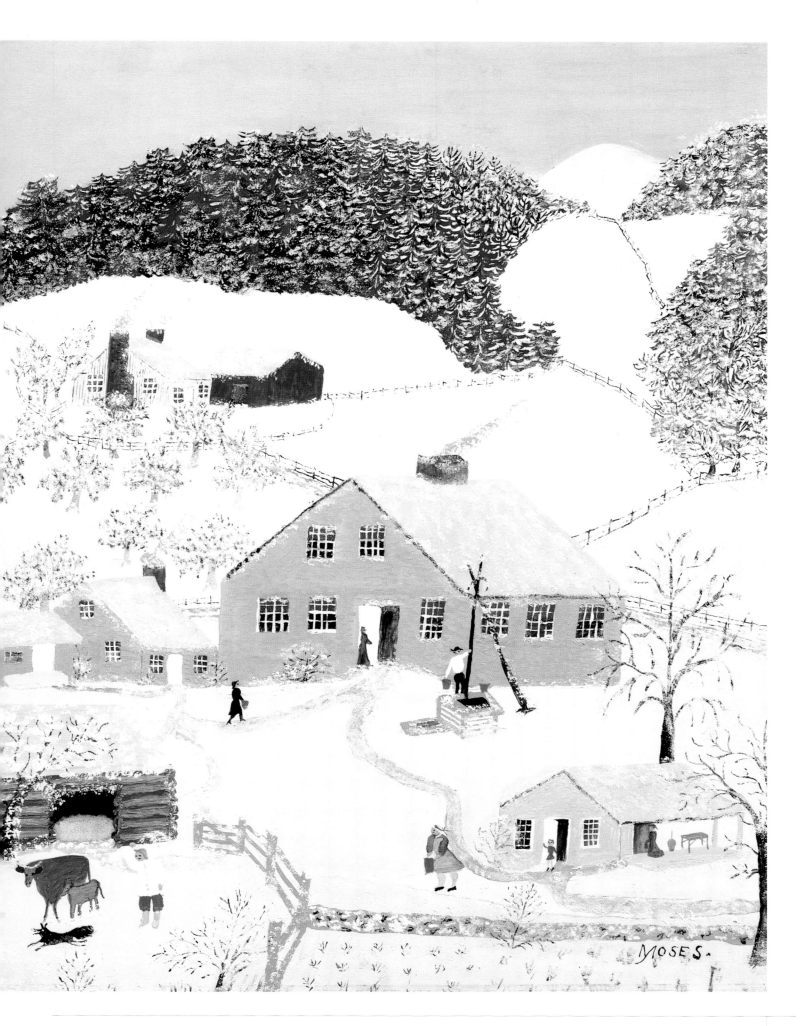

39 The Old Checkered House in 1860

1942. Oil on pressed wood
16 x 20 inches
(40.7 x 50.8 cm)
Signed, lower right
Kallir 144. From the Collection of
Richard D. Della Penna, M.D.,
and Mearl A. Naponic, M.D.,
San Diego, California

Like the Troy fire (plates 11 and 12), the "Checkered House" was a local legend. Located along the Cambridge Turnpike, it was an inn where stagecoach drivers had changed horses as far back as the eighteenth century. During the Revolutionary War, the inn served as General Baum's headquarters and field hospital. Its checkerboard front made the house a distinctive landmark that was remembered long after it burned in 1907.

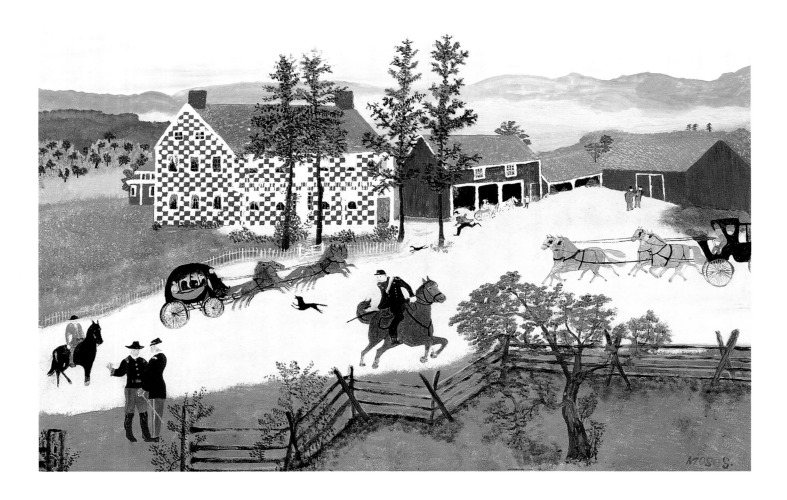

40 **The Old Checkered House**

1944. Oil on pressed wood
23 ^{15}/$_{16}$ x 43 ^{1}/$_{16}$ inches
(60.7 x 109.4 cm)
Signed, lower left
Kallir 367. Seiji Togo Memorial,
Yasuda Kasai Museum of Art,
Tokyo

Moses painted a number of versions of the "Checkered House," in
both winter and summer. When asked how she managed to come up with
a new composition each time, she said she imagined the scene as if she
were looking at it through a window. By then adjusting her viewpoint
slightly, she could cause the elements to fall into place differently. *The Old
Checkered House in 1860*, executed in 1942, is one of the artist's earliest
renditions of the subject. By comparison, the 1944 version is considerably larger, demonstrating Moses' growing confidence as a painter.

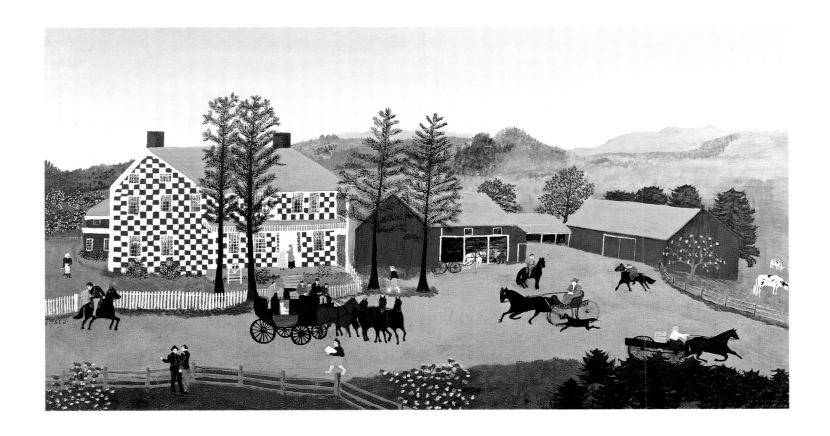

41 The Battle of Bennington

1953. Oil on pressed wood
18 x 30 ½ inches
(45.7 x 77.6 cm)
Signed, lower right
Kallir 1100. The Collection of
G. Arnold Haynes

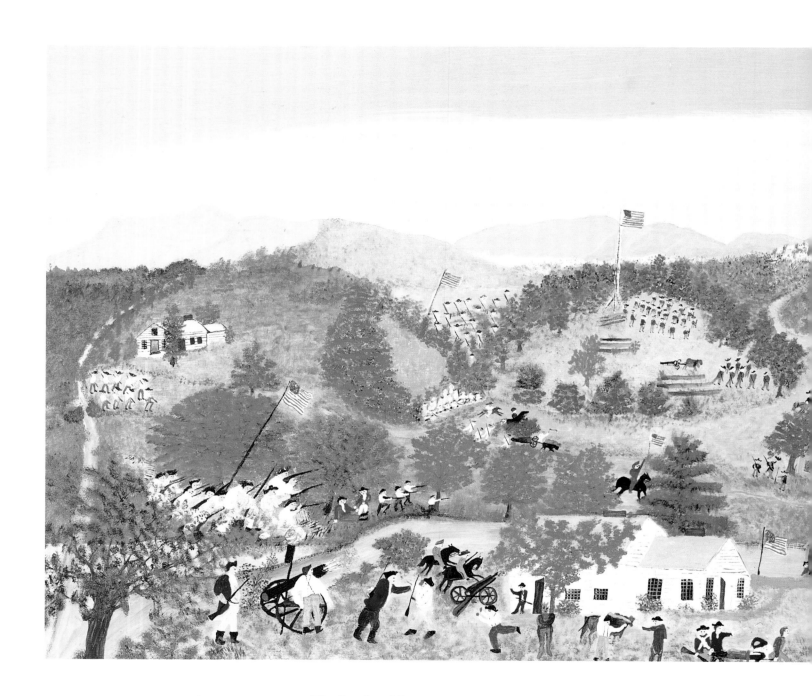

The Battle of Bennington took place during the American Revolution, in upstate New York not far from Moses' birthplace. Vermont claimed the battle by name, and honored it with a monument in Bennington. The actual site of the battle is commemorated with a park just across the state border, in New York.

Several of Moses' ancestors had fought in the Revolutionary War, so the Battle of Bennington held personal as well as historical meaning.

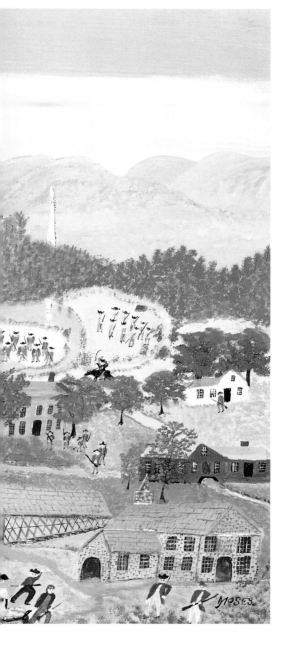

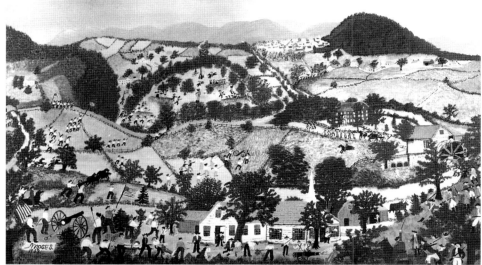

Fig. 16. Grandma Moses, *The Battle of Bennington*, 1953. Oil on pressed wood, 17 ½ x 29 ¼ inches (44.5 x 74.3 cm). Signed, lower left. National Society of the Daughters of the American Revolution Americana Collection (3825.1), Washington, D.C.

The artist was therefore pleased when she received a request to paint the battle from the National Society of the Daughters of the American Revolution (of which she was a proud member). Moses researched the subject at some length to ensure accuracy, only to flub the assignment by including the monument (which obviously did not exist at the time of the battle). She redid the subject, and the corrected version (fig. 16) is today owned by the NSDAR.

**42 Hoosick Valley
(From the Window)**

1946. Oil on pressed wood
19 1/2 x 22 inches
(49.6 x 55.9 cm)
Signed, lower right
Kallir 611. Private collection
Courtesy Galerie St. Etienne,
New York

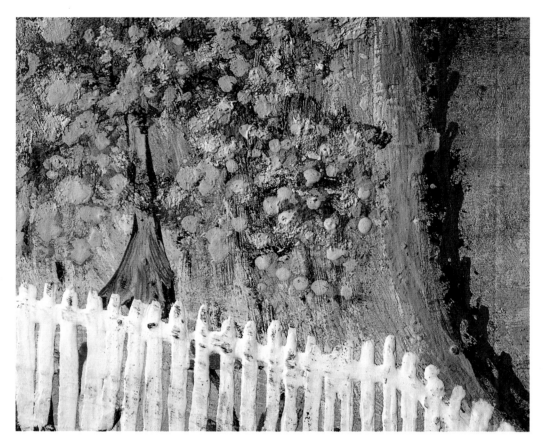

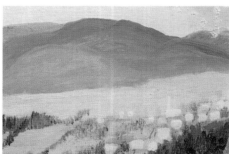

Fig. 17. *Hoosick Valley (From the Window)*, detail of
plate 42

Fig. 18. *Hoosick Valley (From the Window)*, detail of
plate 42

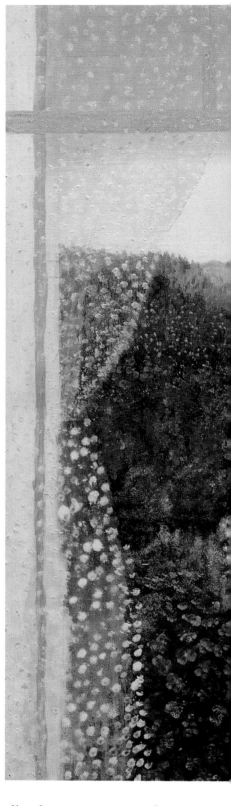

Hoosick Valley (From the Window), with its trompe-l'oeil curtain, is one of
Moses' more unusual compositions, although she claimed that she often
used an imaginary window to frame her landscapes. A view from the
artist's bedroom, the painting is a striking example of Moses' ability to
portray natural detail and color. Employing the "impressionistic" tech-
nique borrowed from embroidery (see plates 2 and 3, and fig. 2), the
artist set varied tones of green and yellow next to one another to evoke
the interplay between parched meadows and verdant hills. The textures

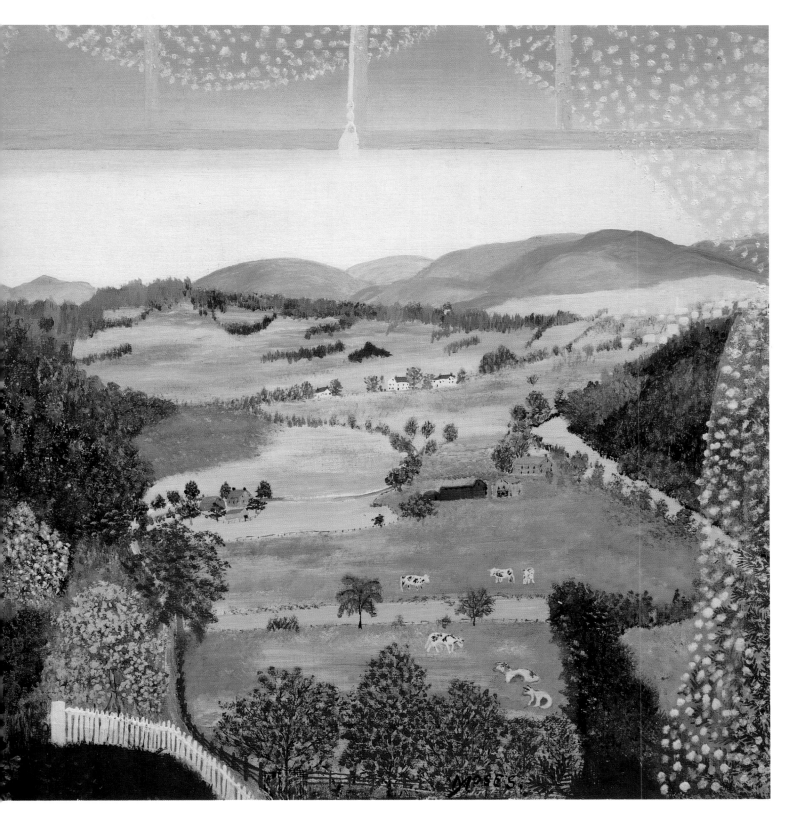

of the paint also mimic embroidery. Fence posts are "stitched" into place, and the blossoming trees resemble little knots of thread (fig. 17). Moses established a series of textural gradations, from flat expanses and isolated blocks of color to more intricate, multicolored configurations. Certain details were executed in raised paint in order to deliberately set them off from the background (fig. 18). Many of Moses' paintings, when viewed up close, are actually composites of abstract forms.

43 The Spring in Evening

1947. Oil on pressed wood
27 x 21 inches
(68.6 x 53.3 cm)
Signed, lower left
Kallir 706. Private collection
Courtesy Galerie St. Etienne,
New York

While Moses' way of piecing together compositions was partly dictated by her sense of abstract design, the arrangements were always subordinated to the requirements of the landscape. As a substitute for academic perspective (which she had never learned), she had recourse not just to a progressive scheme of diminishing sizes, but also to coloristic indicators of space. She was quick to note such qualities as the pale blue of distant hills, or the tonal gradations of the sky. She translated phenomena observed from nature into veils of color and layers of pigment.

The Spring in Evening is notable for the way in which Moses captured both time of year and time of day. The rawness of the freshly plowed earth, the new growth on the hillside, and the lambent pink of the sunset are all recorded with a sure feel for color and a striking verisimilitude. Variations in the physical and tonal density of the paint create a series of transitions between the artist's anecdotal vignettes and the more complex hues of the landscape (fig. 19). The bold silhouettes of the horses (fig. 20) and the houses are spare formal essences embedded in a network of paint. It is, however, the natural landscape that brings the whole to life.

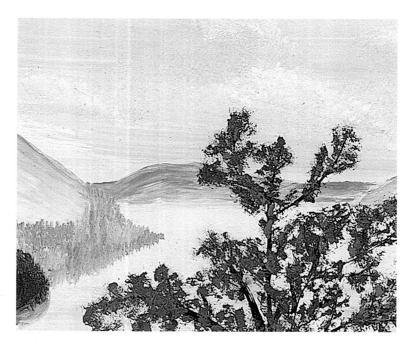

Fig. 19. *The Spring in Evening*, detail of plate 43

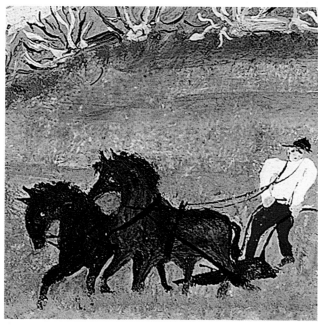

Fig. 20. *The Spring in Evening*, detail of plate 43

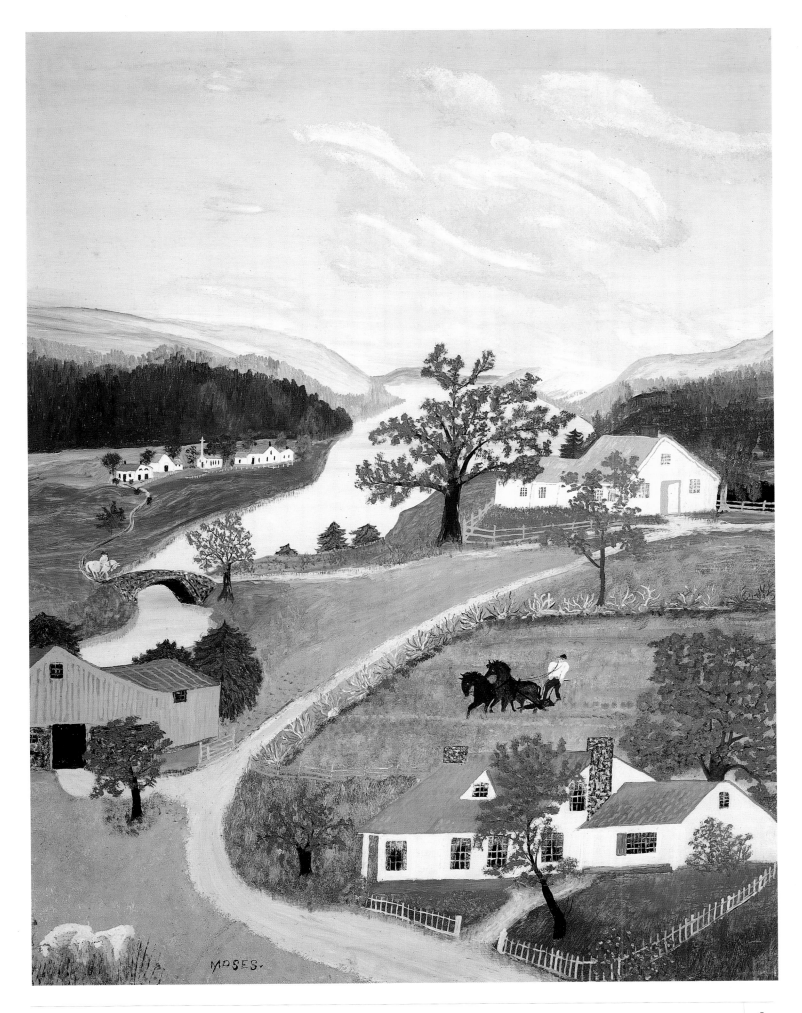

44 Hoosick Falls II

1944. Oil on pressed wood
20 1/16 x 25 7/8 inches
(51.0 x 65.7 cm)
Signed, lower right
Kallir 413. Seiji Togo Memorial,
Yasuda Kasai Museum of Art,
Tokyo

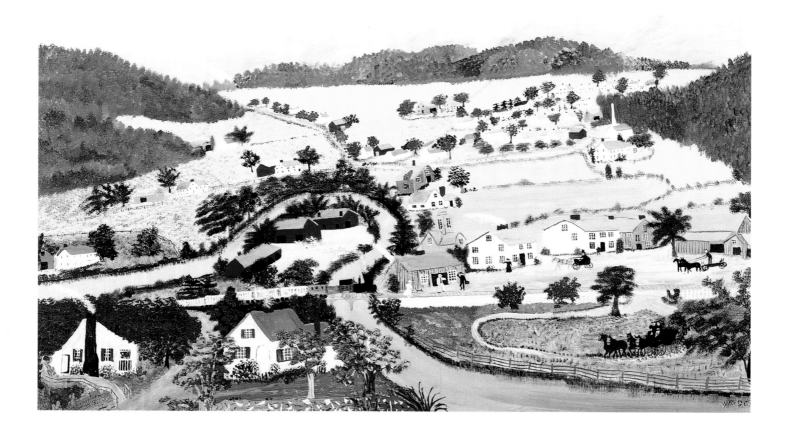

The Village of Hoosick Falls will always have a key place in the biography of Grandma Moses, for it was here that her paintings were first discovered, sitting in Thomas's drugstore window. For Moses herself, however, the importance of Hoosick Falls lay not in its connection to her own career, but in the village's role in American history. Today Hoosick Falls, the closest real town to the Moses farmstead, is a sleepy byway, somewhat passed over by modern economic development. However, until the Great Depression, it was a bustling commercial center, its industrial potential bolstered by its situation at the confluence of the

45 **Hoosick Falls in Winter**

1944. Oil on hardboard
19 ³/₄ x 23 ³/₄
(50.1 x 60.3 cm)
Signed, lower center
Kallir 425. The Phillips Collection,
Washington, D.C.

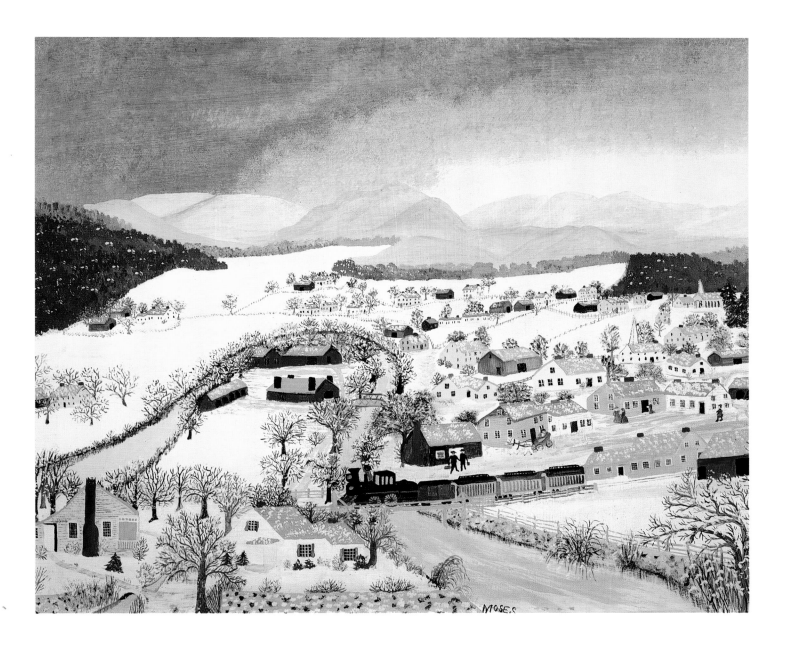

Hoosic and Walloomsack Rivers. Moses associated the area, hunting
grounds of the Mohican Indian tribe, with the tales of James Fenimore
Cooper. "Some say Natty Bumpo sleeps his sleep in an unknown grave in
the village limits," she wrote.

Moses painted a number of versions of Hoosick Falls, showing the
village in various seasons. Most follow the winding path of the Hoosic
River and may be based in part on old prints of the town. The bird's-eye
view—encompassing more than would be visible from any single human
vantage point—is, however, typical of Moses' unique approach.

46 Williamstown in Summer

1948. Oil on pressed wood
15 3/4 x 20 inches
(40 x 50.8 cm)
Signed, lower left
Kallir 760. John and Dorothy Levy

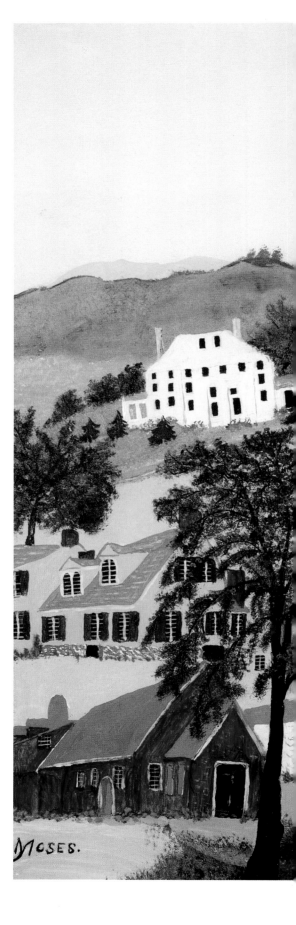

Williamstown, Massachusetts, is, like Hoosick Falls (plates 44 and 45), another larger community not far from Moses' hometown of Eagle Bridge, New York (plate 78). The artist painted towns such as these because they constituted, in effect, the compass points of a life in which travel beyond a certain limited radius was exceptional. Nonetheless, the townscapes stand out in an oeuvre that largely comprises landscapes.

Moses painted three versions of Williamstown, no two of which look alike. Historians have struggled to identify specific buildings in the pictures, with little success. In all likelihood, the buildings in *Williamstown in Summer* are generic abstractions, possibly based on clippings and assembled according to the requirements of design, rather than a realistic road map. However, all the paintings of Williamstown are true to Moses' emotional experience of the place: a quaint New England town set amidst verdant farmland and cradled by mountainous hills.

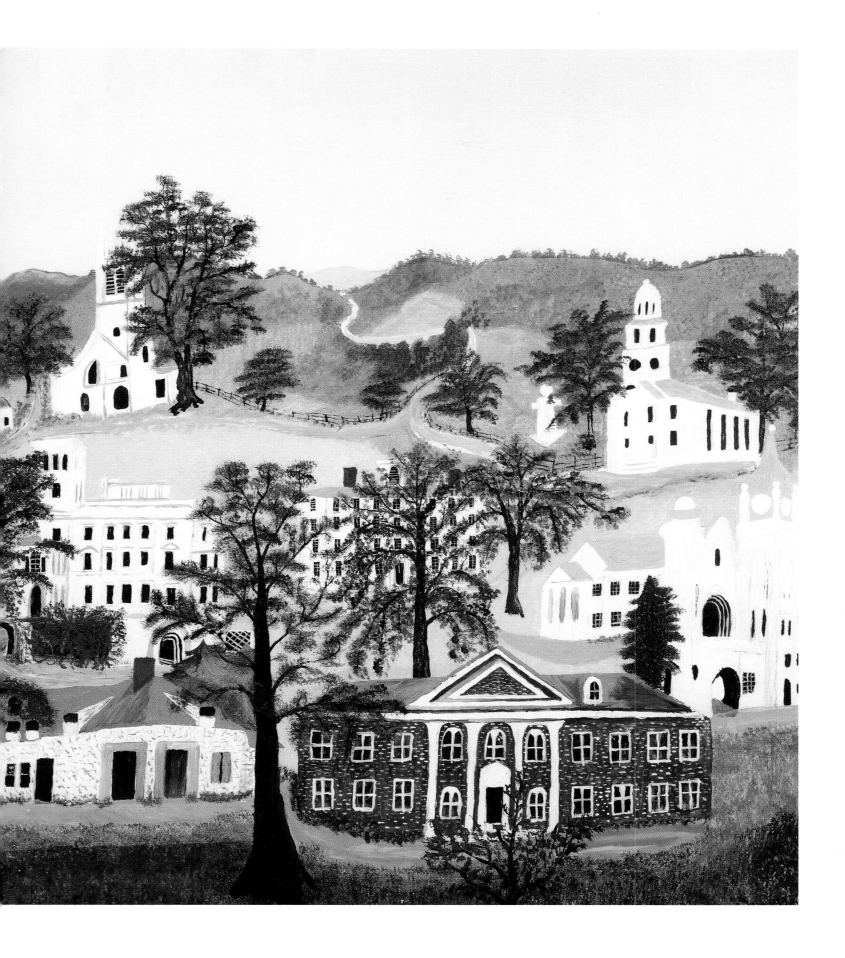

Anna Mary and Thomas Moses had named their farm in Eagle Bridge "Mt. Nebo," after the biblical mountain where Moses disappeared, and the farm is featured in a number of the artist's works (see also plates 3 and 8). *Mt. Nebo in Summer* and *Mt. Nebo in Winter* (plate 48) were painted within days of one another, in August 1943. Obviously, Moses did not need to view an actual snowscape to paint the winter scene, though both versions of the subject are informed by lived experience. Indeed, *Mt. Nebo in Winter* is notable for its dexterous juxtaposition of different shades of white and its masterly solution to the difficult artistic problem of depicting white objects on a white ground (fig. 21).

Placing the focal point of each composition, Mt. Nebo, in the middleground typifies the artist's unconventional approach, which gives equal weight to all areas of a landscape subject. Neither in the foreground nor the background does Moses stint on detail. Rather than glorifying the family farm, she provides it with a rich context, making it at once less personal and more universal: a primordial homestead accessible to all viewers.

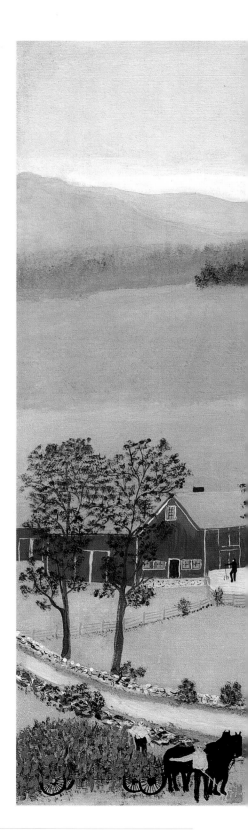

47 **Mt. Nebo in Summer**
1943. Oil on pressed wood
20 x 26 inches
(50.8 x 66 cm)
Signed, lower right
Kallir 274. Private collection

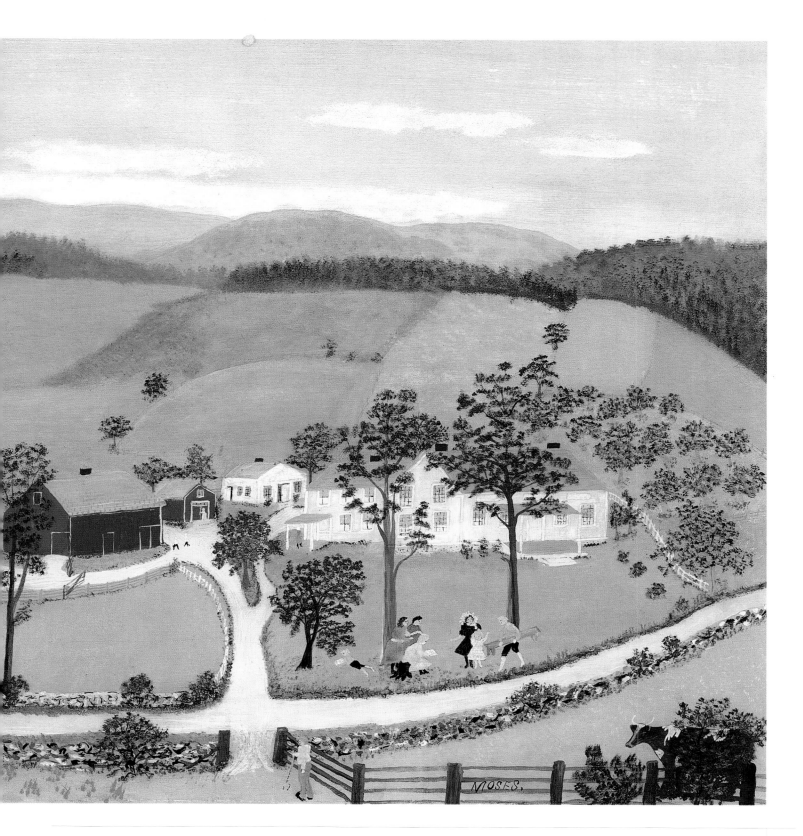

48 Mt. Nebo in Winter

1943. Oil on pressed wood
20 ¹/₂ x 26 ¹/₂ inches
(52 x 67.3 cm)
Signed, lower right
Kallir 275. Private collection
Courtesy Galerie St. Etienne,
New York

Fig. 21. *Mt. Nebo in Winter*, detail of plate 48

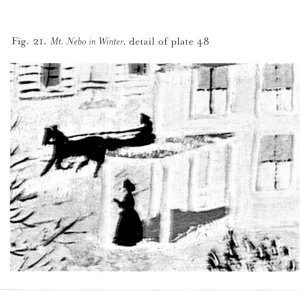

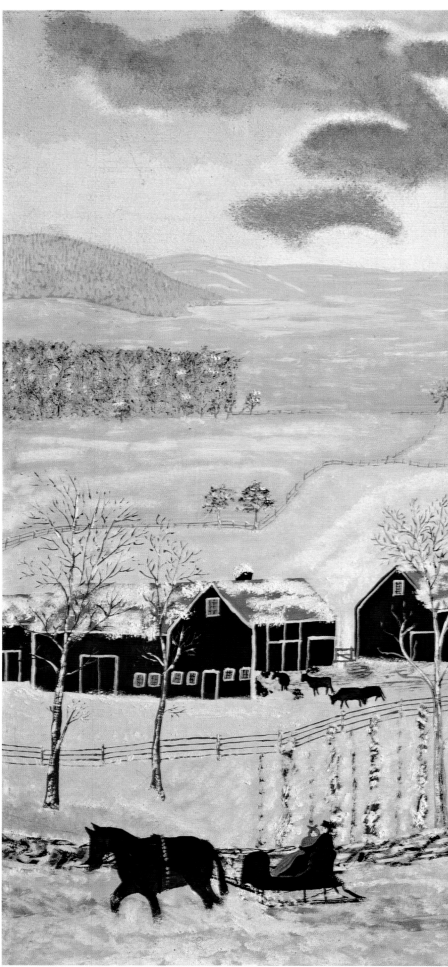

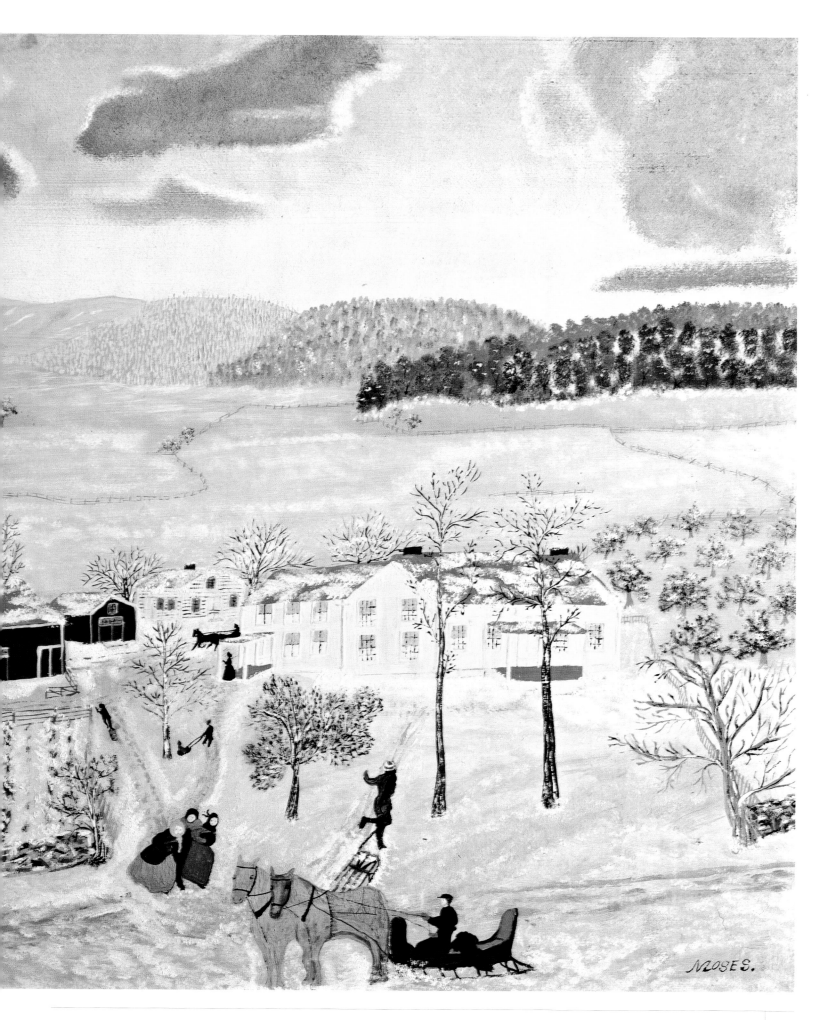

Moses frequently painted versions of the same subject in different seasons (see also plates 44 and 45; 47 and 48; 37, 38, and 80). *Hoosick River, Summer* and *Hoosick River, Winter* (plate 50) depict a section of the river not far from the Moses farm. Comparison of these two closely related scenes allows a keen analysis of the way Moses used color to record precise natural phenomena. The summer scene is full of promise: rich, dark, freshly plowed earth, children playing on and beneath a blooming tree, new green growth poking up through the golden loam in the middle distance.

The winter view, by comparison, is stark and cold: one of the few Moses snow scenes in which the trees are barren, rather than laden with fresh fallen snow. As with many of Moses' best paintings, *Hoosick River, Winter* functions almost like an animation: one can practically hear the crack of the hunters' guns, and then watch as the two pheasants scramble into the air (fig. 22). Like the *Mt. Nebo* paintings (plates 47 and 48), the two versions of *Hoosick River* were painted at roughly the same time, in March. Possibly this is the reason that, of the two, the winter variation is the more strongly redolent of its season. One can also imagine the pleasure the artist took, envisioning summer at the end of a long, cold winter.

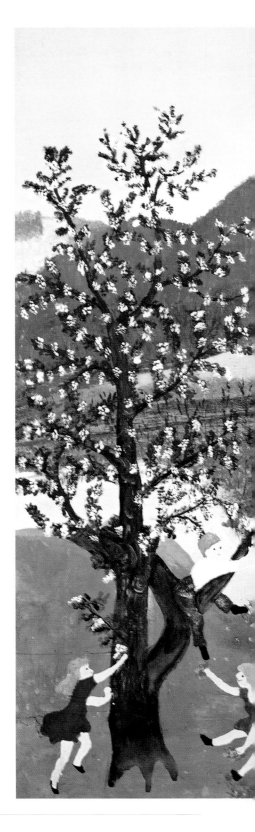

49 **Hoosick River, Summer**
1952. Oil on pressed wood
18 x 24 inches
(45.7 x 60.9 cm)
Signed, lower right
Kallir 1032. Private collection
Courtesy Galerie St. Etienne,
New York

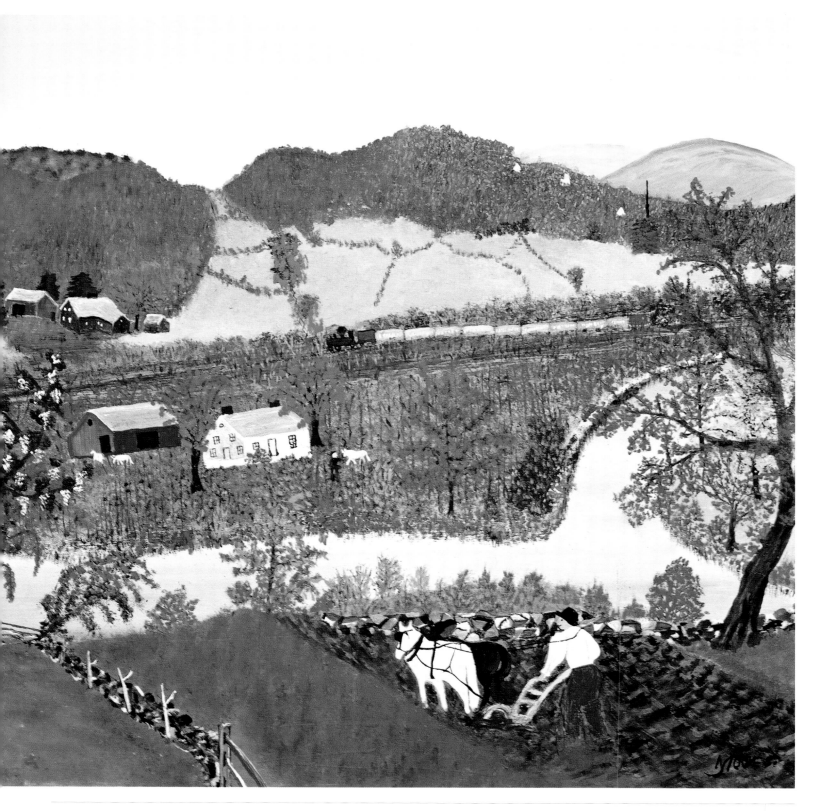

50 Hoosick River, Winter

1952. Oil on pressed wood
18 x 24 inches
(45.7 x 60.9 cm)
Signed, lower right
Kallir 1031. Private collection
Courtesy Galerie St. Etienne,
New York

Fig. 22. *Hoosick River, Winter*, detail of plate 50

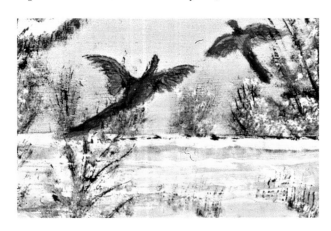

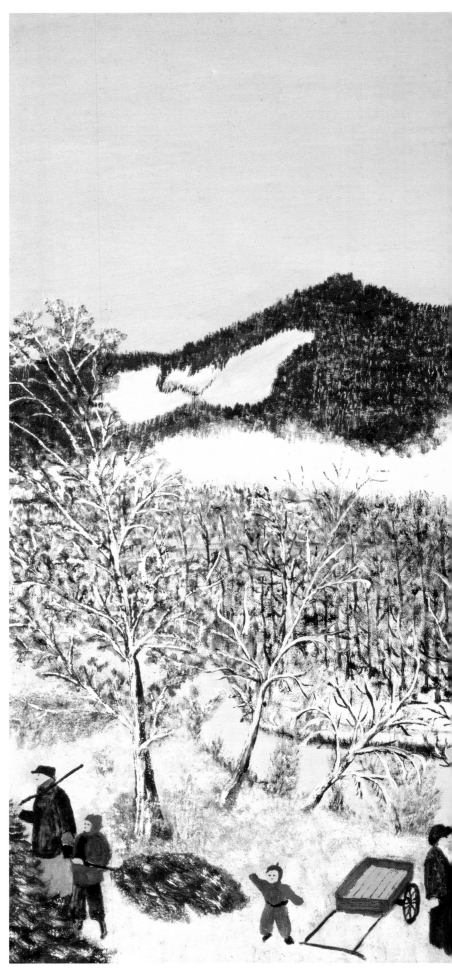

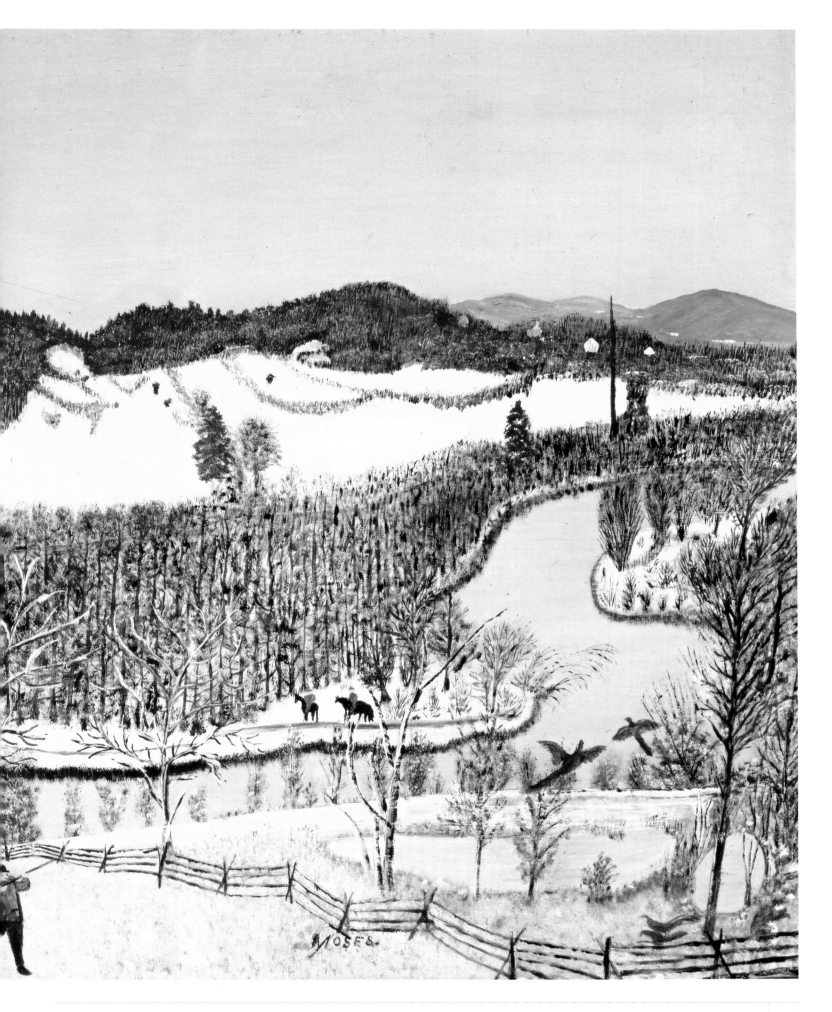

51 Forrest Moses' Home

1952. Oil on pressed wood
11 7/8 x 16 inches
(30.3 x 40.7 cm)
Signed, lower right
Kallir 1048. Private collection

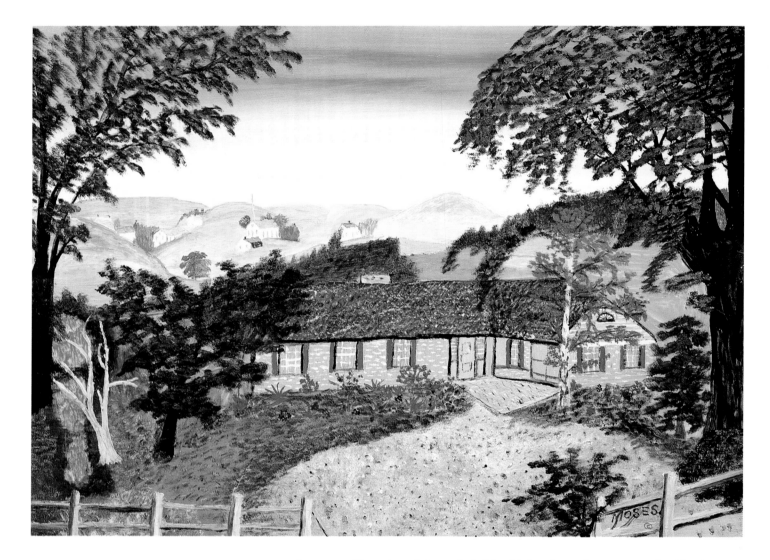

In 1951, Grandma Moses left Mt. Nebo (see plates 47 and 48), the old, rambling farmhouse in which she had lived since returning from the South in 1905, for a new, more comfortable ranch home across the street. The house had been built for her by her sons Forrest and Loyd, and the artist would live there for the remainder of her life, first with her daughter Winona, and then with Forrest and his wife, Mary. Nevertheless, Moses always referred to Mt. Nebo as "home." And the new house, though it had been built specially for her, in fact belonged to Forrest, and in her mind, it was always his.

52 **Early Springtime on the Farm**

1945. Oil on pressed wood
16 x 25 3/4 inches
(40.7 x 65.4 cm)
Signed, lower right
Kallir 500. Private collection
Courtesy Galerie St. Etienne,
New York

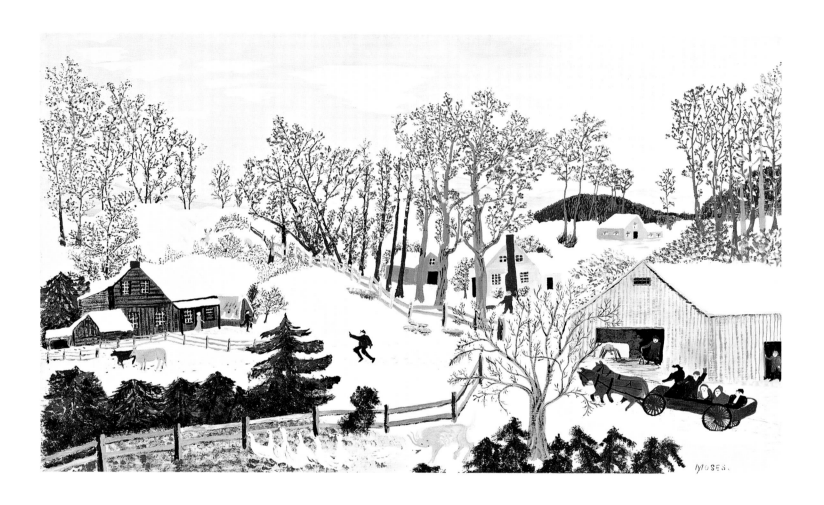

The title *Early Springtime on the Farm* is an example of Moses' dry Yankee
humor. The calendar may say it's spring, but in the North there is still
plenty of snow on the ground. Nonetheless, signs of a thaw are evident
in the foreground of the painting, where a flock of geese waddles along
on fresh turf. "These are the damp snow days," Moses wrote, "when
we love to go to the woods and look for the first bloom of the trailing
arbutus, which sometimes blooms beneath the snow, or gather the pussy
willow. Those are the days of childhood."

53 The Thunderstorm

1948. Oil on pressed wood
20 3/4 x 24 3/4 inches
(52.7 x 62.8 cm)
Signed, lower right
Kallir 729. Private collection
Courtesy Galerie St. Etienne,
New York

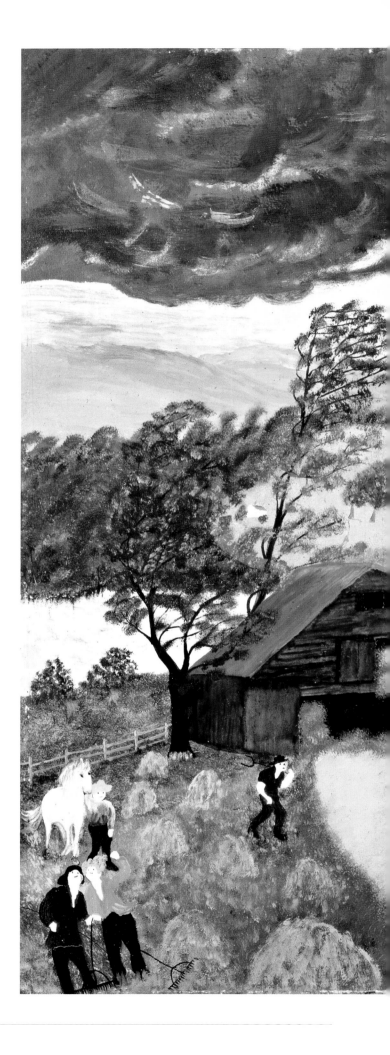

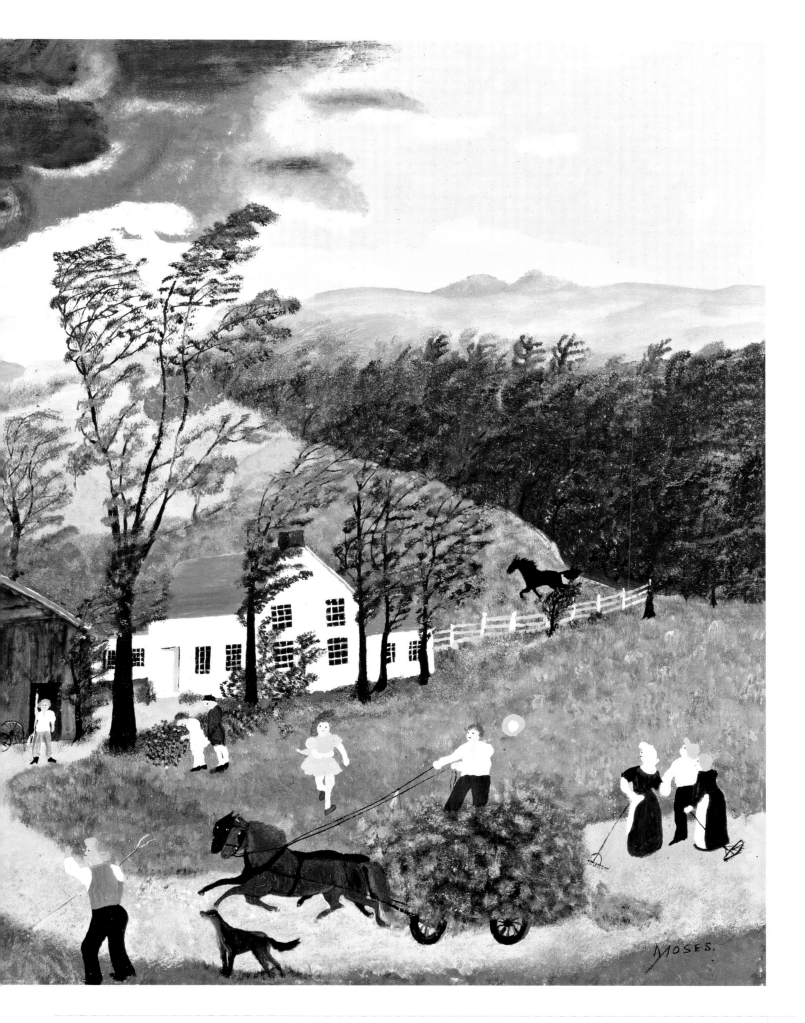

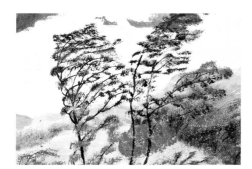

Fig. 23. *The Thunderstorm*, detail of plate 53

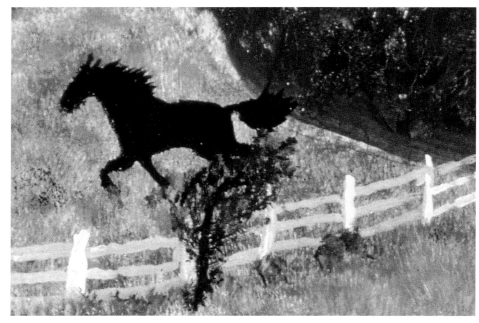

Fig. 24. *The Thunderstorm*, detail of plate 53

Grandma Moses' ability to capture the shifting moods of the local landscape is perhaps most readily demonstrated by her storm scenes, for here the various forces and colors of nature of necessity appear in exaggerated form. *The Thunderstorm* (plate 53) and *Wind Storm* (plate 54) illustrate poignantly how Moses managed to combine intensely evocative renditions of natural phenomena with anecdotal detail. Her deployment of color in these paintings is extraordinarily acute: the parched browns and yellows of a late summer meadow, the varied greens of the trees, and the shifting colors of the sky before the advancing storm are all keenly observed. The abstract forms used to render all the human and animal activity stand in sharp contrast to the impressionistic interplay of colors in the landscape elements of the composition. This juxtaposition of abstraction and realism was one of the principal cornerstones of the "Grandma Moses style."

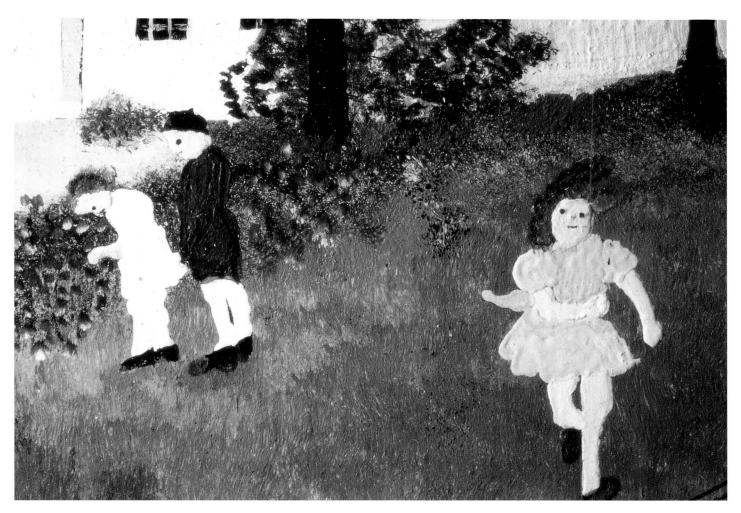

Fig. 25. *The Thunderstorm,* detail of plate 53

The Thunderstorm is also a good example of Moses' "cinematic" approach to storytelling, which combines several levels of action that can be imagined as playing out either simultaneously or in sequence. The full impact of the approaching torrent is most evident in the distant landscape, with its lowering clouds and wildly whip-lashed trees (fig. 23). At middle distance, a black horse bolts in terror (fig. 24), and in the foreground the farmers are rushing madly to get the hay into the barn. The girl in the yellow dress is frozen in mid-run, but strangely, behind her to the left, two other children seem oblivious to the commotion (fig. 25).

54 Wind Storm

1956. Oil on pressed wood
16 x 24 inches
(40.7 x 60.9 cm)
Signed, lower right
Kallir 1250. Private collection

Wind Storm lacks the pseudo-cinematic effects of *The Thunderstorm* (plate 53), since the human players appear remarkably oblivious to the approaching threat. The drama is instead conveyed solely through the natural elements. The darkening, glowing sky is cut through with streaks of lightning. This harsh light seems to sparkle on the parched golden fields, while all else has already fallen into comparative darkness.

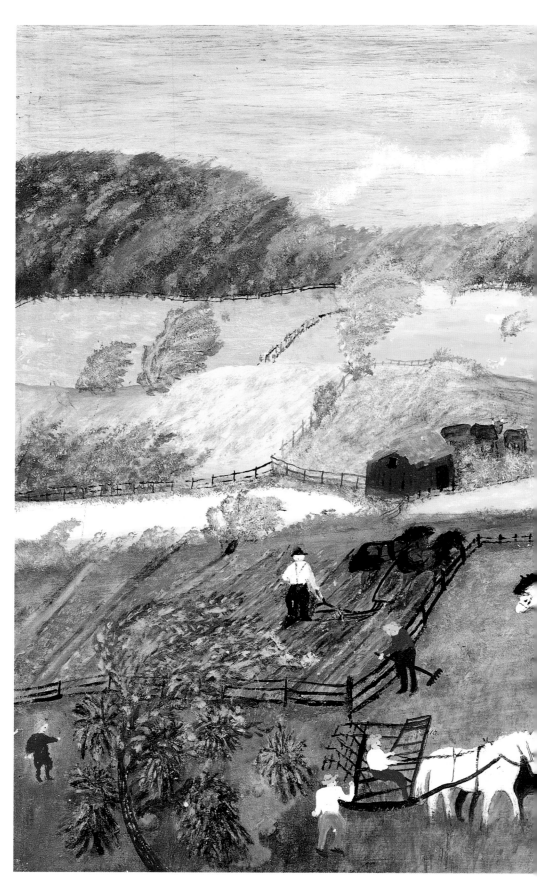

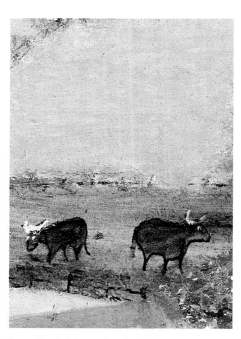

Fig. 26. *Wind Storm*, detail of plate 54

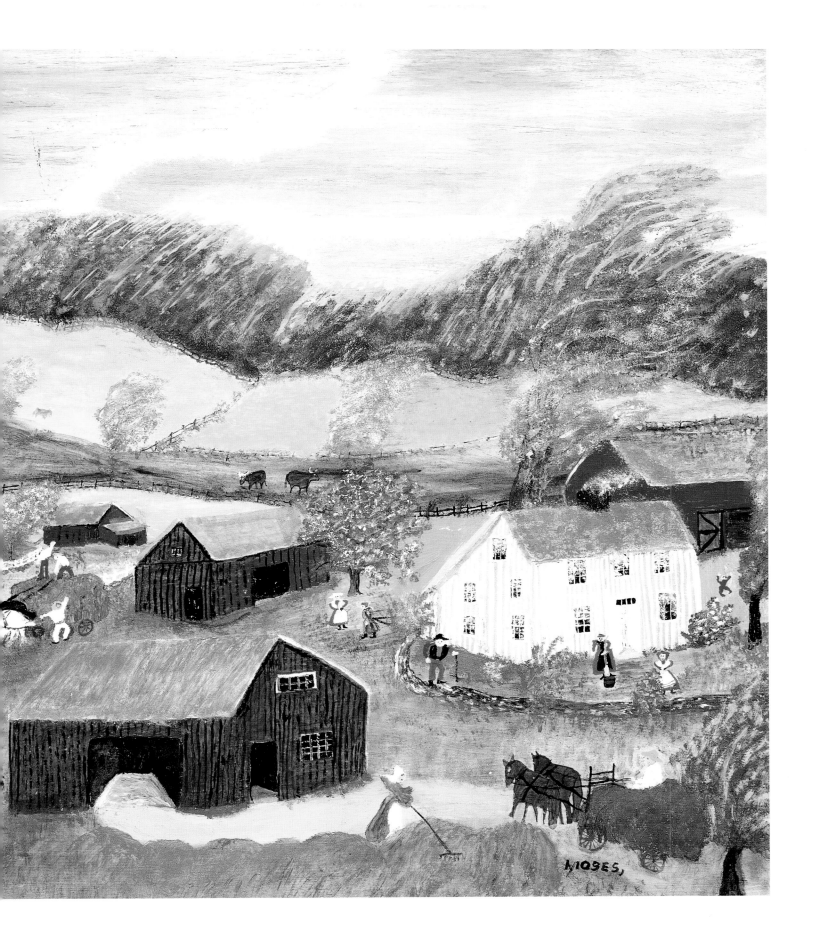

55 For This Is the Fall of the Year

1947. Oil on pressed wood
16 x 21 3/4 inches
(40.7 x 55.3 cm)
Signed, lower left
Kallir 711. Private collection

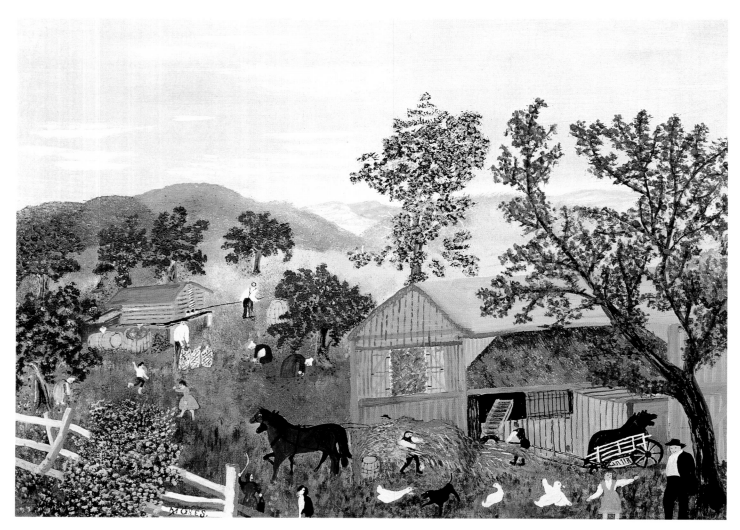

Autumn is the least frequently depicted season in Grandma Moses'
paintings. This may seem surprising, given that upstate New York and
New England are renowned for their fall foliage. Perhaps, however, this
palette did not appeal to the artist. Possibly the season, after the drama
of the late summer's harvest and before the excitement of the winter holidays, was lacking in anecdotal interest. Nevertheless, Moses' autumnal
scenes are no less successful than her other seasonal pictures. *For This Is
the Fall of the Year* is certainly rife with appropriate activity: apples are
being gathered, hay stored for the winter. The colors are richer and
duskier than Moses' customary palette. Greens are leavened by reddish
browns and yellow, as the landscape gradually prepares to go into its
annual hibernation.

56 **Grey Day**
1952. Oil on pressed wood
18 x 24 inches
(45.7 x 60.9 cm)
Signed, lower left
Kallir 1051. Hallmark Fine Art
Collection, Hallmark Cards, Inc.,
Kansas City, Missouri

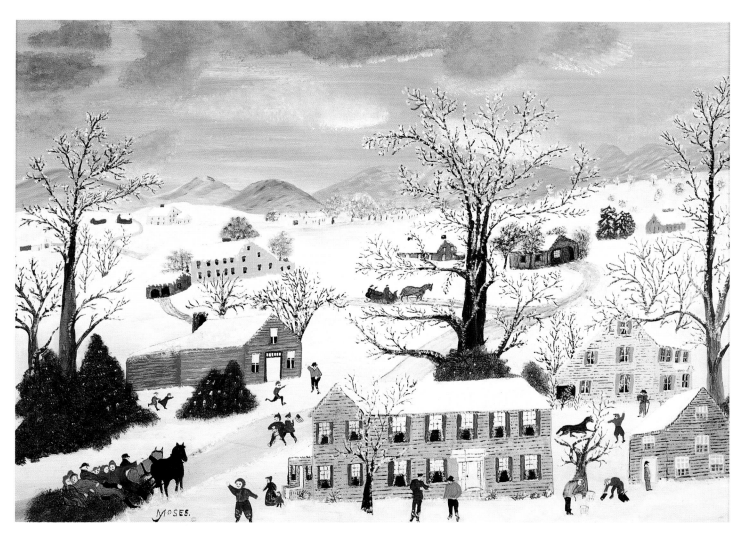

Grandma Moses was best known for her winter paintings, in part because, starting in 1946, they were regularly reproduced on best-selling Thanksgiving and Christmas cards. She was, in fact, a master at capturing the varied aspects of a season that many people find merely cold and dreary.

The sky in *Grey Day* is decidedly leaden, and in *December* (plate 57) one can almost smell the moist air and approaching snow. Yet these scenes also vibrate with productive and pleasurable activity: a cheery hayride, children playing, sheep being herded to safety in a barn. In *A Blizzard* (plate 58), a storm has hit in all its fury, but here too, the mood is largely one of exhilaration. Order is quickly restored in *A Frosty Day* (plate 59), when the entire community seems drawn outdoors to admire the sparkling trees and pristine powder.

57 December

1943. Oil on pressed wood
18 $^1/_2$ x 21 $^3/_4$ inches
(47 x 55.2 cm)
Signed, lower center
Kallir 287. Private collection
Courtesy Galerie St. Etienne,
New York

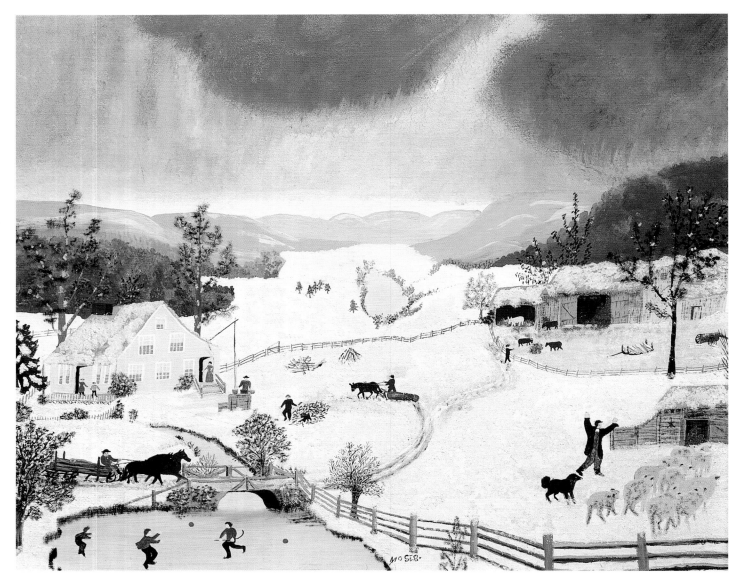

Fig. 27. *December,* detail of plate 57

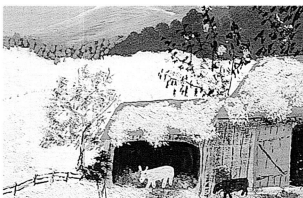

58 **A Blizzard**
1958. Oil on pressed wood
16 x 24 ¹/8 inches
(40.7 x 61 cm)
Signed, lower right
Kallir 1343. Private collection

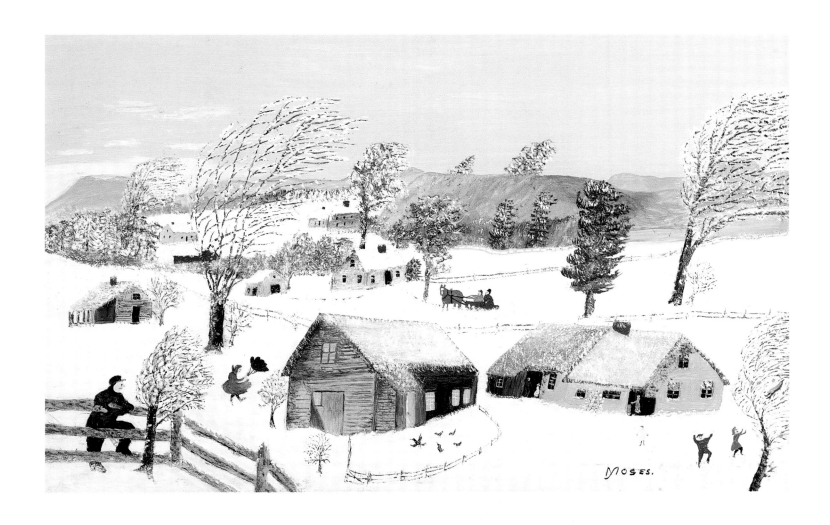

If Moses' winter scenes are, in part, idealized, they are also intensely realistic, employing a complex palette of whites, grays, and blues to render the season's shifting moods. Once again, it is this intense realism, combined with the abstraction of the figural elements (figs. 27–29), that accounts for the power of these paintings. Grandma Moses' snow paintings are a universalized homage to the season and to the restorative powers of nature (see plate 59).

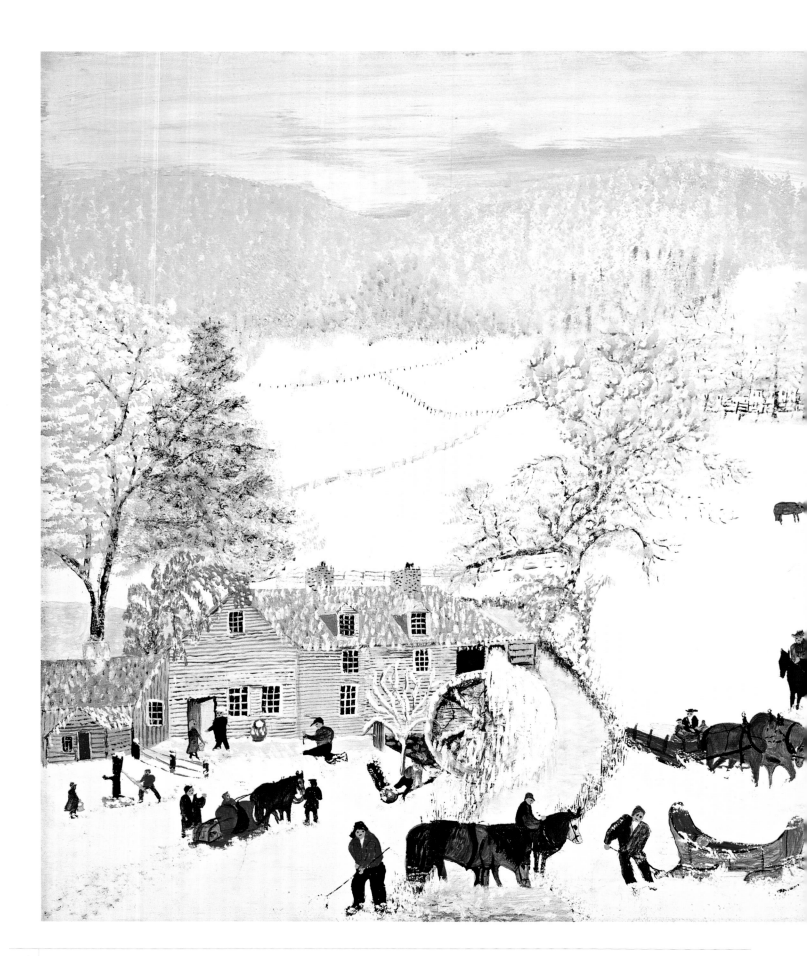

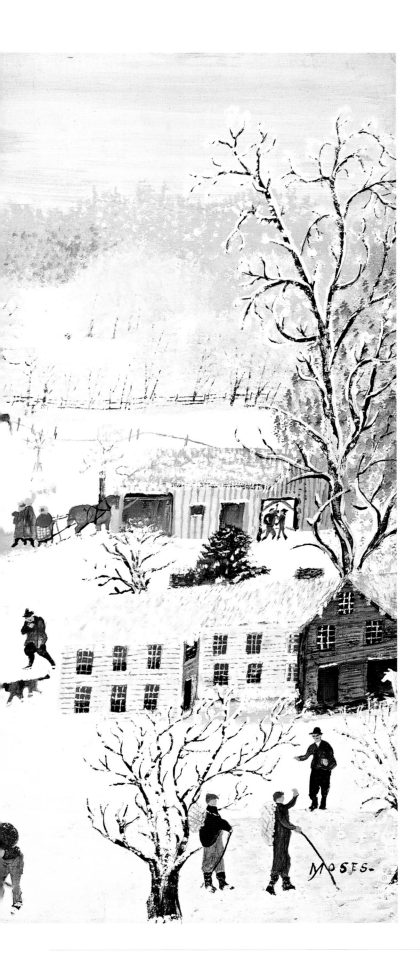

59 A Frosty Day

1951. Oil on pressed wood
18 x 24 inches
(45.7 x 60.9 cm)
Signed, lower right
Kallir 985. Private collection
Courtesy Galerie St. Etienne,
New York

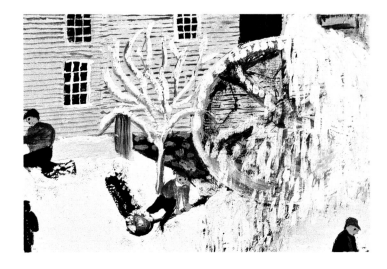

Fig. 28. *A Frosty Day*, detail of plate 59

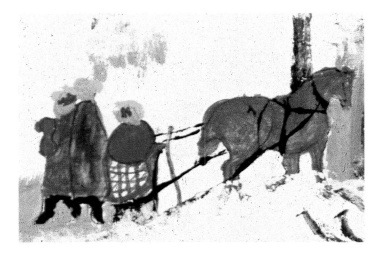

Fig. 29. *A Frosty Day*, detail of plate 59

Play and Celebration

*Despite—or perhaps because of—*her emphasis on work and duty, Moses was not a particularly strict parent. "I didn't bring up the children," she recalled, "they kind of come up. They were always with me in the house helping, till they started into school." The family was viewed as a communal enterprise to which everyone contributed, and play was fair recompense for a job well done. Discipline was not truly necessary. "The children were always full of pranks, always in mischief with their young friends," Moses wrote. "It was a rollicksome, happy house, and their father would join in with them, he really was one of them." In tandem with the flow of the seasons and the rhythms of work, the family's calendar was enlivened by periodic celebrations and by a constant sense of fun.

Today, we experience the summer months as vacation time and winter as a working period, but on the Moses farm, these priorities were inverted. Planting, tending, and then harvesting the crops consumed all of the warmer months, while winter permitted relative repose. What little schooling young Anna Mary received also took place in summer. It is thus no coincidence that winter provides the setting for so many of Grandma Moses' celebratory scenes. In addition to the traditional cold-weather holidays, Thanksgiving and Christmas, every heavy snow seems to provide occasion for a "joy ride" in the horse-drawn sleigh (see plates 61 and 62). Summer or winter, "fun" in Moses' paintings always revolves around communal activities and the simple natural pleasures of the pre-modern era.

60 **It Snows, Oh It Snows**
1951. Oil on pressed wood
24 x 30 inches
(60.9 x 76.2 cm)
Signed, lower left
Kallir 971. Private collection
Courtesy Galerie St. Etienne,
New York

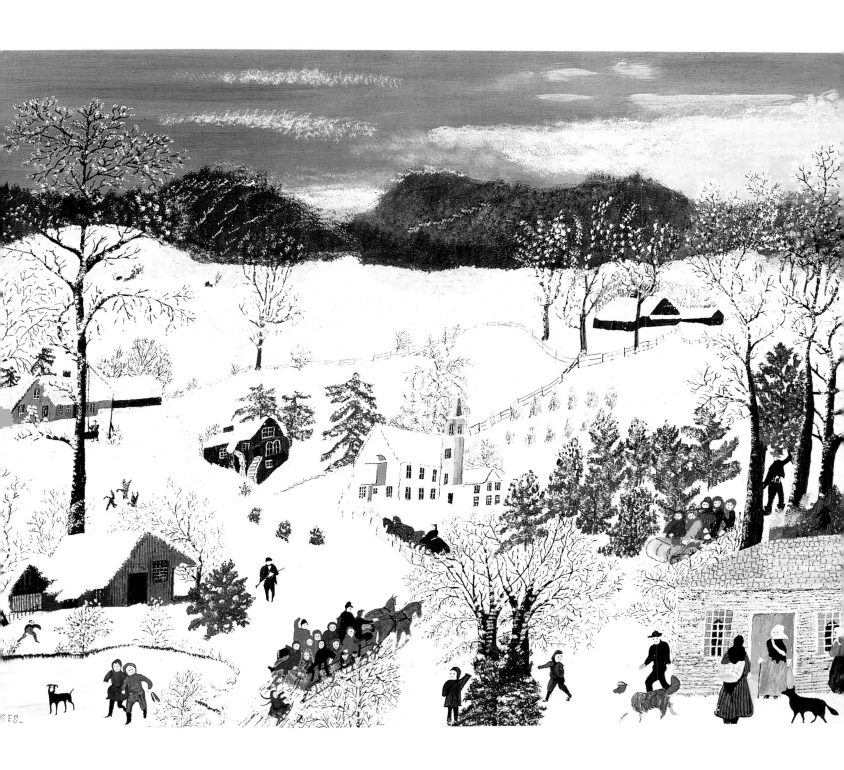

61 Sleigh Ride

1957. Oil on pressed wood
16 x 24 inches
(40.7 x 60.9 cm)
Signed, lower right
Kallir 1291. From the Collection
of Richard D. Della Penna, M.D., and
Mearl A. Naponic, M.D.,
San Diego, California

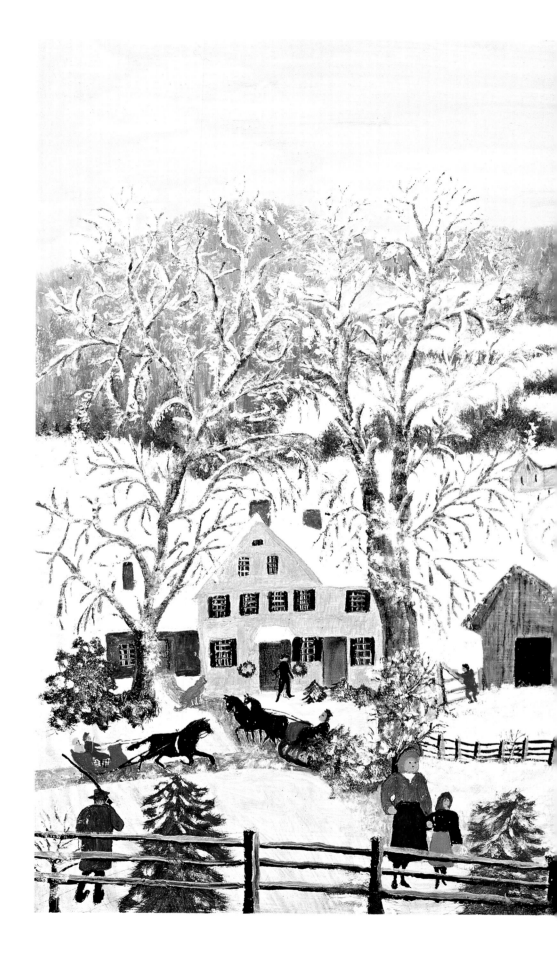

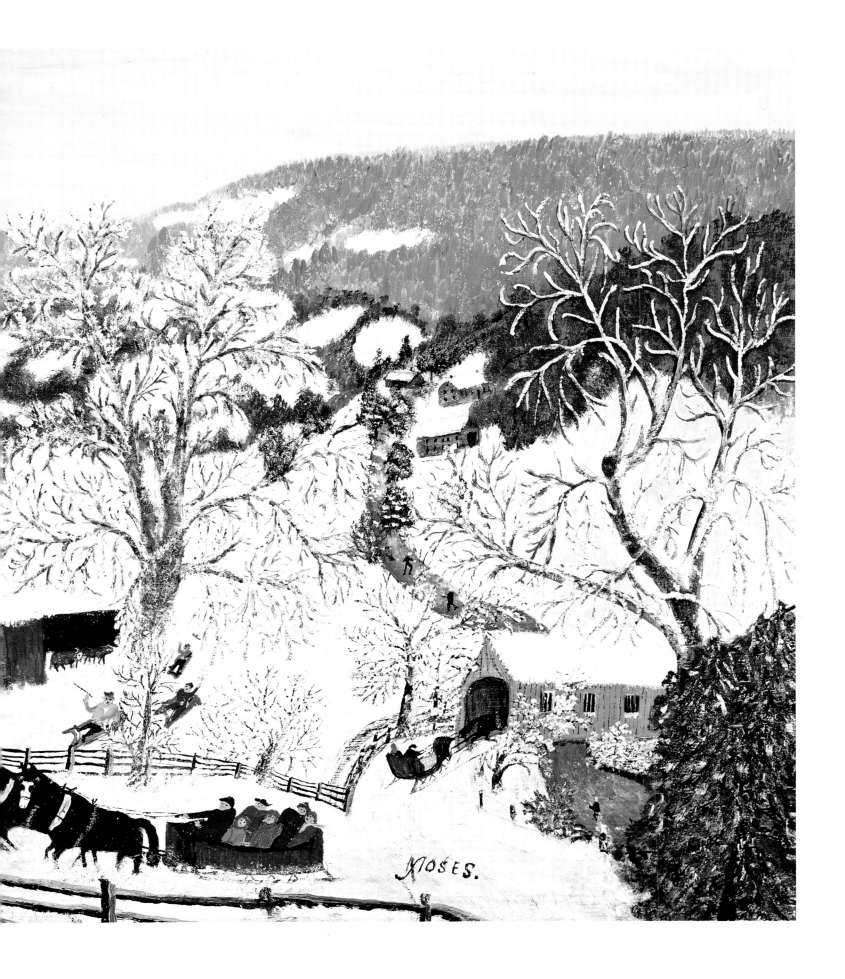

62 Joy Ride

1953. Oil on pressed wood
18 x 24 inches
(45.7 x 60.9 cm)
Signed, lower right
Kallir 1079. Private collection
Courtesy Galerie St. Etienne,
New York

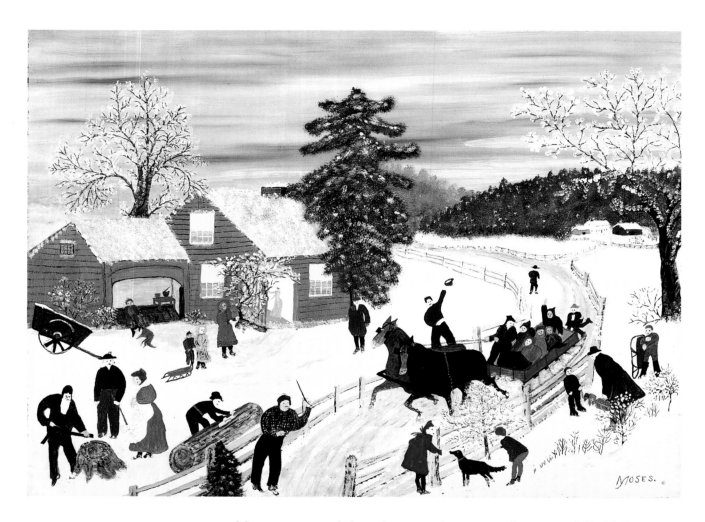

Moses recounted that whenever there was a deep snowfall, "father
would hitch up the horses to the old big red sleigh and break out all of
the roads, as we lived back in the fields, probably half a mile from the
main road, and father had to keep the road open."

*He would drive up to the kitchen door, and we would all climb in the sleigh on a lot of
straw and blankets, and away we would go, out to the main road, then on through the
woods; and oh! that was grand to drive under the hemlocks and have the snow fall on us!
Then back home and around the barn, back to the house. Oh, those happy days!
Then the sun came out and melted the snow on top, and then it froze so hard, it would
almost hold up a horse. It was so cold, my brothers could not go to school, and we played
on the crust on the snow. We would go up a field above the orchard, get on our sleighs,
and away we would go! Lester had a sleigh with cast iron runners, Horace had an old
wash bench, upside down, but very safe, Arthur a dust pan, and I an old scoop shovel.
Oh, what fun! We would play out for hours, and the thermometer at 25 below zero.*

My Life's History, p. 28

63 **We Are Resting**

1951. Oil on pressed wood
24 x 30 inches
(60.9 x 76.2 cm)
Signed, lower left
Kallir 970. Private collection
Courtesy Galerie St. Etienne,
New York

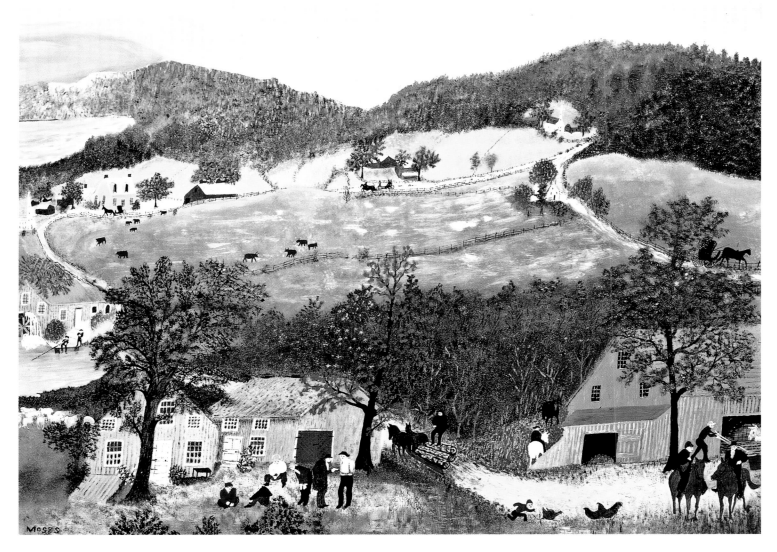

In Moses' world, spring and summer provided comparatively few
opportunities for relaxation. Therefore the majority of her "green"
paintings are work-oriented. The title of *We Are Resting* apparently refers
to the group loafing in the center foreground. However, the rest of the
painting—buzzing with productive activity—belies its name.

64 Balloon

1957. Oil on pressed wood
15 3/4 x 24 inches
(40 x 60.9 cm)
Signed, lower right and lower left
Kallir 1289. Private collection

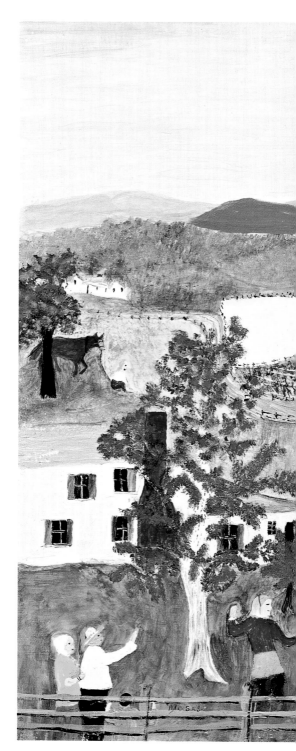

Balloon is one of the artist's few summer pictures in which all work has momentarily ceased—for the farmers are witnessing a truly exceptional event. Moses painted this work at the request of her dealer and biographer, Otto Kallir, who was intensely interested in the history of early aviation. When the artist told him that she had once seen a hot-air balloon, he urged her to record the memory, which she did both in paint and in her autobiography.

> *It was the year of 1907, I remember seeing a balloon going over from Argyle to Cambridge, New York, there was a man, woman and child in it. They landed in Cambridge. In 1911 there was a lot of talk about a new invention, airplanes. Sometime later I saw my first.*
>
> My Life's History, p. 110

It was in part their mutual awareness of living within history that united Moses and Kallir, an Austrian refugee from Hitler who would seem to have had little in common with the Yankee artist. *Balloon* expresses the sense of promise and exhilaration aroused by the prospect of human flight. While Moses recognized that "progress" might dampen and eventually kill the simple life she loved, she also saw innovations like air travel as triumphs of human ingenuity.

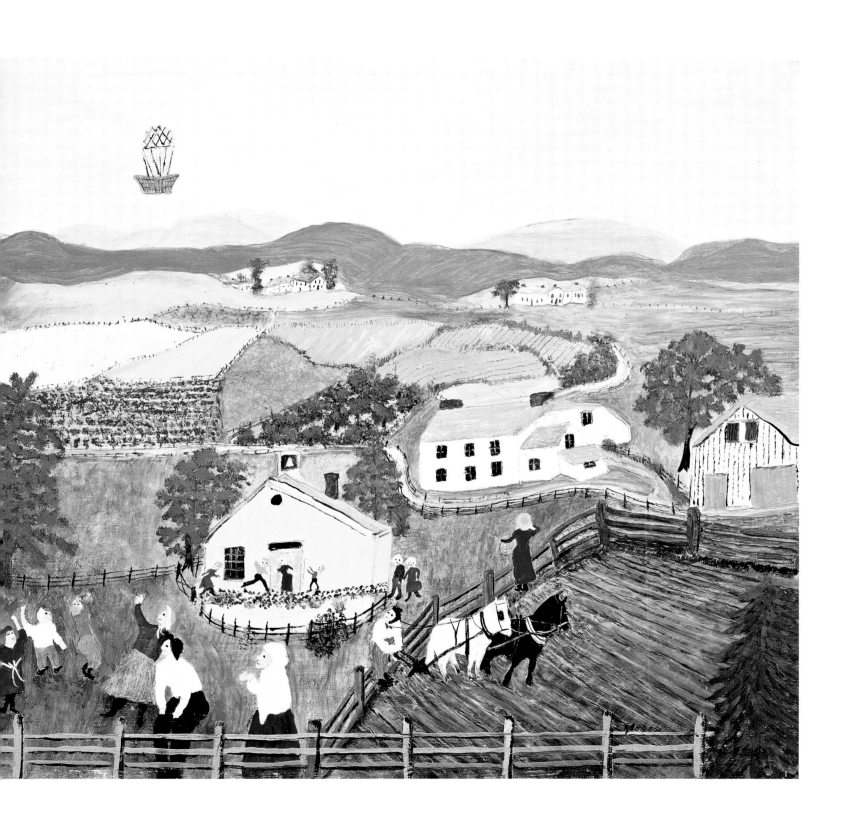

65 The Family Picnic

1951. Oil on pressed wood
16 3/4 x 22 inches
(42.5 x 55.8 cm)
Signed, lower left
Kallir 966. Private collection

Picnics were among the ritual events that offered a respite from the summer work routine. The picnic, Moses recalled, "was one of the days that children looked forward to through the year. Then it was when they could have all the cake and lemonade they wanted, watermelon and peanuts were a wonderful treat." *The Family Picnic* recapitulates some of the artist's favorite themes: play as the province principally of children, leisure as a reward sanctioned by labor, food as one of life's great indulgences, and community as the entity binding all together.

Of course, by the 1950s, most people would have found it hard to accept such relatively simple enjoyments as adequate recompense for a year's hard physical labor and drudgery. Nostalgia for a lost America was one of the things that fueled Grandma Moses' popularity. With her deep memories of by-gone customs, the artist seemed like an emissary from the past. "In my childhood days life was different," she wrote. "In many ways, we were slower, still we had a good and happy life, I think, people enjoyed life more in their way, at least they seemed to be happier, they don't take the time to be happy nowadays." However, the artist was not preaching a return to the past, and her paintings, with their abstracted figures, were not historical re-creations, but distillations of what Moses perceived to be eternal values. Her compositional methods, too, served to distance her subjects, thereby enhancing their iconic, universalized qualities.

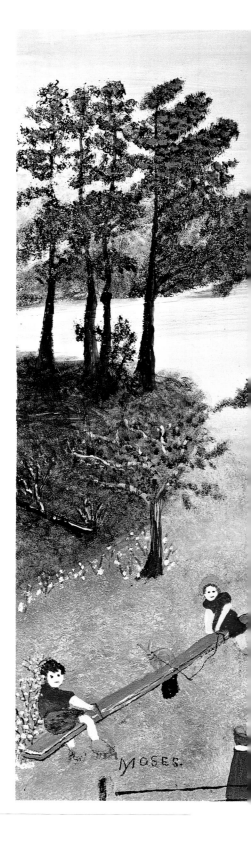

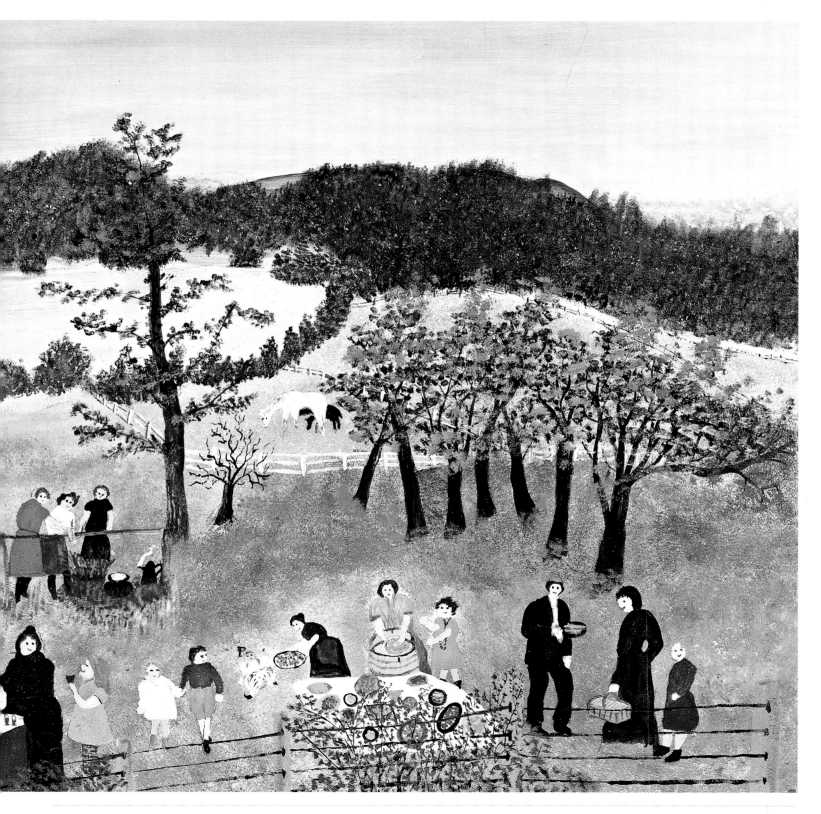

66 The Quilting Bee

1950. Oil on pressed wood
20 x 24 inches
(50.8 x 60.9 cm)
Signed, lower right
Kallir 883. Private collection
Courtesy Galerie St. Etienne,
New York

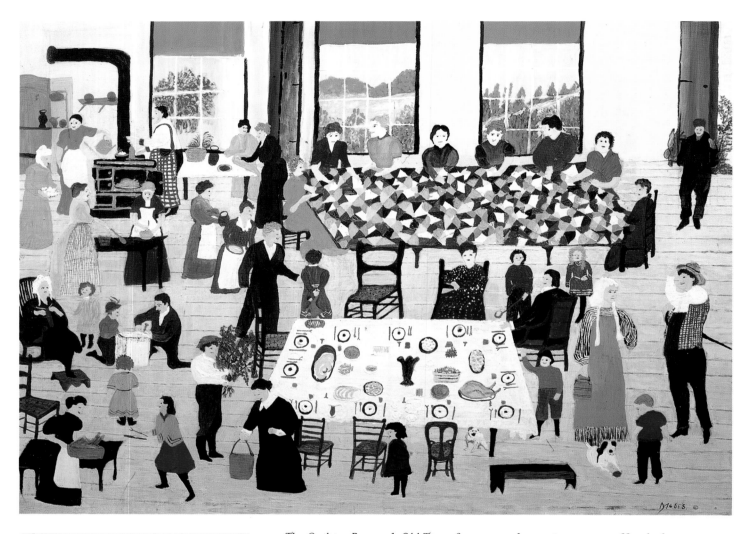

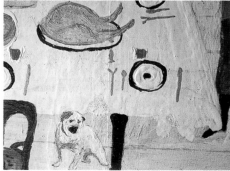

Fig. 30. *The Quilting Bee*, detail of plate 66

The Quilting Bee and *Old Times* focus on the enjoyments afforded women on the farm. In both cases, pleasure is tied to serving the family and the community. Quilting bees provided an opportunity to socialize, but they also had a practical function. Feasts, such as that portrayed in *Old Times*, might have fostered happy gatherings, but they entailed a lot of hard work for the (typically female) cook. However, since Moses never viewed work as a negative, she was able to see such occasions as purely joyful. It is evident that the tasks of quilting and cooking were pleasurable not only because of the comradery they fostered, but also in their own right.

Nevertheless, given that the feminine domain was largely indoors, while men worked the land, it is interesting to note that interiors are relatively rare in Moses' oeuvre. She was primarily a landscape painter, and it was obviously nature, more than domesticity, that thrilled her. She pursued interiors partly because she recognized that certain themes

67 **Old Times**

1957. Oil on pressed wood
16 x 24 inches
(40.7 x 60.9 cm)
Signed, lower left
Kallir 1296. Private collection

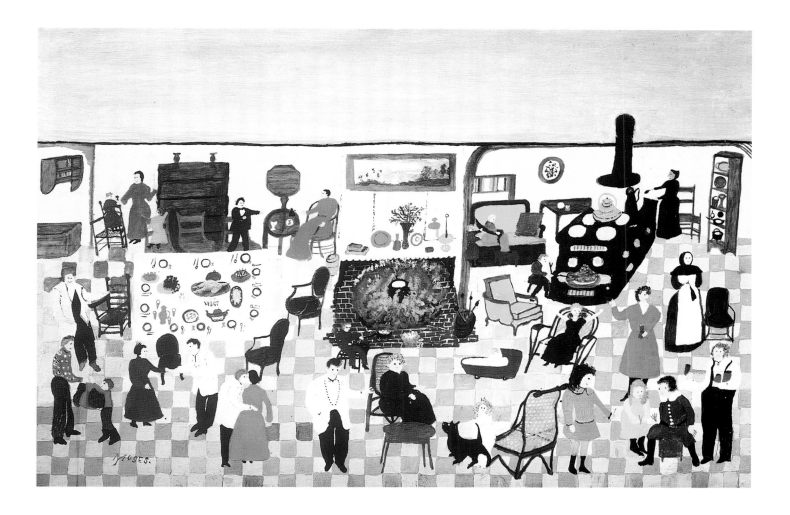

demanded an indoor setting, and partly at the request of her patrons.
But such subjects did not come easily to her. "I tried that interior but
did not like it, so I erased it," she wrote on one occasion. "That doesn't
seem to be in my line. I like to paint something that leads me on and on
into the unknown, something that I want to see away on beyond. Well,
maybe I'll try again." In spite of her difficulties with these subjects,
Moses did paint a number of striking interiors. Without the landscape
to anchor the scene and provide an element of realism, her interiors rely
almost wholly on the artist's command of abstract form (fig. 30). These
qualities are used to maximum advantage in *The Quilting Bee* and *Old Times*,
wherein the patterns of (respectively) the quilt and the flooring play off
neatly against the elaborate table settings and bright clothing of the
numerous bustling characters.

68 Halloween

1955. Oil on pressed wood
18 x 24 inches
(45.7 x 60.9 cm)
Signed, lower right
Kallir 1188. Private collection
Courtesy Galerie St. Etienne,
New York

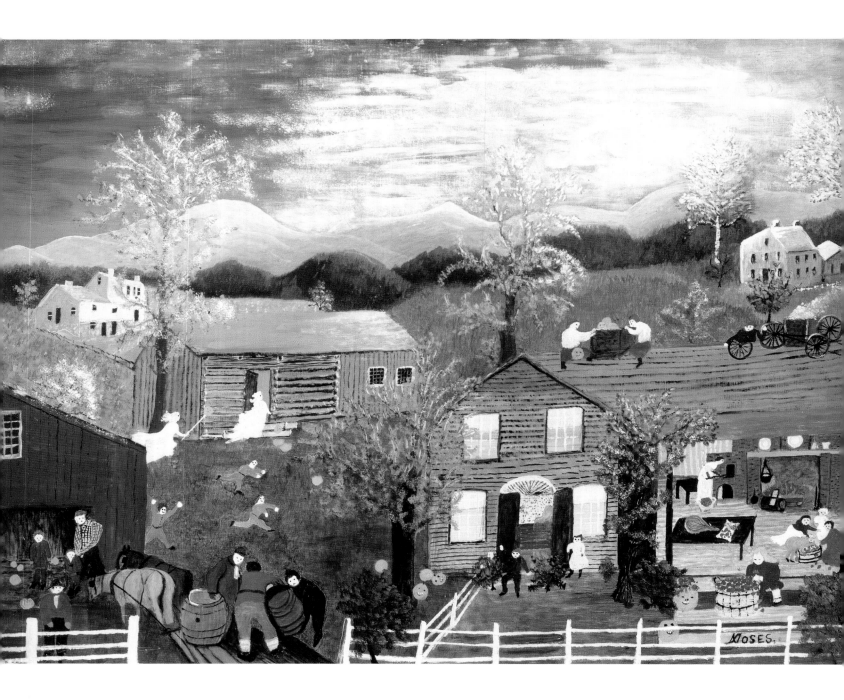

As a parent, Moses had no aversion to such shenanigans as water fights, and she considered Halloween to be a holiday celebrating the boisterous aspects of family life: the one day a year which indulged pranks that would normally be frowned upon. At the same time, she was capable of being spooked, as when once, on a Virginia farm, she thought she saw a ghost. *Halloween* combines these two aspects of the holiday: the good-spirited and the bad-spirited, as it were.

Halloween records a number of typical Halloween escapades: little girls dressed as ghosts, boys on the roof, stuffing pumpkins down the chimney and rattling a cart of coals to make scary noises. Downstairs, the adults are preparing more sedate entertainment. Men are unloading barrels of cider, and a woman stokes the fire while children bob for apples. However, the slightly discordant palette of white, gray, green, and orange creates a sense of subliminal unease, which contrasts sharply with the merry goings-on. The distant landscape is downright frightening. Clouds scud across the moon, trees glow silver in the darkness, and the houses in the background look decidedly haunted (fig. 31).

Never entirely comfortable painting interiors (see plates 66 and 67), Moses here used a cutaway, dollhouse-like view of the house to depict interior and exterior at once. She was always happier if she could imagine a scene in a natural setting.

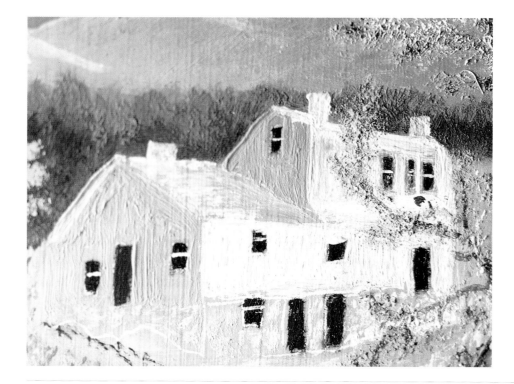

Fig. 31. *Halloween,* detail of plate 68

69 Catching the Turkey

1940. Oil on pressed wood
12 x 16 inches
(30.5 x 40.7 cm)
Kallir 64. Private collection
Courtesy Galerie St. Etienne,
New York

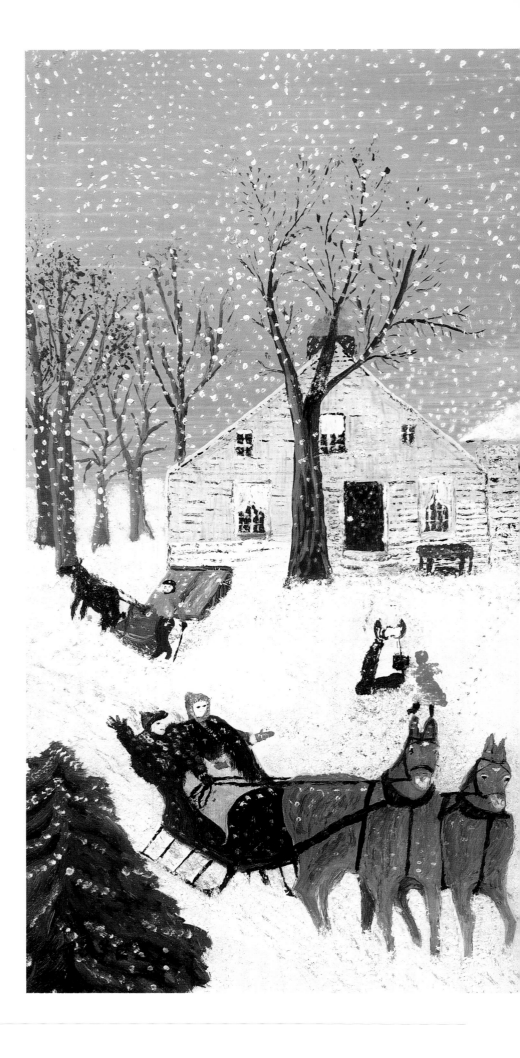

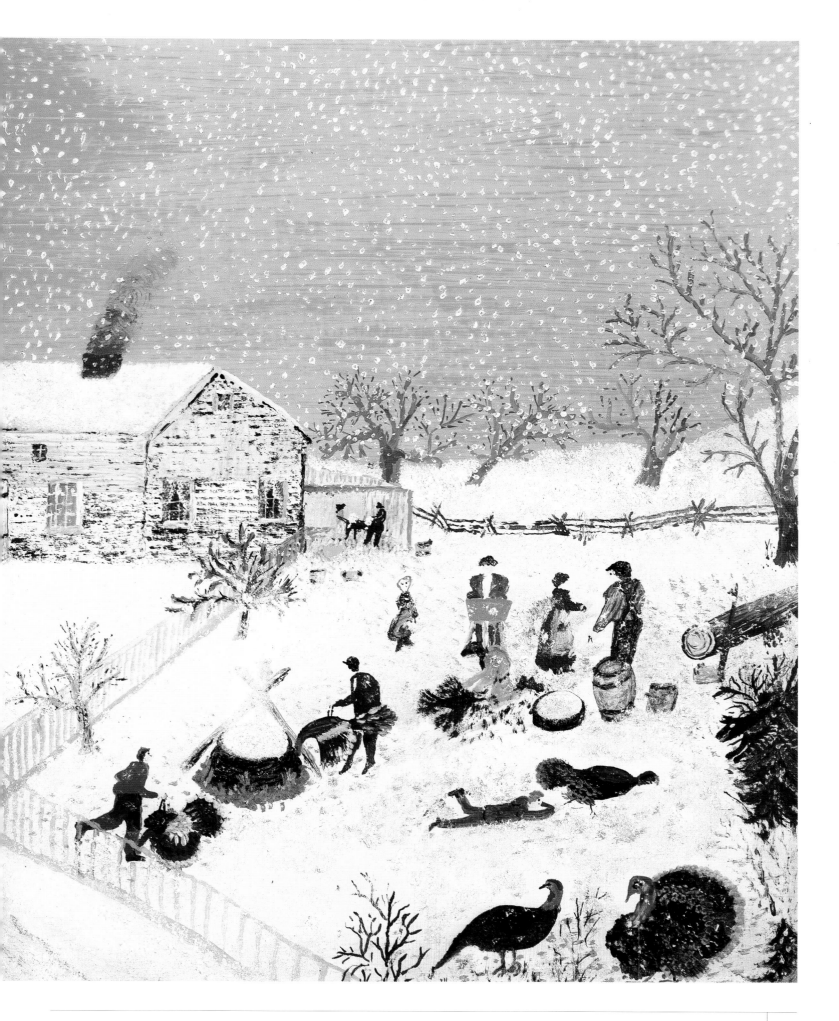

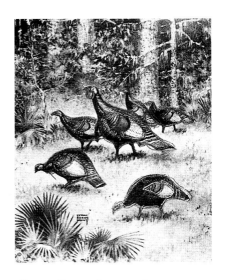

Fig. 32. Four-color magazine illustration with Moses' pencil notations

Fig. 33. Two-color magazine illustration with Moses' pencil notations

Particularly in the early years of her career, Moses frequently chose subjects that were staples of nineteenth- and early-twentieth-century illustration (see plate 15). "Catching the turkey"—part of the annual Thanksgiving ritual—was one such theme that Moses painted numerous times (see also plate 69), drawing on an array of printed sources (figs. 32 and 33). By tying the holiday feast to its origins in the barn-yard, Moses' turkey paintings (like their historical prototypes) certify Thanksgiving as a rural American tradition.

However, as Judith Stein notes elsewhere herein, Thanksgiving only became a regular holiday when Moses was a child, and it is interesting that the artist actually questioned the pre-ordained composition of the meal. "Why do we think we must have turkey for Thanksgiving?" she asked. "Just because our forefathers did. They had it because turkeys were plentiful, and they did not have other kinds of meat. Now we have abundance of other kinds of luxuries. Poor Turkey, he has but one life to give to his country."

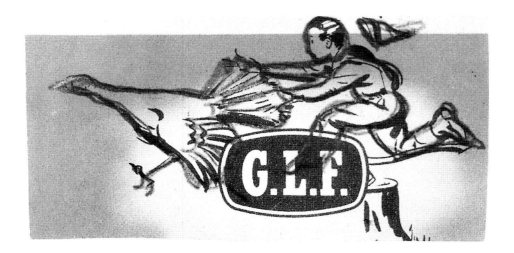

70 Turkeys

1958. Oil on pressed wood
16 x 24 inches
(40.7 x 60.9 cm)
Signed, lower right
Kallir 1325. Private collection
Courtesy Galerie St. Etienne,
New York

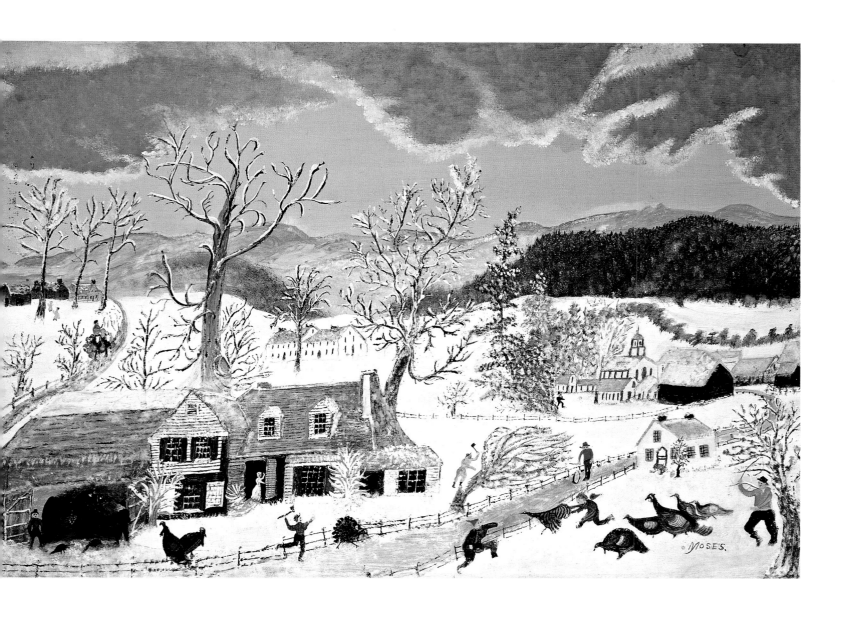

71 Over the River to Grandmother's House

1945. Oil on pressed wood
12 x 20 inches
(30.5 x 50.8 cm)
Signed, lower left
Kallir 529b. Private collection

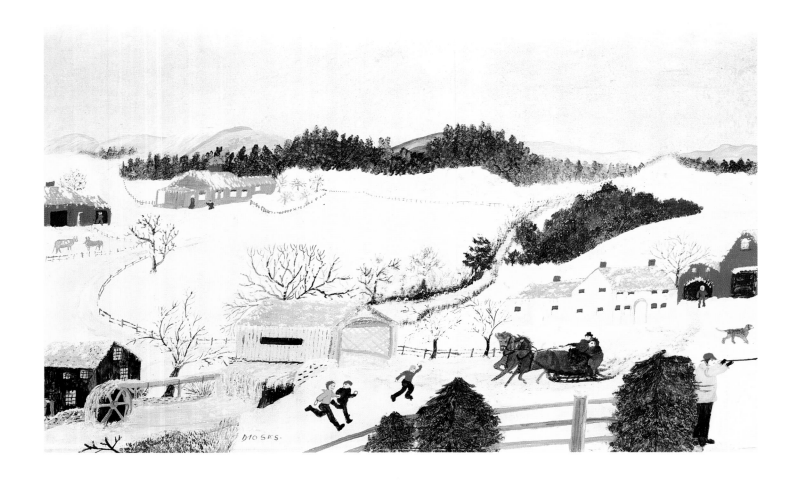

As with the *Old Oaken Bucket* (see plates 37 and 38), Moses took the title of this painting from a traditional American song that was dense with personal associations. The journey "over the river and through the woods" to Thanksgiving dinner at Grandmother's house was cherished principally because the holiday reunited family members who did not regularly see one another. "When Thanksgiving came, we were all expected home to dinner," she noted. "There were so many young people like ourselves, and we would have a grand time in playing sports of all kinds, as we were of different ages, some old, some young." Even though most of Anna Mary's family were settled in Washington County and the immediate vicinity, travel in the late nineteenth century was difficult, and get-togethers were thus reserved for special occasions. This sense of specialness adds poignancy to Grandma Moses' holiday paintings.

72 Out for Christmas Trees
1946. Oil on pressed wood
26 x 36 inches
(66.1 x 91.5 cm)
Signed, lower right
Kallir 606. Private collection
Courtesy Galerie St. Etienne,
New York

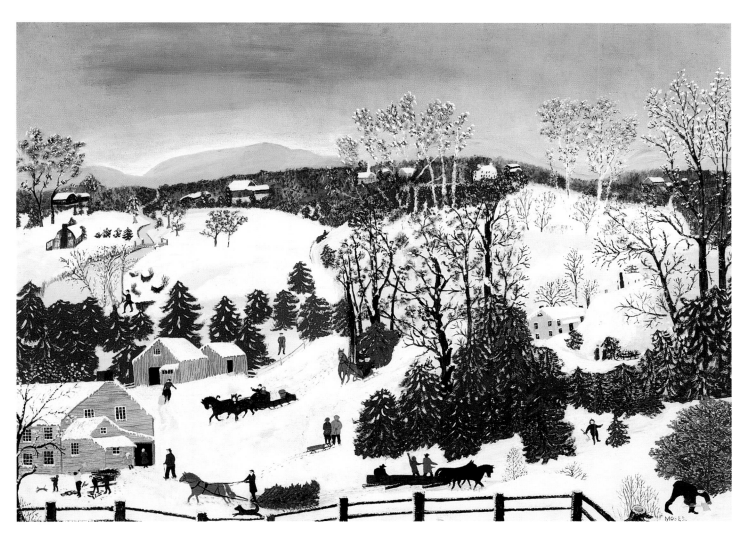

Grandma Moses was closely associated with Christmas, in part because
of the ubiquitous Moses Christmas cards and in part because that holiday—with its combination of wintry cheer, evergreen trees, and joyful
celebration—mirrors many of Moses' own favorite preoccupations (see
also plate 73). Christmas is a beloved children's holiday, but Moses saw
no reason why adults should not vicariously share in the pleasures of
the season. In addition to re-investing adult life with childhood gaiety,
Christmas releases the stored energy of a year's anticipatory glee. As a
long-awaited annual indulgence, Christmas underscores Moses' belief
that delayed gratification is ultimately more satisfying than immediate
gratification, an earned reward better than a windfall.

73 Christmas

1958. Oil on pressed wood
16 1/8 x 20 1/8 inches
(40.9 x 51.1 cm)
Signed, lower right
Kallir 1366. Anne C. Brower,
Brock H. Brower, and
Charles N. Brower

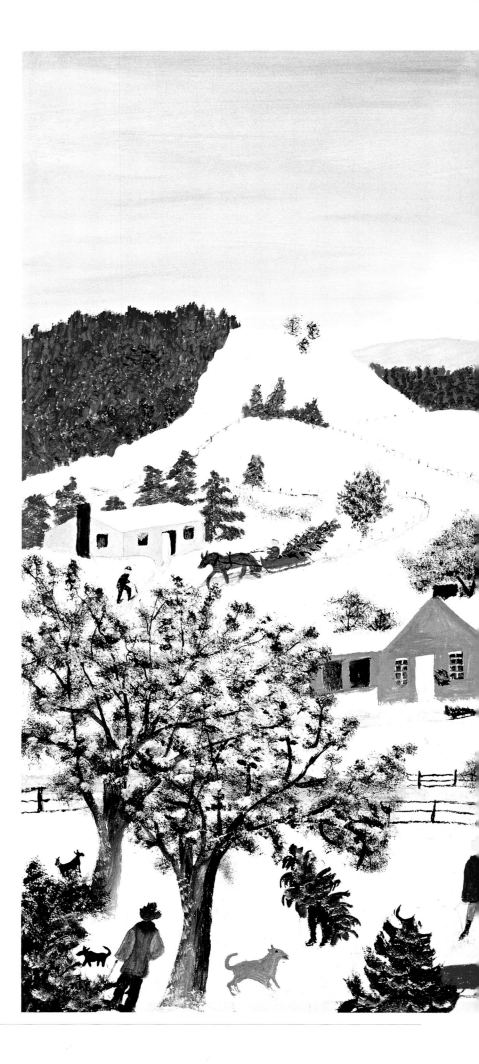

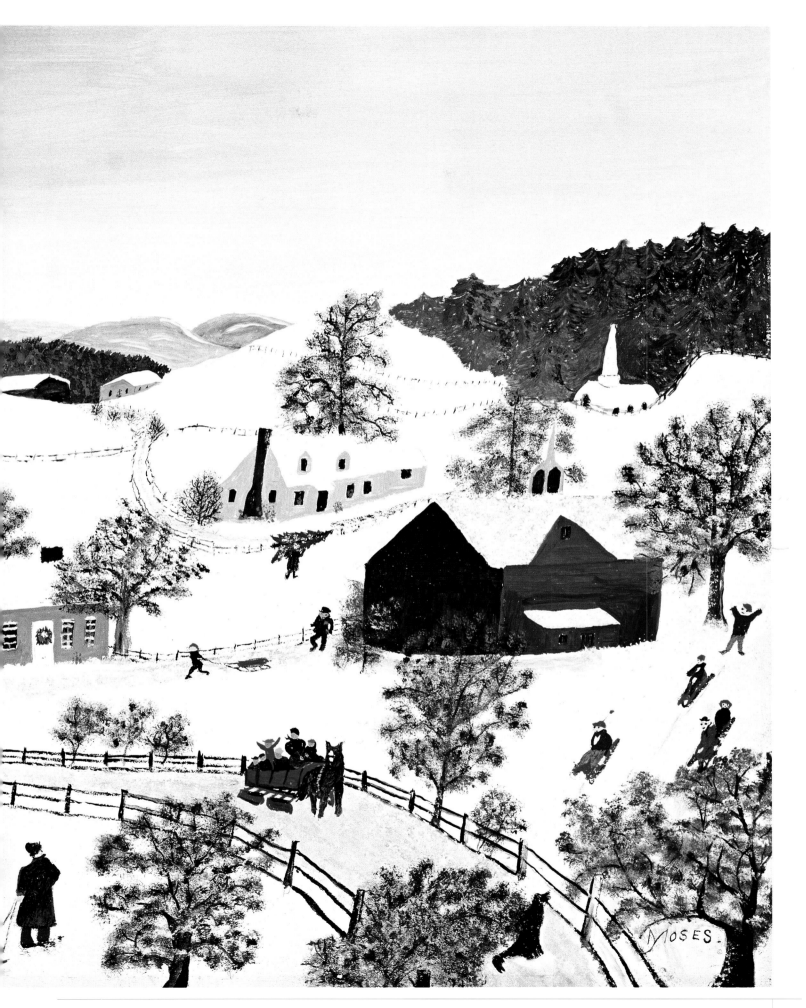

Down the Chimney He Goes

1960. Oil on pressed wood
16 x 23 3/4 inches
(40.7 x 60.3 cm)
Signed, lower right
Kallir 1460. Grandma Moses
Properties Co., New York

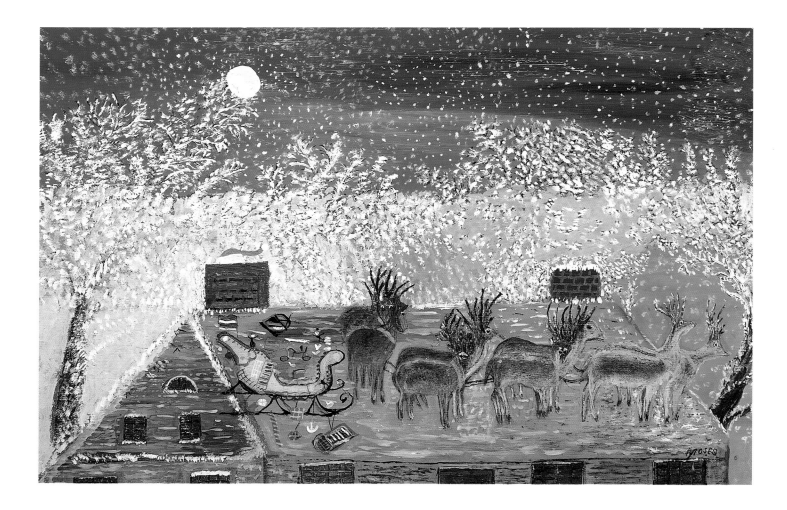

In 1960, Bennett Cerf, the head of Random House, asked Grandma Moses to illustrate Clement C. Moore's classic children's poem, "The Night Before Christmas." At first she resisted, for her art had always been drawn from lived experience, never fantasy or imaginary events. However, Moses liked the poem and knew it by heart. Although nearing her 100th birthday and in failing health, she agreed to take on the project.

Moses had, in effect, come full circle: instead of replicating stereotypical American scenarios, such as Currier & Ives's *Maple Sugaring* (fig. 6), she was now herself reformulating a classic subject. Moses' version of "The Night Before Christmas" did indeed become part of the iconography of the generation born in the last decade of the artist's life. The book, issued in 1962 shortly after Moses' death, remained in print for decades and was an annual staple on the *Captain Kangaroo* television show. A redesigned edition was published in 1991.

75 Waiting for Santa Claus

1960. Oil on pressed wood
12 x 16 inches
(30.5 x 40.7 cm)
Signed, lower left
Kallir 1463. Grandma Moses
Properties Co., New York

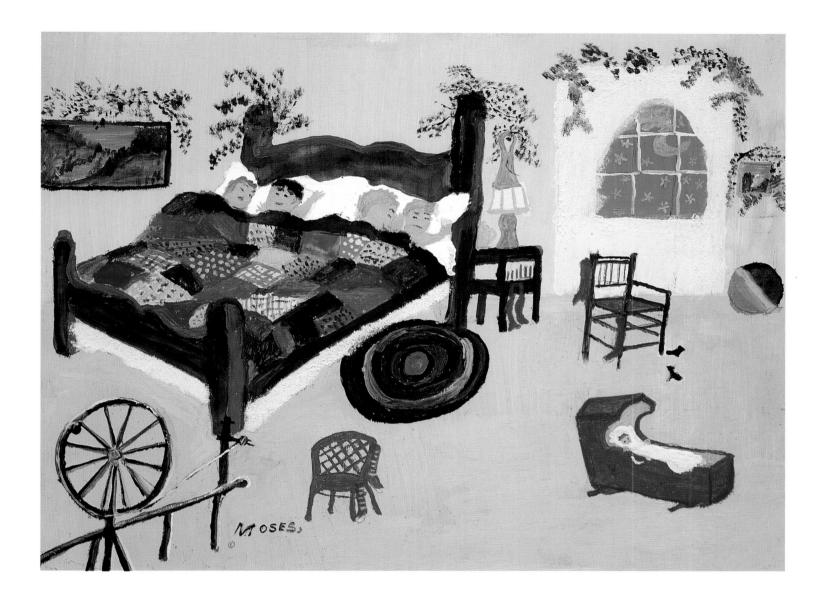

Late Work and "Old-Age Style"

Success can be devastating for self-taught artists, offering pressures and exposure to an alien lifestyle that they are ill prepared to accommodate. Grandma Moses, however, never let fame change her life, and more to the point, she never allowed it to affect her art. To be sure, she received many requests to repeat popular subjects, but no matter how many versions she did, she always managed to come up with a fresh approach (see plates 11–15, 18, 37, 38, 44, 45, and 47–50). Nor did she succumb to the temptation to turn out marketable clones of the style that had made her famous. Instead, her work developed and changed considerably over the course of her twenty-year career. It might even be said that success became a spur to creative growth, permitting Moses to take seriously a hobby she might otherwise have seen as frivolous.

It may seem ironic to speak of an "old-age style" in an artist whose career did not effectively start until she was 80, but, in fact, the last works of Grandma Moses display a conceptual kinship with the later work of other long-lived painters, such as Rembrandt. There is a comparable loosening of brushwork and a similar shorthand approach to form in Moses' paintings from the late 1950s and early 1960s. The human and animal figures are painted with far less precision than one finds in works from the 1940s. The foliage is daubed erratically onto the trees, and a narrower horizontal format forces more compression of detail. As a result, the artist's message is telegraphed with far greater immediacy than formerly. The overall impression is far more spontaneous, more expressionistic.

✤

Although Moses created iconic works throughout her career, the famous "Grandma Moses" style is probably most closely associated with the paintings that she did in the early- to mid-1940s. She hit her stride with pictures such as *Black Horses* (plate 17) and *Sugaring Off* (plate 15), both of which are notable for squarish, quiltlike formats, punctuated by crisp anecdotal detail.

By the early 1950s, however, Moses had begun to abandon squarish proportions, and by mid-decade, the pressed-wood boards she painted on were generally cut to significantly tighter horizontals. This new shape was somewhat more limiting than the squarish one had been. If, as in *The Lake*, the artist chose to concentrate the action in the foreground, there was less room for background detail. In *Callers* (plate 77), conversely, Moses achieved a full landscape panorama, but at the expense of foreground detail.

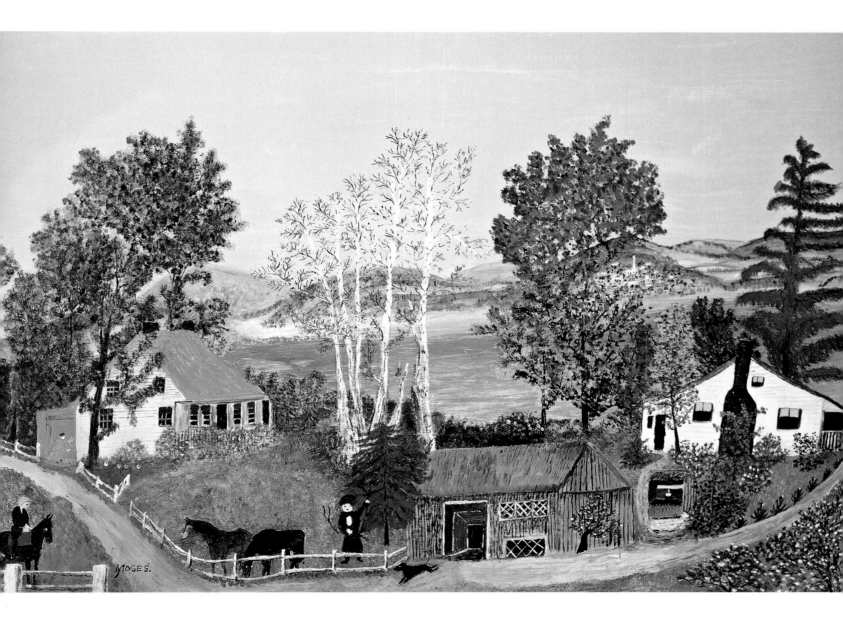

76 The Lake

1957. Oil on pressed wood
15 7/8 x 23 7/8 inches
(39.7 x 59.5 cm)
Signed, lower left
Kallir 1279. Private collection
Courtesy Galerie St. Etienne,
New York

77 Callers

1959. Oil on pressed wood
16 x 24 inches
(40.7 x 60.9 cm)
Signed, lower right
Kallir 1373
The Montclair Art Museum
Gift of The William Lightfoot
Schultz Foundation (1970.17)

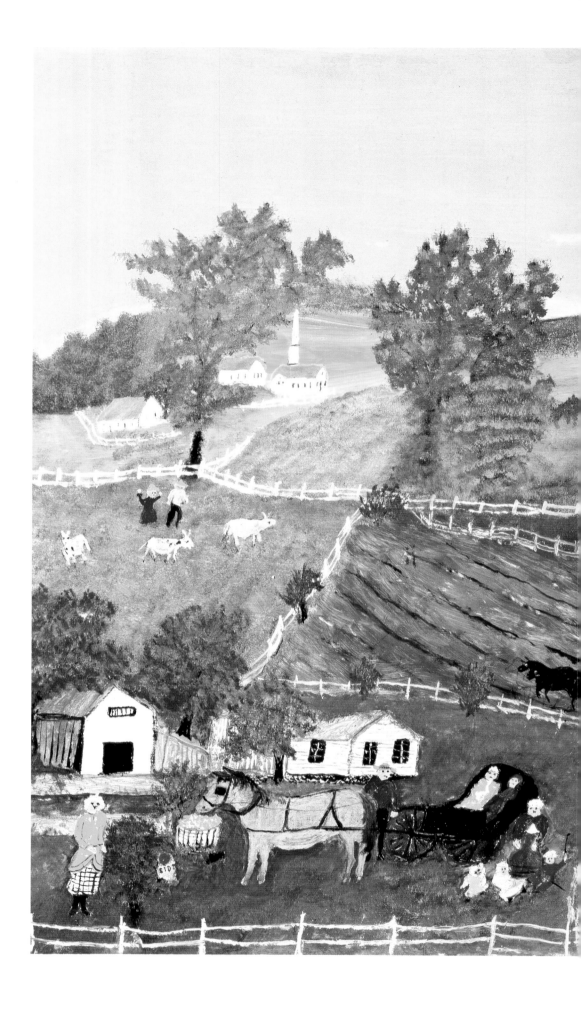

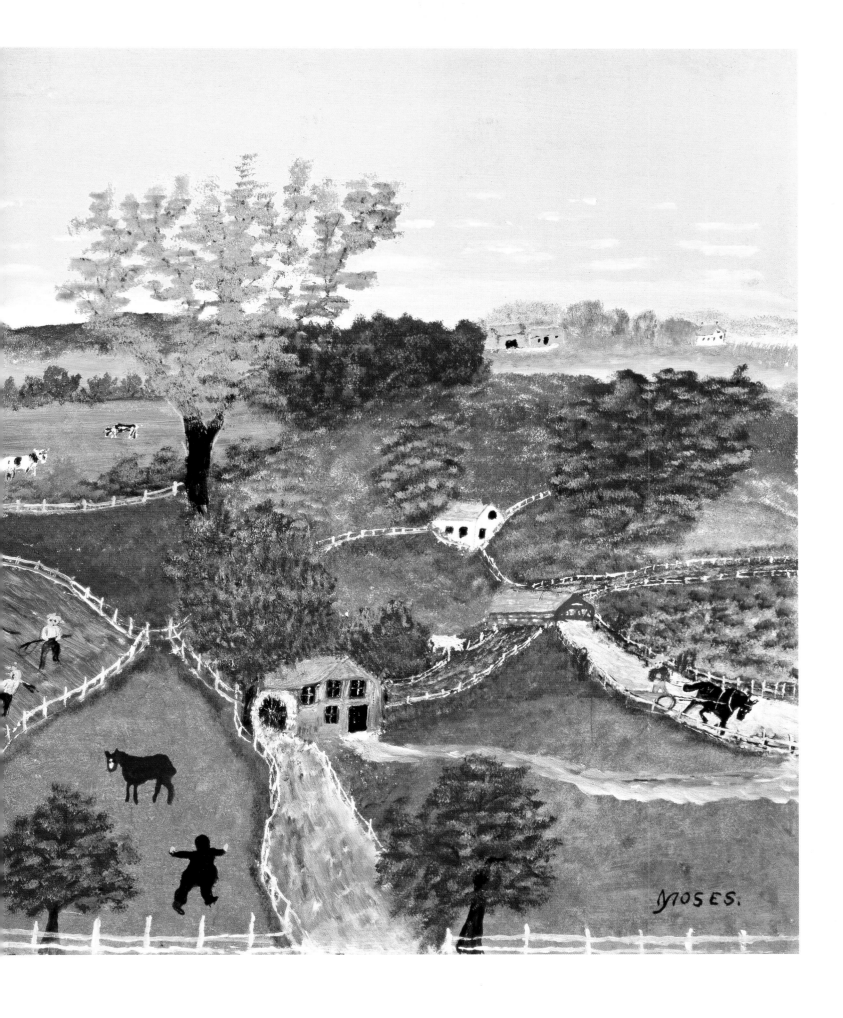

78 Eagle Bridge Hotel

1959. Oil on pressed wood
16 x 24 inches
(40.7 x 60.9 cm)
Signed, lower right
Kallir 1387. Private collection

Along with the compositional changes occasioned by Moses' switch to a more horizontal format came a coarsening of detail. Her last works invite comparison with those done in the early days, when lack of proper tools had hampered the clarity of the artist's rendering (see fig. 4). A similar looseness is seen in the artist's late drawings (figs. 34 and 35). As with any old artist, it is tempting to attribute these changes to the aging process: a shaky hand, diminished eyesight. These explanations, however, are less than fully convincing for an artist who was already in her seventies and suffering from arthritis when she began to paint seriously. Furthermore, Moses herself was conscious of her own stylistic metamorphosis. "I'm changing my style," she said in a 1956 interview, "getting modern in my old age, with a head full of ideas." Perhaps the best explanation for Grandma Moses' "old-age style" is that, like other artists who suffered from physical infirmity, such as Lovis Corinth or Willem de Kooning, she managed to make a virtue of her limitations. The aging process and the creative process became one.

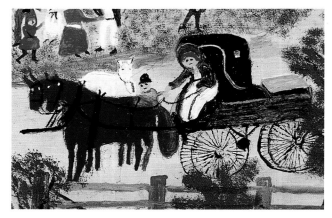

Fig. 34. *Eagle Bridge Hotel*, detail of plate 78

Fig. 35. Grandma Moses, *Horse and Carriage*. Pencil on tracing paper, 3 ¼ x 5 ¼ inches (8.3 x 13.3 cm). Courtesy Grandma Moses Properties Co., New York

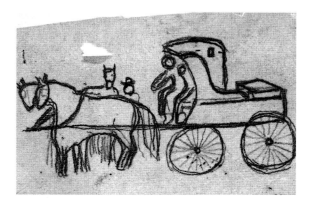

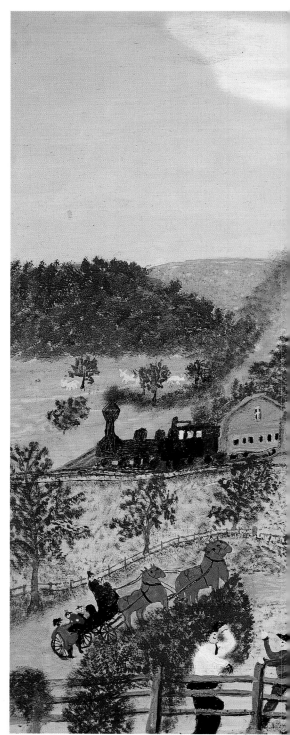

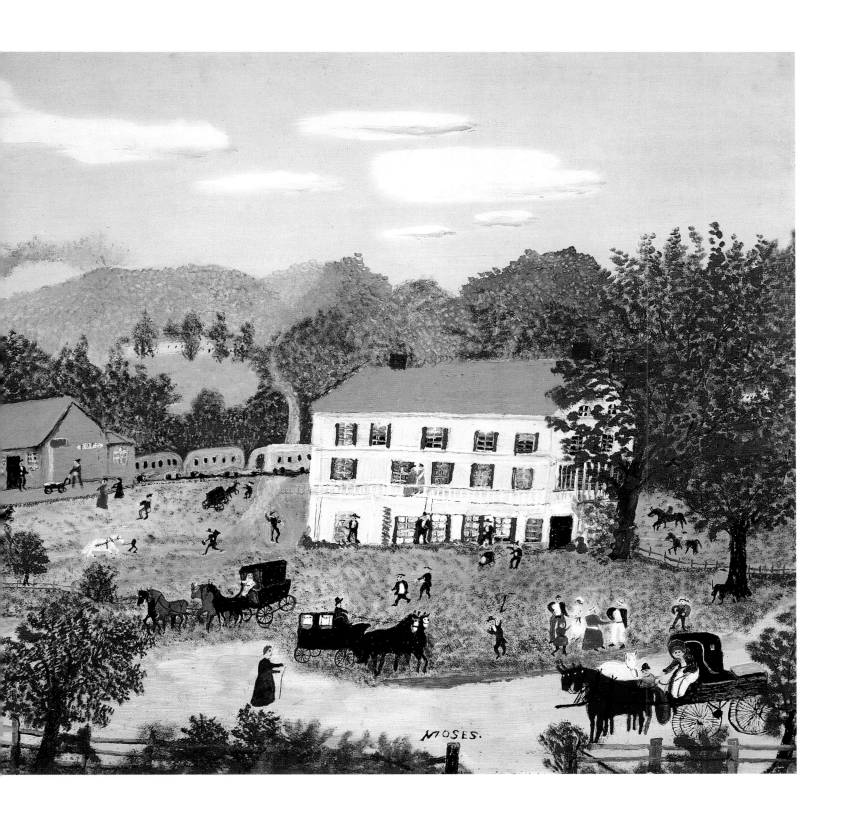

79 **Grandma's Birthplace**
1959. Oil on pressed wood
12 x 16 inches
(30.5 x 40.7 cm)
Signed, lower right
Kallir 1395. Private collection

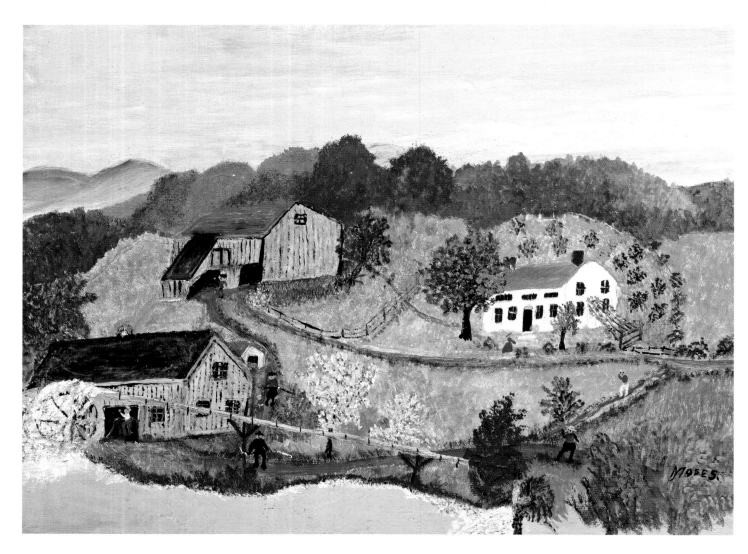

To the end of her life, Moses was willing to tackle new challenges, such as illustrating "The Night Before Christmas" (see plates 74 and 75). However, she also remained loyal to certain favorite subjects. Comparison of *Grandma's Birthplace*, *Vermont Sugar* (plate 82), *The Old Bucket*, and *Witches* (plate 81) with earlier versions of the same or similar subjects (see fig. 8 in Lynda Hartigan's essay and plates 15, 18, 37, 38, and 68) vividly illustrates the changes which the artist had undergone. In addition to looser paint handling and more compositional compression, the later paintings all employ a noticeably brighter palette. What Moses sacrificed in the way of detail, she gained in color and expressive freedom (fig. 36).

80 The Old Bucket

1960. Oil on pressed wood
15 15/16 x 24 inches
(40.4 x 60.9 cm)
Signed, lower right
Kallir 1466. Seiji Togo Memorial,
Yasuda Kasai Museum of Art, Tokyo

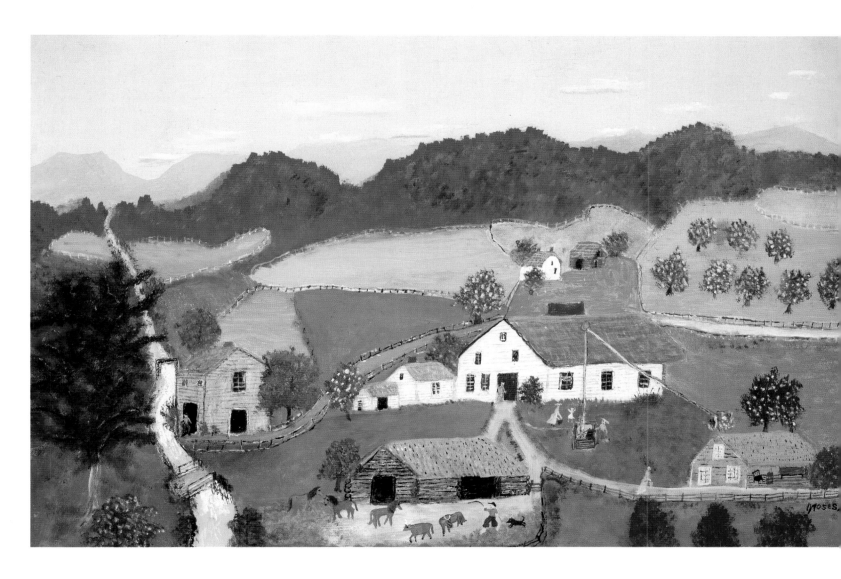

81 Witches

1960. Oil on pressed wood
16 x 24 inches
(40.7 x 60.9 cm)
Signed, lower right
Kallir 1477. Private collection

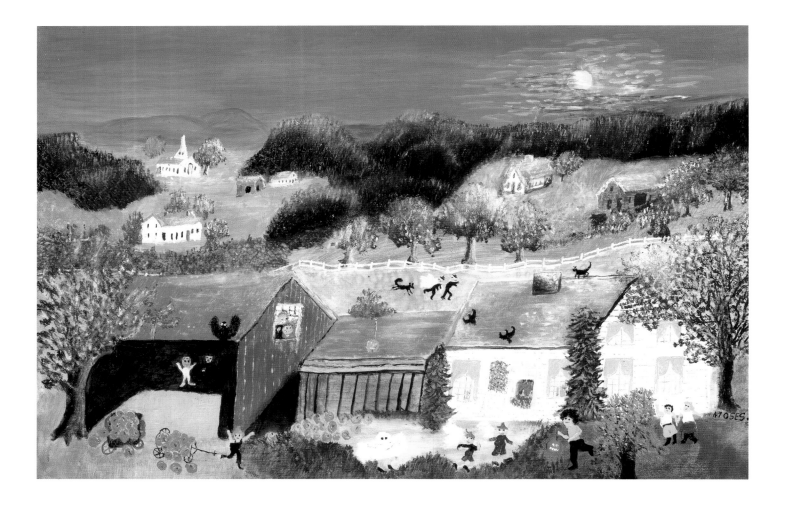

82 Vermont Sugar

1961. Oil on pressed wood
16 x 24 inches
(40.7 x 60.9 cm)
Signed, lower right
Kallir 1496. Private collection

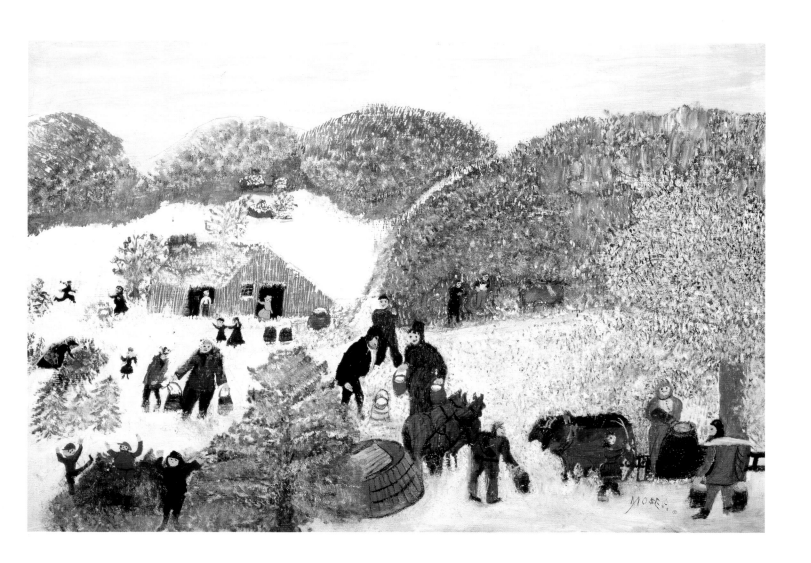

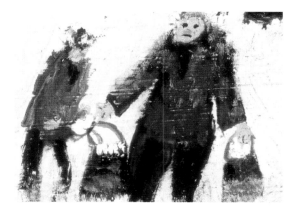

Fig. 36. *Vermont Sugar,* detail of plate 82

83 Green Sleigh

1960. Oil on pressed wood
16 x 24 inches
(40.7 x 60.9 cm)
Signed, lower right
Kallir 1449. Private collection

Moses' substitution of expressive intensity for anecdotal precision
had a multifaceted impact on her style. Pattern was now less important
than painterly unity. Hue and texture became dominant, with increased
emphasis on atmospheric effects. The figural elements, rendered with
fluid brushwork rather than as flat shapes, began to merge with the
background, so that both became integral components in a network
of pigment and color (see plates 84–86).

Aging seems to have turned Moses more inside herself, prompting her
to rely more on memory and less on direct observation, and to regard
her art more exclusively in terms of her immediate materials: the color,
the paint, and the painter herself. The critic Emily Genauer called
Moses' last work "a statement about the inner artist."

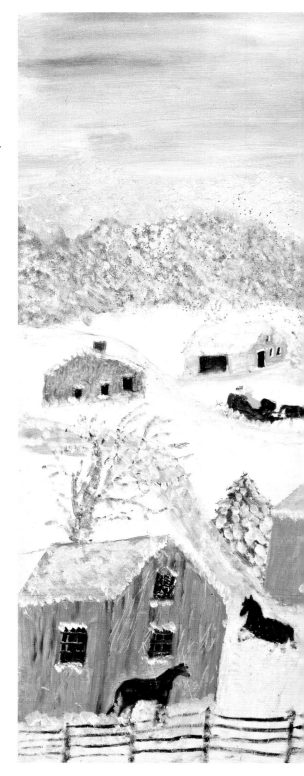

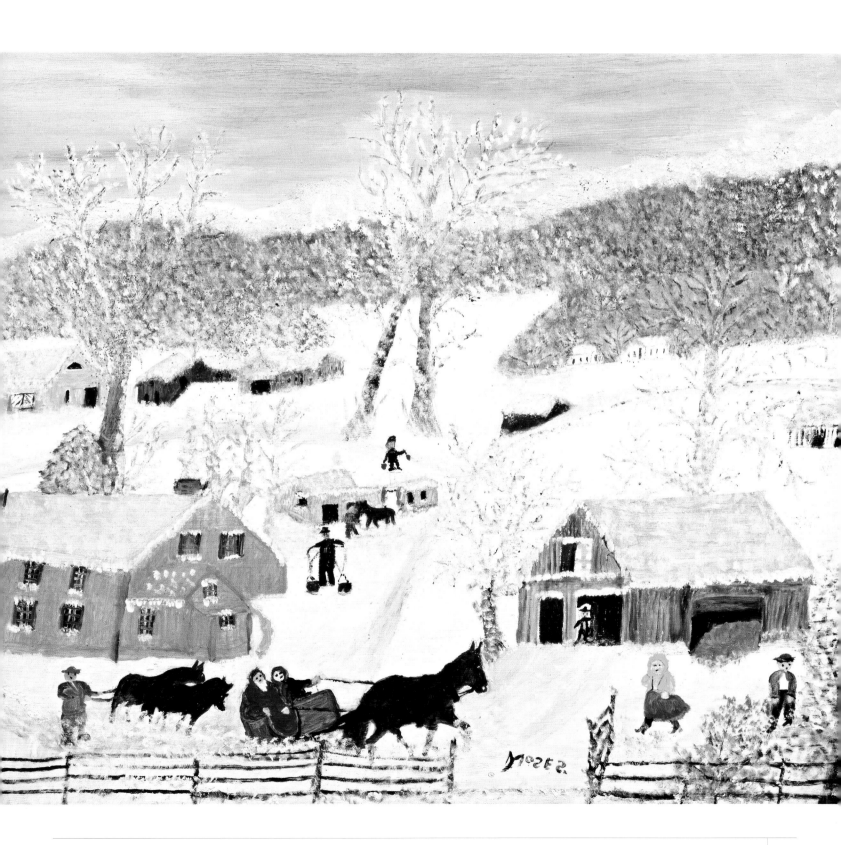

84 Get Out the Sleigh

1960. Oil on pressed wood
16 x 24 inches
(40.7 x 60.9 cm)
Signed, lower right
Kallir 1474. Private collection

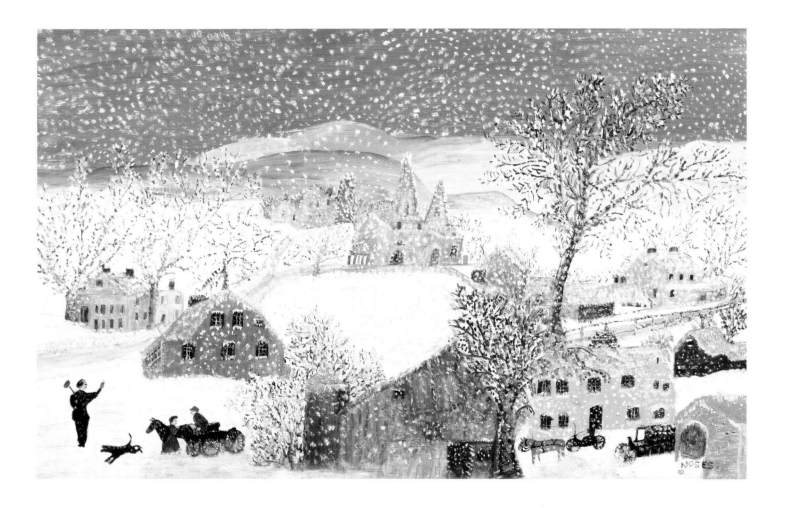

85 White Birches

1961. Oil on pressed wood
16 x 24 inches
(40.7 x 60.9 cm)
Signed, lower center
Kallir 1489. Private collection

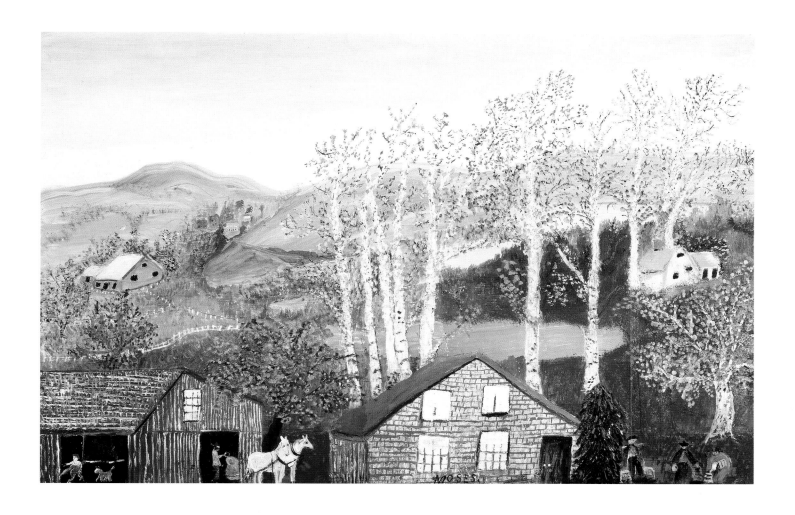

86 The Ice Is Good

1961. Oil on pressed wood
16 x 24 inches
(40.7 x 60.9 cm)
Signed, lower left
Kallir 1499. Private collection

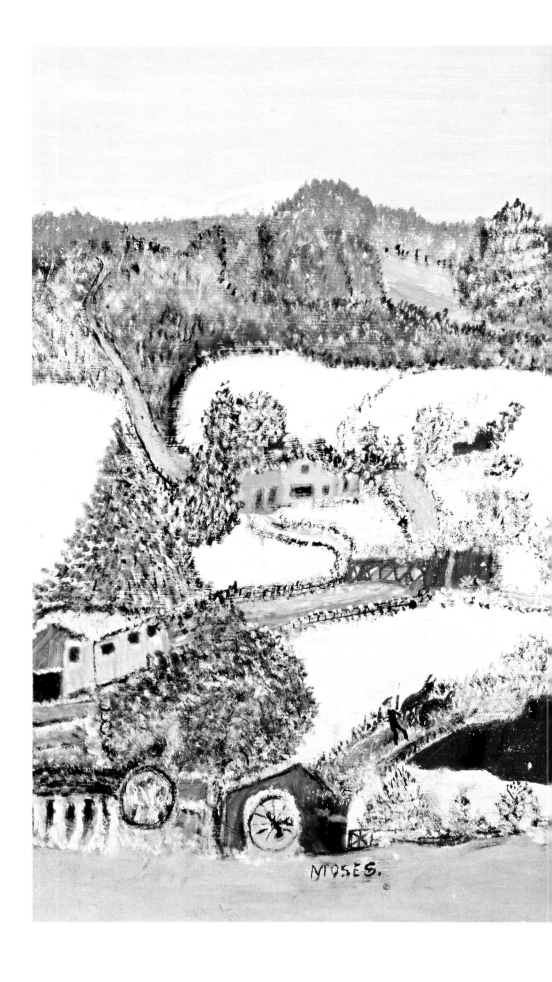

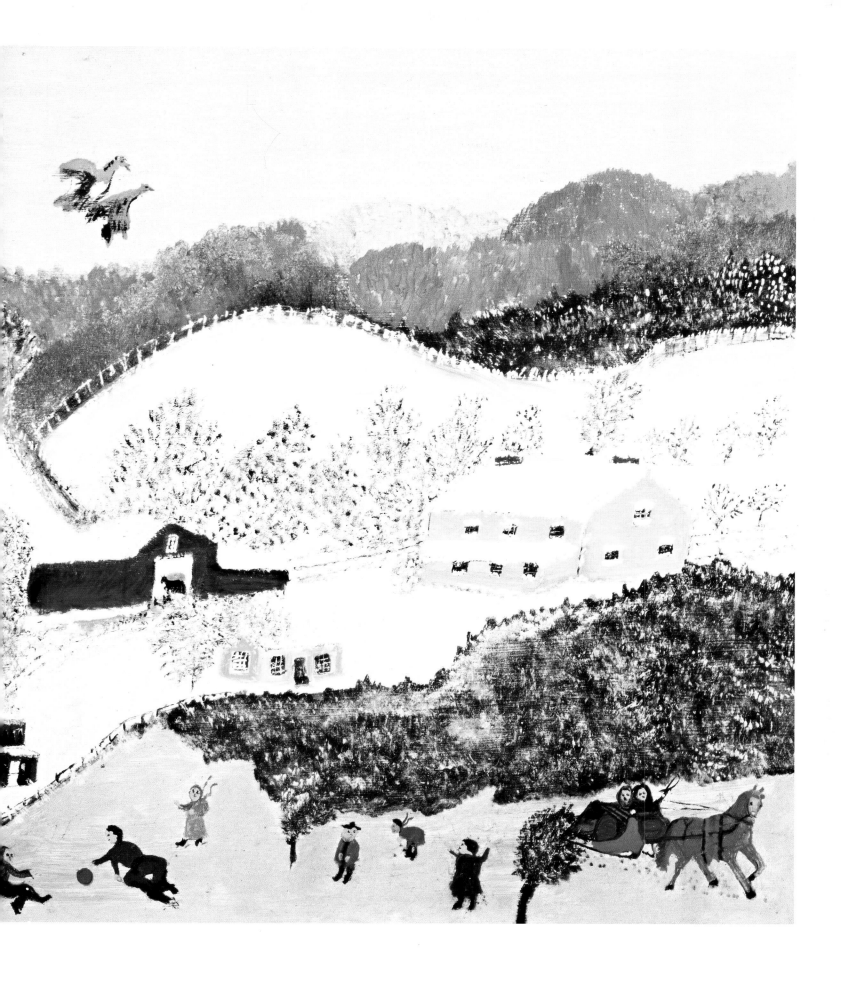

87 Rainbow

1961. Oil on pressed wood
16 x 24 inches
(40.7 x 60.9 cm)
Signed, lower right
Kallir 1511. Private collection
Courtesy Galerie St. Etienne,
New York

Fig. 37. *Rainbow,* detail of plate 87

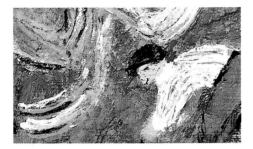

Fig. 38. *Rainbow,* detail of plate 87

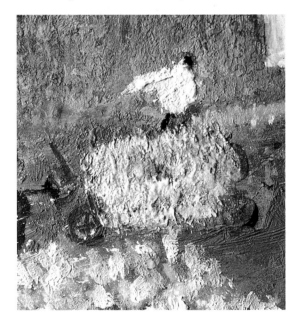

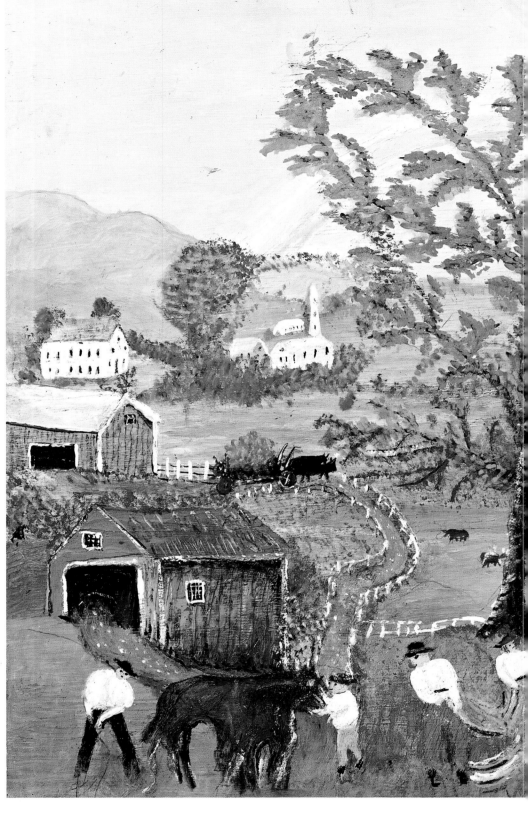

Grandma Moses continued to paint well into her 101st year, although during the final months of her life she was too weak to do much work. *Rainbow,* executed in June 1961, is generally considered her last finished picture. As such, it is an amazing distillation of the artist's worldview. *Rainbow* represents Moses "old-age style" in all its glory. The wild paint handling facilitates a joyous free-for-all of color. Figural vignettes merge

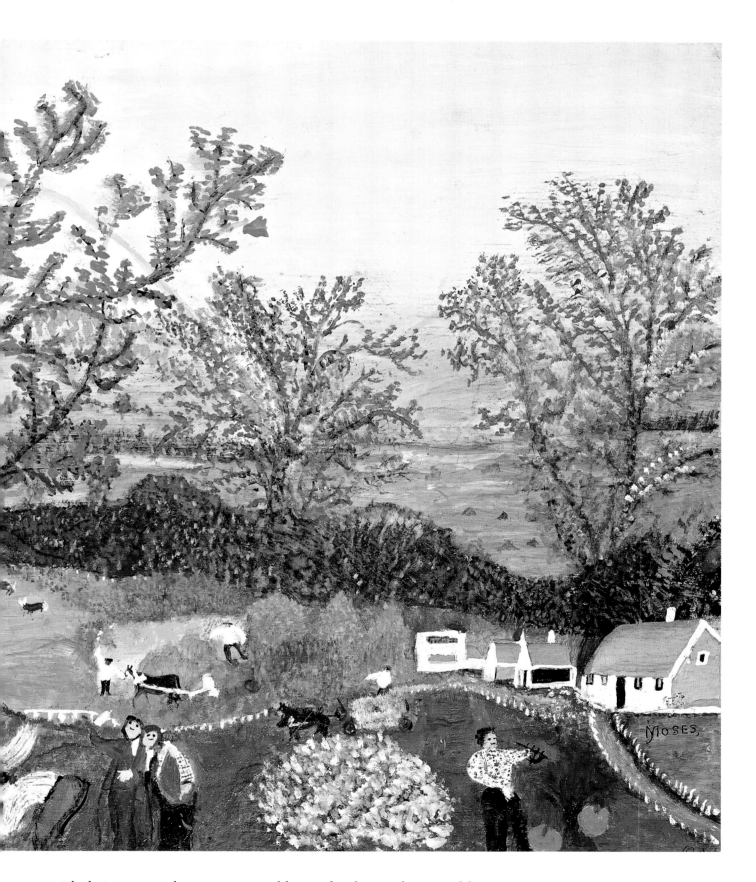

with their surroundings: nature and humankind are at last one. Moses is
no longer terribly concerned with representational accuracy in her use
of color; the emotional impact is paramount. The glorious rainbow, the
exuberant swish of candy-striped scythes (fig. 37), and the triumphant,
nearly airborne hay wagon (fig. 38) are presented as bright symbols in
paint, tokens of peace, a final offering of hope.

Biographical Chronology

Including a selection of major exhibitions and publications

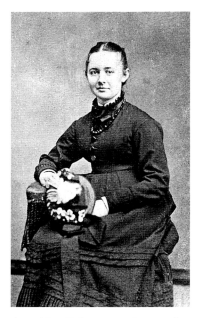

Anna Mary Robertson at the age of 15

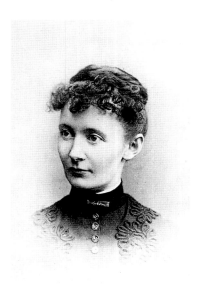

Anna Mary Robertson Moses as a bride, 1887

1860 Anna Mary Robertson is born on September 7 in Greenwich, New York, the third of ten children of Mary Shannahan and Russell King Robertson, a farmer.

1872–1887 Leaves home to work as "hired girl" on neighboring farm. Anna Mary will spend most of the next 15 years in this manner, learning how to sew, cook, and keep house for various wealthier neighbors.

1870s Obtains a few years of schooling along with children of family for whom she works.

1887 On November 9, marries Thomas Salmon Moses, the "hired man" on farm where she is then employed.

1887–1905 The couple move to Virginia, where they work as tenant farmers for a number of years until they save enough to buy their own place. Mrs. Moses contributes to family's income by producing butter and potato chips. Gives birth to ten children, of whom five die in infancy.

1905 The family returns to upstate New York, purchasing farm in Eagle Bridge, not far from Anna Mary's birthplace.

1909 Moses' mother dies in February, her father in June.

1918 Paints first large picture (plate 1) on fireboard in parlor.

1920s Paints landscapes on panels of "tip-up" table and occasional pictures for relatives and friends.

1927 On January 15, Thomas Salmon Moses dies of heart attack.

1932 Goes to Bennington, Vermont, to assist daughter Anna, who is ill with tuberculosis. At Anna's suggestion, makes first "worsted" embroidered pictures (plates 2 and 3). After Anna's death, Moses stays on to care for her two grandchildren.

1935 Returns to her farm in Eagle Bridge, where she lives with youngest son Hugh, his wife Dorothy, and their children. Begins to paint in earnest and exhibits pictures at local events, such as fairs and charity sales. Moses later recalls receiving prizes for her preserves at the county fair, but nothing for her paintings.

1938 A display of her pictures at Thomas's drugstore in Hoosick Falls, New York, is discovered by Louis Caldor, a traveling engineer and amateur collector. Caldor vows to make Moses famous, but her family scoffs at the idea; he sends her first professional artist's paints and canvases.

1939 At Caldor's instigation, three Moses paintings are included in show *Contemporary Unknown American Painters* in Members' Rooms of Museum of Modern Art in New York (October 18–November 18). Exhibition not open to the general public and thus has little impact. Most art dealers whom Caldor approaches refuse to commit to a 79-year-old artist.

1940 Otto Kallir, owner of Galerie St. Etienne in New York, is taken with the Moses paintings Caldor shows him and mounts artist's first one-woman show, *What a Farm Wife Painted* (October 9–31). In November, Gimbel's department store features Moses' work in a "Thanksgiving festival." She attends and captivates press and public alike.

1941 Receives New York State Prize for *Old Oaken Bucket* at Syracuse Museum of Fine Arts (now Everson Museum of Art), Syracuse, New York. The painting is purchased by Thomas J. Watson, founder of IBM. Celebrities such as Katherine Cornell and Cole Porter begin to collect her work.

1942 Chapter devoted to Grandma Moses in *They Taught Themselves* by Sidney Janis (New York: The Dial Press), and three paintings included in exhibition of same title (Marie Harriman Gallery, New York; February 9–March 7). American British Art Center, New York, presents *Anna Mary Robertson Moses: Loan Exhibition of Paintings* (December 7–22).

1944 Galerie St. Etienne cements its commitment to Moses, presenting two exhibitions of her work (*New Paintings by Grandma Moses: The Senior of the American Primitives,* in February, and *Grandma Moses,* in December).

1944–1963 Otto Kallir organizes extensive traveling exhibition program, which during the next two decades brings Moses' work to innumerable cities throughout the United States (Alabama, California, Connecticut, Delaware, District of Columbia, Florida, Illinois, Indiana, Iowa, Kansas, Louisiana, Maryland, Massachusetts, Minnesota, Missouri, Montana, Nebraska, New Hampshire, New York, North Carolina, Ohio, Oklahoma, Pennsylvania, South Carolina, Tennessee, Texas, Vermont, Virginia, Washington, Wisconsin).

1945 Moses is featured artist at the "Women's International Exposition: Woman's Life in Peacetime," held in Madison Square Garden, New York (November 13–18).

1945–1950 Represented in every annual juried exhibition of the Carnegie Institute, Pittsburgh, Pennsylvania.

1946 Gains significant national exposure through publication of first Moses greeting cards and best-selling monograph, *Grandma Moses: American Primitive* (autobiographical notes by Grandma Moses, edited by Otto Kallir, and with an introduction by Louis Bromfield; New York: The Dryden Press). Sixteen million Grandma Moses Christmas cards sold. Moses painting featured in ad for Richard Hudnut lipstick, "Primitive Red."

1947 Second, expanded edition of *Grandma Moses: American Primitive* is published (Garden City, N.Y.: Doubleday & Co.), and Hallmark Company takes over Moses Christmas- and greeting-card license. One-woman exhibition at Galerie St. Etienne, New York (May 17–June 14).

1948 First large color reproductions of Moses' paintings produced by Arthur Jaffe Heliochrome Company, New York. Exhibition *Ten Years—Grandma Moses*, at Galerie St. Etienne, New York (Thanksgiving–Christmas).

1949 Moses' son Hugh dies in February. Meets President Harry S. Truman in May, when she travels to Washington, D.C., to receive Women's National Press Club Award "For Outstanding Accomplishment In Art." Simultaneous exhibition, *Paintings by Grandma Moses,* at Phillips Gallery, Washington (May 8–June 9). Receives Honorary Doctorate from Russell Sage College, Troy, New York, in June. Included in *Pictorial Folk Art in America, New England to California* by Alice Ford (New York and London: The Studio Publications). Riverdale Fabrics begins producing line of drapery fabrics based on Moses' paintings, and Atlas China Company issues series of plates featuring four Moses paintings.

1950 Documentary color film produced by Jerome Hill, with narration by Archibald MacLeish and photography by Erica Anderson, nominated for Academy Award. First European Moses exhibition, sponsored by the U.S. Information Service (Vienna, Munich, Salzburg, Berne, The Hague, Paris; June–December). The artist's birthday is celebrated in the national press for first time; Albany Institute of History and Art, Albany, New York, mounts commemorative exhibition, *Grandma Moses: Exhibition Arranged on the Occasion of Her 90th Birthday* (September 7–October 15). Included in *Primitive Painters in America* by Jean Lipman and Alice Winchester (New York: Dodd, Mead & Co.). Otto Kallir establishes umbrella organization, Grandma Moses Properties, to administer artist's copyrights and trademarks; subsequent licensing program revolves around print reproductions and items of domestic use.

1951 In April, moves from her old farm to more comfortable one-story house across the road, and daughter Winona Fisher takes over running of household. Receives Honorary Doctorate from Moore College of Art, Philadelphia, Pennsylvania, in March.

1952 Publication of autobiography, *My Life's History*, by Grandma Moses, edited by Otto Kallir (New York: Harper & Row; London: André Deutsch; Frankfurt am Main: Ullstein Verlag, 1957; Utrecht: A.W. Brauna & Zoon, 1958.) Lillian Gish portrays artist in televised "docudrama" based on the autobiography. In December, Galerie St. Etienne issues brief memoir, *Christmas*, by Grandma Moses.

1953 Guest speaker at the *New York Herald Tribune* forum in New York, October 20. Featured on cover of *Time* magazine. Crown Potteries produces dinnerware based on the painting *Home for Thanksgiving*.

1954–1955 Five paintings included in *American Primitive Paintings from the 17th Century to the Present*, exhibition circulated in Europe by the Smithsonian Institution for the U.S. Information Agency (Lucerne, Vienna, Munich, Dortmund, Stockholm, Oslo, Manchester, London, Trier).

1955 Interviewed by Edward R. Murrow for *See It Now* television series, broadcast December 13. *A Tribute to Grandma Moses*, on the occasion of her 95th birthday, presented by Thomas J. Watson and the Fine Arts Department of the IBM Corp., IBM Gallery, New York (November 28–December 31). Moses travels to New York to attend opening; her birthday again gets national press coverage.

1956 Painting specially commissioned by President Eisenhower's Cabinet is given to him on third anniversary of his inauguration. Publication of set of four color reproductions, *The Four Seasons* (Port Chester, N.Y.: Donald Art Company).

1957 *Grandma Moses: New York Showing of an Exhibition Presented in Europe During 1955–1957*, at Galerie St. Etienne, New York (May 6–June 4).

1958 Moses' daughter, Winona Fisher, dies on October 14. Son Forrest and his wife Mary move into house to take care of her.

1959 Included in *Modern Primitives: Masters of Naïve Painting* by Otto Bihalji-Merin (New York: Harry N. Abrams). Publication of portfolio of six color reproductions, *Six of My Favorite Paintings* (New York: Catalda Fine Arts).

1960 Governor Nelson A. Rockefeller proclaims artist's 100th birthday "Grandma Moses Day" in New York State. The IBM Gallery in New York celebrates with *My Life's History: A Loan Exhibition of Paintings by Grandma Moses* (September 12–October 6), and artist herself dances a decorous jig with her physician. *LIFE* magazine publishes cover story, with photographs by Cornell Capa.

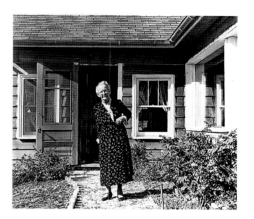

Grandma Moses in front of her home in Eagle Bridge, New York, 1952

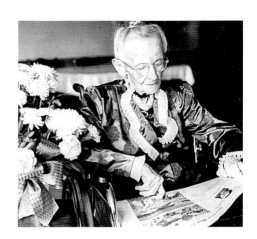

Grandma Moses on her 101st birthday,
September 7, 1961

1960–1961 *My Life's History*, exhibition circulated by the Smithsonian Institution (Milwaukee, Washington, D.C., Chattanooga, Baton Rouge, Seattle, Laguna Beach, Fort Worth, Winnipeg, Chicago).

1961 Grandma Moses taken to Health Center in Hoosick Falls, New York, on July 18. New York Governor Nelson A. Rockefeller again proclaims artist's birthday "Grandma Moses Day." Publication of *The Grandma Moses Storybook*, illustrated by Grandma Moses (containing stories and poems by 28 writers, edited by Nora Kramer, and with a biographical sketch by Otto Kallir; New York: Random House). Grandma Moses dies, aged 101, at Health Center on December 13 and is buried in Maple Grove Cemetery, Hoosick Falls.

Selected Posthumous Publications, Honors, and Exhibitions

1962 Publication of Clement C. Moore's *The Night Before Christmas*, with illustrations painted by Grandma Moses in 1960–1961 (New York: Random House); the book becomes an annual holiday staple on the children's television show *Captain Kangaroo. Grandma Moses: Memorial Exhibition*, at Galerie St. Etienne, New York (November–December).

1962–1964 *A Life's History in 40 Pictures*, traveling exhibition circulated in Europe (Vienna, Paris, Bremen, Hamburg, Hameln, Fulda, Düsseldorf, Darmstadt, Mannheim, Berlin, Frankfurt, Oslo, Stockholm, Helsinki, Gothenburg, Copenhagen, Moscow) and concluded at Hammer Galleries, New York.

1964 Two paintings included in exhibition *De Lusthof der Naïven/Le Monde des Naifs*, Museum Boymans-van Beuningen, Rotterdam; Musée National d'Art Moderne, Paris (July–October).

1966 Eleven paintings included in *1st Triennial of Insitic Art*, Slovenska Národná Galéria, Bratislava (July 26–October 2).

1966–1972 Forrest and Mary Moses acquire one-room schoolhouse attended by Anna Mary and have it moved to old Moses farm in Eagle Bridge; they remodel interior and exhibit Moses mementos.

1967 Publication of portfolio of eight color reproductions, with appreciation by John Canaday (New York: Art in America).

1968–1972 *The Grandma Moses Gallery*, permanent display of paintings and documentary material, at Bennington Museum, Bennington, Vermont.

1969 *Art and Life of Grandma Moses,* loan exhibition of 151 pictures, the "tip-up" table, and documentary material, Gallery of Modern Art, New York (February 20–March 30). United States Government issues six-cent Grandma Moses commemorative postage stamp, depicting detail of painting *July Fourth,* owned by White House. Publication of *Grandma Moses, Favorite Painter* by Charles Graves (Champaign, Ill.: Garrard Publishing Co.).

1971 Publication of *Barefoot in the Grass: The Story of Grandma Moses* by William H. Armstrong (Garden City, N.Y.: Doubleday & Co.). Syracuse China issues series of plates featuring eight Moses paintings.

1972 Fifteen paintings included in *Four American Primitives: Edward Hicks, John Kane, Anna Mary Robertson Moses, Horace Pippin,* A.C.A. Galleries, New York (February 22–March 11).

1973 Publication of *Grandma Moses* by Otto Kallir, including catalogue raisonné (New York: Harry N. Abrams). Publication of four color reproductions (New York: American Heritage Publishing Company).

1973– present Bennington Museum annexes Grandma Moses schoolhouse as supplement to continuing display of paintings and related memorabilia.

1974–1975 Five paintings included in *Die Kunst der Naïven,* Haus der Kunst, Munich; Kunsthaus, Zurich (November–March).

1975 Publication of concise edition of Otto Kallir's *Grandma Moses* (New York: Harry N. Abrams and New American Library; Cologne: M. DuMont Schauberg; pocketbook edition, DuMont Buchverlag, 1979; Amsterdam: Meulenhoff). Ridgewood China issues Christmas plate reproducing the painting *The Old Checkered House in Winter.*

1979 *Grandma Moses, Anna Mary Robertson Moses (1860–1961),* exhibition of 43 paintings, National Gallery of Art, Washington, D.C. (February 11–April 1). Calhoun Collector's Society issues series of plates featuring four Moses paintings.

1980 *Grandma Moses: 1860–1961,* exhibition at Hammer Galleries, New York (May 23–June 7).

1982 Publication of *Grandma Moses: The Artist Behind the Myth* by Jane Kallir (New York: Crown), and exhibition of the same title at Galerie St. Etienne, New York (November 16, 1982–January 8, 1983).

1983 *Grandma Moses: The Artist Behind the Myth* exhibition travels to Danforth Museum, Framingham, Massachusetts, and New York State Museum, Albany. Japanese edition (translated by Kyoko Kato) of Moses' autobiography *My Life's History* (Tokyo: Miraisha). Bennington Museum begins publishing reproductions featuring Moses paintings from its collection. Paragon Needlecraft issues series of kits and "how-to" booklets featuring needlework reproductions of Moses' paintings.

1984 The Seiji Togo Memorial, Yasuda Kasai Museum of Art in Tokyo, Japan, installs permanent display of the artist's paintings; now numbering 33 works, this remains one of the largest public collections of her work in the world. New York Graphic Society inaugurates line of Moses reproductions.

1984–1985 Traveling exhibition, *The World of Grandma Moses,* circulated under auspices of International Exhibitions Foundation (Museum of American Folk Art, New York; Baltimore Museum of Art; Norton Gallery, Palm Beach; Cheekwood Fine Arts Center, Nashville; Joslyn Art Museum, Omaha; Lakeview Museum of Art, Peoria). Second edition of *Grandma Moses* by Otto Kallir (New York: Harrison House/Harry N. Abrams)

1986 Japanese edition (translated by Kyoko Kato) of *Grandma Moses* by Otto Kallir (Tokyo: Sanrio).

1987 First Japanese exhibition, *Grandma Moses* (Isetan Museum, Tokyo; Daimaru Museum, Osaka). Publication of *Grandma Moses: Painter of Rural America* by Zibby O'Neal (New York: Puffin Books).

1989 Seventeen paintings included in Japanese traveling exhibition *Masters of Naive Art* (Daimaru Museum, Kyoto; Yamagataya Art Gallery, Yamagataya; Daimaru Art Gallery, Hakata; Daimaru Art Gallery, Tokyo). Publication of *Grandma Moses, Painter* by Tom Biracree, with an introduction by Martina S. Horner (New York: Chelsea House), and second edition of *Grandma Moses: The Artist Behind the Myth* by Jane Kallir (Secaucus, N.J.: Wellfleet Press). *Grandma Moses: An American Primitive,* a play starring Cloris Leachman and produced by Bob Banner Associates, presented at 14 regional American theaters.

1989–1992 Cleo Publishing Company issues line of Moses greeting cards and calendars.

1990 Second Japanese exhibition, *Grandma Moses* (Isetan Museum, Tokyo; Daimaru Museum, Osaka; Daimaru Museum, Kyoto; Funabashi Art Forum, Funabashi; Takashimaya Museum, Yokohama). *Grandma Moses (1860–1961): An American Treasure*, exhibition at Hammer Galleries, New York (September 17–October 27). Second tour of the play *Grandma Moses: An American Primitive*, seen at 11 American theaters.

1990–present The Seiji Togo Memorial Yasuda Kasai Museum of Art in Tokyo, Japan, publishes annual Grandma Moses calendars.

1991 Publication of *Grandma Moses* by Margot Cleary (New York: Crescent Books), and of redesigned edition of *The Night Before Christmas* (New York: Random House).

1993–1996 Cedco Publishing issues annual Moses calendars.

1994 Third tour of the play *Grandma Moses: An American Primitive*, seen at 24 American theaters.

1995 Third Japanese exhibition, *Grandma Moses* (Daimaru Museum, Osaka; Yasuda Kasai Museum, Tokyo; Shimonoseki Museum, Yamaguchi; Sogo Museum, Chiba).

1996 *Grandma Moses: Pictures from the Past*, exhibition at Fort Lauderdale Museum of Art, Florida (February 2–May 19). Publication of *Grandma Moses: An American Original* by William C. Ketchum (New York: Smithmark Publishers).

1997 Publication of *Grandma Moses: 25 Masterworks* by Jane Kallir (New York: Harry N. Abrams).

1998 *Grandma Moses (1860–1961): An American Treasure*, exhibition at Hammer Galleries, New York (January 20–February 28).

1998–1999 The Bennington Museum circulates an exhibition of Moses paintings from its collection (Ronald Reagan Library, Simi Valley, California; Gerald R. Ford Museum, Grand Rapids, Michigan; New Britain Museum of Art, Connecticut; Newport Art Museum, Rhode Island; Society of the Four Arts, Palm Beach, Florida; Lyndon B. Johnson Museum and Library, Austin, Texas). Five paintings included in *Self-Taught Artists of the Twentieth Century: An American Anthology* (Philadelphia Museum of Art; High Museum of Art, Atlanta; Amon Carter Museum, Forth Worth; Memorial Art Gallery, Rochester; Wexner Center for the Arts, Columbus, Ohio).

2000 Publication of *The Year with Grandma Moses* by W. Nikola-Lisa (New York: Henry Holt).

Selected Bibliography

"About Grandma Moses." *The New York World-Telegram*, 21 May 1947.

Bihalji-Merin, Otto. *Modern Primitives: Masters of Naïve Painting.* New York: Harry N. Abrams, 1959.

Biracree, Tom. *Grandma Moses, Painter.* New York and Philadelphia: Chelsea House, 1989.

Bishop, Robert. *Folk Painters of America.* New York: E. P. Dutton, 1979.

Breuning, Margaret. "Grandma Moses." *Art Digest*, 1 December 1944.

Canaday, John. "Art of Grandma Moses—An Appraisal Shows She Captured and Relayed the Magic of Being Alive." *The New York Times*, 14 December 1961.

Capa, Cornell. "100 Candles for a Gay Lady." *LIFE*, 19 September 1960, 105–12.

Chaliapin, Boris. "Presents from Grandma." *Time*, 28 December 1953, 38–42.

Clark, Gregory. "'I Just Follow Nature' Says Grandma Moses." *Weekend Picture Magazine*, 16 February 1952.

Cleary, Margot. *Grandma Moses.* New York: Crescent Books, 1991.

Devree, Howard. Untitled article. *The New York Times*, 13 October 1940.

Eisenstein, Ruth, and Lois Brown, eds. *The Grandma Moses American Songbook.* New York: Harry N. Abrams, 1985.

Erskine, John. "Author John Erskine Reviews Grandma Moses' Autobiography." *The New York Journal American*, 12 January 1947.

Evans, Ernestine. "Untaught, She Painted What She Loved." *The New York Herald Tribune Weekly Book Review*, 22 December 1946.

Genauer, Emily. "This Week in Art—Granny Gains Stature as Painting Marvel." *The New York World-Telegram*, 1 June 1948.

———. "Grandma Moses: A Lovely Spirit." *The New York Herald Tribune*, 10 September 1961.

———. "The Passing of Grandma Moses at 101." *The New York Herald Tribune*, 14 December 1961.

Grandma Moses, *see also* Moses, Anna Mary Robertson.

Grandma Moses: Anna Mary Robertson Moses (1860–1961). Exh. cat. National Gallery of Art, Washington, D.C. (11 February–1 April 1979). Washington, D.C.: National Gallery of Art, 1979.

"Grandma Moses Just Paints and Makes No Fuss About It." *The New York World-Telegram*, 15 November 1940.

"Grandma Moses, Painting at 87, Is 'Working Up Some Mischief'." *The New York Herald Tribune*, 23 August 1948.

Grandma Moses. Exh. cat. Isetan Museum (Tokyo), 1–17 March 1987; Daimaru Museum, Umeda (Osaka), 22 April–10 May, 1987. Tokyo: Hata International, 1987.

Grandma Moses. Exh. cat. Isetan Museum (Tokyo), 1–24 July 1990; Daimaru Museum, Umeda (Osaka), 5–17 September 1990; Daimaru Museum (Kyoto), 20 September–2 October 1990; Funabashi Art Forum (Funabashi), 10–30 October 1990; Yokohama Takashimaya Gallery (Yokohama), 8–20 November 1990. Tokyo: Nippon Television Network, 1990.

Grandma Moses. Exh. cat. Daimaru Museum, Umeda (Osaka), 19 April–8 May 1995; Seiji Togo Memorial, Yasuda Kasai Museum of Art (Tokyo), 3 June–30 July 1995; Shimonoseki Daimaru Art Gallery (Yamaguchi), 30 August–11 September 1995; Chiba Sogo Museum of Art (Chiba), 13–30 October 1995. Tokyo: Hata Stichting, 1995.

Hemphill, Herbert Waide, Jr., and Julia Weissman. *Twentieth-Century American Folk Art and Artists.* New York: E. P. Dutton, 1974.

Janis, Sidney. *They Taught Themselves: American Primitive Painters of the 20th Century.* New York: Dial Press, 1942. Reprint, New York: Hudson River Press, 1999.

Kallir, Jane. "Grandma Moses." In *Self-Taught Artists of the 20th Century: An American Anthology.* New York: Museum of American Folk Art, 1998.

———. *Grandma Moses: The Artist Behind the Myth.* New York: C. N. Potter, 1982.

———. *The Folk Art Tradition.* New York: Viking Press, 1981.

———. *Grandma Moses: 25 Masterworks.* New York: Harry N. Abrams, 1997.

Kallir, Otto. *Grandma Moses.* New York: Harry N. Abrams, 1973.

———. "Grandma Moses." *The Studio,* CLI No. 757 (April 1956): 97–101.

———. *Grandma Moses: American Primitive.* New York: The Dryden Press, 1946; 2nd ed. Garden City, N.Y: Doubleday, 1947.

Kallir, Otto, ed. *Art and Life of Grandma Moses.* Exh. cat. Gallery of Modern Art, New York (20 February–30 March 1969). South Brunswick and New York: A. S. Barnes, 1969; London: Thomas Yoseloff, 1969.

Ketchum, William C. *Grandma Moses: An American Original.* New York: Smithmark, 1996.

Kramer, Nora, ed. *The Grandma Moses Storybook.* New York: Random House, 1961.

Moore, Clement C. *The Night Before Christmas,* with illustrations painted by Grandma Moses. New York: Random House, 1962.

Moses, Anna Mary Robertson. *The Grandma Moses Storybook.* Illustrated by Grandma Moses, edited by Nora Kramer. New York: Random House, 1961.

———. *My Life's History.* Edited by Otto Kallir. New York: Harper and Row, 1952.

My Life's History: A Loan Exhibition of Paintings by Grandma Moses. Exh. cat. IBM Gallery of Arts and Sciences, New York, 12 September–6 October 1960. New York: Galerie St. Etienne, 1960.

Nikola-Lisa, W. *The Year with Grandma Moses.* New York: Henry Holt, 2000.

Oneal, Zibby. *Grandma Moses: Painter of Rural America.* New York: Viking Penguin, 1986.

Schonberg, Harold C. "Grandma Moses: Portrait of the Artist at 99." *The New York Times Magazine,* 6 September 1959.

Sullivan, Frank. "An Afternoon with Grandma Moses." *The New York Times Magazine,* 9 October 1940.

[Updike, John]. "Notes and Comments: The Talk of The Town." *The New Yorker,* 23 December 1961, 56.

Vlach, Michael. "The Twentieth Century: Grandma Moses, American 'Primitive'." In *Plain Painters.* Washington, D.C., and London: Smithsonian Institution Press, 1988.

Index of Exhibited Works

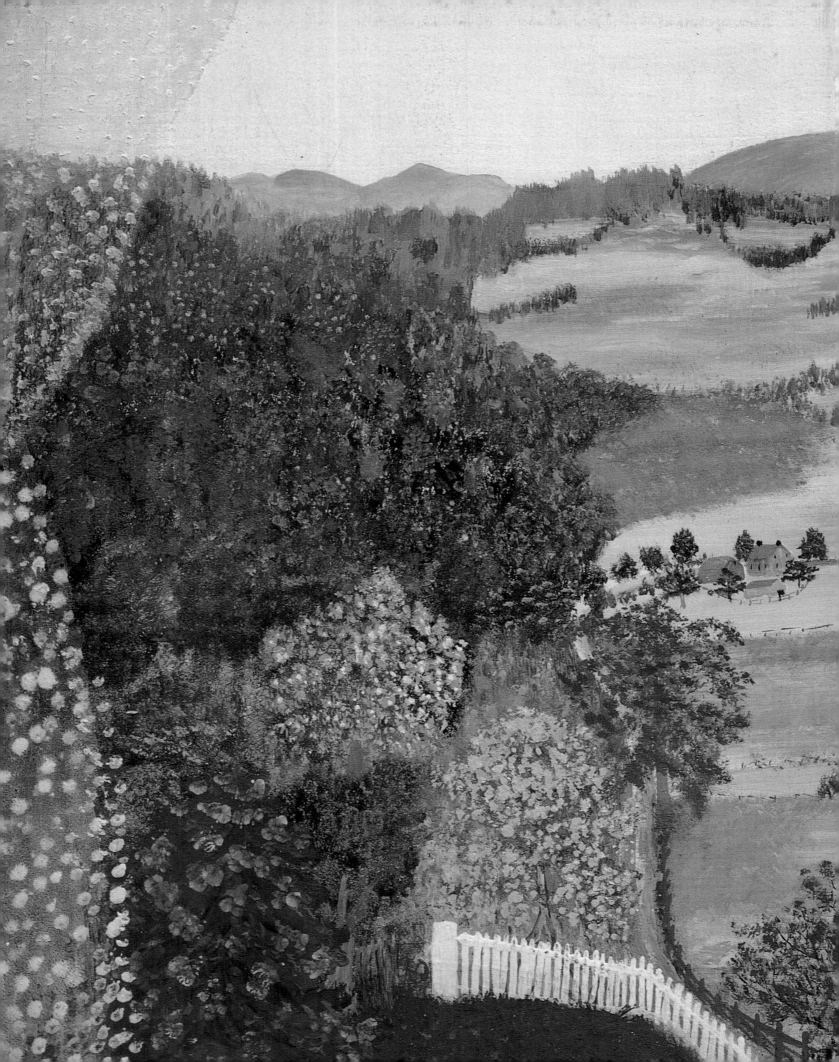